REGULARS AND THE
SECULAR REALM

REGULARS AND THE SECULAR REALM:

THE BENEDICTINES
OF THE CONGREGATION OF SAINT-MAUR
IN UPPER NORMANDY
DURING THE EIGHTEENTH CENTURY
AND THE FRENCH REVOLUTION

By
MARY KATHRYN ROBINSON

UNIVERSITY OF SCRANTON PRESS
SCRANTON AND LONDON

Library of Congress Cataloging-in-Publication Data

© Robinson, Mary Kathryn, 1974-

Regulars and theSecularRealm:
the Benedictines of the Congregation of Saint-Maur
in Upper Normandy
during the Eighteenth Century and the French Revolution
by Mary Kathryn Robinson.

p. cm.

Includes Bibliographical References and Index.

ISBN 978-1-58966-175-2 (cloth : alk. paper)
ISBN 978-1-58966-176-9 (pbk. : alk. paper)

1. Maurists--France--Normandy--History--18th century.
2. France--Normandy--Church history--18th century. I. Title.

BX3050.M3R63 2008
271'.104424--dc22
2008031066

Distribution:
UNIVERSITY OF SCRANTON PRESS
Chicago Distribution Center
11030 S. Langley
Chicago, IL 60628

PRINTED IN THE UNITED STATES OF AMERICA

An academic is in some sort a public man who by his very title becomes accountable to his fellow citizens by the use of his talents, the fruit of his vigilance. In this association he indeed contracts the obligation to offer to them the tribute of his work. Thus, the savant and the literary man are no longer free to hide their efforts and their success in modest but useless obscurity, like those authors who desire that no one knows that they even lived.

Dom François Philippe Gourdin, 1816

ACKNOWLEDGEMENTS

MANY PEOPLE HAVE HELPED ME IN THIS ENDEAVOR, and I wish to thank everyone who graciously assisted me in bringing this work to fruition. First of all, Jeffery L. Gainey, John Hunckler and the staff of the University of Scranton Press for their confidence in me and for their continued support throughout the last two years. To my colleagues at Lourdes College and elsewhere, I am most grateful for their feedback and empathy over the years; most especially, I am indebted to Dr. Donald Horward for his continued guidance and to Lourdes College for providing me with research funds to complete this work.

During my research trips to France, the staff of the Archives Nationales de France, the Archives departemetales de l'Eure, the Archives departementales de Seine-Maritimem the Bibliotheque municipale de Rouen and the Archives municipales de Yvetot not only helped me immeasurably with my work but also welcomed me with hospitality and generosity which made my research experience so enjoyable. I am also grateful to the monks of the abbey of Bec-Hellouin and Free Herve and the monks of Saint-Wandrille. They shared with me not only their libraries and invaluable documents but also their food and prayers. They are truly worthy heirs of Saint Benedict, Saint Anselm, and the monks of the Congregation of Saint-Maur.

The steadfast love and unyielding encouragement of all my family and friends have brought me joy, comfort and love throughout the completion of this book, and for this I am truly grateful. I offer my heartfelt appreciation and affection to my parents, Thomas and Sharon Cooney, and my parents-in-law, Gene and Janet Robinson. My mother deserves special acknowledgement for once again displaying her talents as the best of proofreaders. With love, I wish to thank my husband Michael, who willingly served as my research assistant at the Archives Nationales, even on our honeymoon. Lastly, I dedicate this book to my Eoghan and Madeleine whose births accompanied this work. The past holds more meaning when ones sees the future. The unfailing love and prayers of these loved ones have sustained me in this project and throughout all my professional endeavors.

CONTENTS

INTRODUCTION

IN 1807, DOM FRANÇOIS PHILIPPE GOURDIN wrote to his fellow ex-monk Dom Grappin for the first time since 1789. Having learned only recently that his friend and fellow scholar had survived the tumultuous years of the last two decades, Dom Gourdin seemed eager to hear Dom Grappin's story and share his own: "How have you passed the Revolutionary storm? What became of you during those unfortunate times? Did you leave your fatherland? Did you remain here? If so, did you suffer from the persecution? . . . . As for me, from the moment the Revolution began, I have been charged with the library and I am still the librarian of the city [of Rouen]. I hid during the tempest, but, thanks be to God, I have not compromised myself in anything."[1]

As historians, Doms Gourdin and Grappin, like priests and monks throughout France, no doubt wondered how the French Revolution, which began with the promise of greater equality and popular sovereignty for all Frenchmen, subsequently turned against a significant portion of the population. The various regimes which governed France from 1789 to 1799 passed legislation detrimental to the clergy, and sometimes religious practice in general. Beginning shortly after the fall of the Bastille, the national government began assuming control of the Catholic Church in France by confiscating its lands, suppressing the religious orders, and putting the clergy on state salaries. During the Reign of Terror, the Committee of Public Safety tried to eliminate Catholicism altogether and to abolish all signs of the nation's 1,400-year-old Christian tradition. While some of the most stringent measures relaxed in 1795 and 1796, a new wave of anticlericalism in the final years of the 1700s again treated the clergy like second-class citizens, or worse, outlaws. Contemporaries of the Revolution and historians since have sought to explain the motivation behind these religious policies and to understand their real impact on those affected.

In 1798, Abbé Augustin Barruel concluded that the catastrophic events of the French Revolution resulted from a plot hatched by the anticlerical *philosophes*, Jacobins, and freemasons to topple their sworn enemy, the Catholic Church.[2] This former Jesuit's conspiracy theory (*thèse du complot*) became popular in the

---

1. Dom François Philippe Gourdin to Dom Grappin, 19 March 1807, Dantier, ed., *Rapports sur la correspondance,* 195.
2. Barruel, *Mémoires,* I–V.

XI

nineteenth century as it resonated with the ultra-Catholic political faction which came to power after the fall of Napoleon. Barruel's explanation enjoyed somewhat of a resurgence in the twentieth century, first with the work of Auguste Cochin and then, most notably, with that of François Furet. While the latter did not completely accept the idea of a well-planned conspiracy, he argued that the deism and anticlericalism of the Enlightenment *philosophes* fostered negative attitudes toward the clergy that later manifested themselves in the Revolution's policies.[3] Furet's contention showed the influence of the eminent historian of the French Revolution, François-Alphonse Aulard. He disputed Barruel's *thèse du complot* and argued instead that the circumstances of the time (*thèse des circonstances*)— such as invasion, civil war, and the economic crisis—dictated the Revolutionary governments' stances vis-à-vis the Catholic Church. Desperate times called for desperate measures. For example, with the state facing bankruptcy, the Revolutionary government in 1789 and 1790 needed cash fast. So, it confiscated all the Church's lands and sold them off to raise money. Again, when France's neighbors declared war in 1792 and parts of the countryside became embroiled in civil strife, the more radical National Convention and Committee of Public Safety needed a ready means of distinguishing friend from foe. Thus, laws against the clergy, the Church, and religious practice were intended to tell who truly supported the new regime and who did not. As Aulard interpreted these instances, the events—not an insidious, concerted plot to undermine the Church in France—dictated the actions of the government .[4]

Both the *thèse du complot* and the *thèse des circonstances* attributed the religious crisis of the Revolution to the machinations of external, ambivalent forces. Nineteenth- and early-twentieth-century religious authors, on the other hand, have tended to blame the Catholic Church itself for its fate during the last decade of the eighteenth century. Abbé Augustin Sicard, who exemplified this school, blamed the corruption, apathy, and lack of discipline of the French clergy throughout the eighteenth century for weakening the Gallican Church to such a degree that it could not resist the onslaught of the anticlerical legislators at the century's end. He saved some of his harshest criticism for the religious orders which he described as having degenerated beyond hope of reform.[5]

Historians since the mid twentieth century have built on the methodology of Sicard by investigating the state of religion and the Church in pre-Revolutionary France for clues to the origins of the Revolution's effect on Catholicism and the clergy. Michel Vovelle, one of the most influential of these contemporary historians, argued that the intellectual, social, and political roots of the Revolutionary policies could be traced at least to the mid eighteenth century, if not earlier. In his various works, Vovelle concluded that the measures taken to break

---

3. Cochin, *La Révolution et la libre-pensée,* 164–204.
4. Aulard, *Christianity and the French Revolution,* 13–14, 97–100.
5. Sicard, *Le Clergé,* I, 276–308.

the Church's position of authority in society during the Revolution merely made official an escalating secular attitude which had begun to permeate French society long before 1789. For example, his study of wills and bequests in Southern France during the seventeenth and eighteenth centuries indicated a change in language. Fewer testaments included invocations to God and the saints for eternal salvation or generous donations to religious establishments than in previous centuries. He interpreted this as the germination of the secularization that came into full bloom with the Revolution's religious policies.[6]

One of the aspects of Vovelle's work that rendered it so seminal to the study of religion during the French Revolution was its emphasis on the importance of regional studies to the understanding of the complexity of this topic. Writers in the nineteenth century viewed the Revolution through Parisian eyes, but Aulard's forays into the archives of the provinces sparked the interests of regional authors in the role that their areas played in these events.[7] Surveying data from various departments was one of the hinges of Vovelle's argument; if different regions of France witnessed the same decrease in clerical support and the same increase in secular terminology in wills, then his thesis could perhaps apply to France as a whole.[8]

More recent scholars have questioned the conclusions of Vovelle and Sicard. While agreeing that looking backward provides insight into Revolutionary attitudes toward the Church, historians like Dale Van Kley and Nigel Aston have not perceived either Sicard's complete ecclesiastical degeneration or Vovelle's progressive secularization. On the contrary, Van Kley and Aston acknowledge that the Church faced serious challenges to its authority from both inside and outside its ranks, but the very fact that these controversies existed attests to the influence which the Church still possessed in eighteenth-century France.[9]

Vovelle's insistence on analyzing the French Revolution from the view-point of various regions of France, and not just from the capital, has found wide acceptance among historians. At the same time though, they have challenged his assertion that such research will render a homogeneous picture for the entire nation. Most notably, Timothy Tackett's assessment of regional acceptance or rejection of one piece of Revolutionary religious legislation, the Civil Constitution of the Clergy, confirmed that attitudes toward religion and the Church before 1789

---

6. Vovelle, *Piété baroque,* 610; Vovelle, *The Revolution against the Church,* 1–24
7. Vovelle, The Revolution against the Church, 3.
8. See Ibid., 183–95 for Michel Vovelle's charts on his de-Christianization data for the various departments.
9. Van Kley, *The Religious Origins of the French Revolution,* 4–6; Aston, *Religion and Revolution,* 54–56. For Catholic opposition to the Enlightenment, see McMahon, *Enemies of the Enlightenment.*
10. Tackett, *Religion, Revolution, and Regional Culture,* 287–300.
11. Clergy who belong to a religious order which follows a monastic rule are called *regulars,* from the Latin word *regula* meaning rule. Diocesan clergy who minister to parishes are called *seculars.*

were reflected in the events which followed. However, the extent of that influence and the experiences beyond Paris were hardly uniform.[10]

In discussing the Catholic Church during the French Revolution, historians for the most part have devoted little research to the fate of the male members of the religious orders; the female religious have received much greater attention. Yet, the men of the cloisters were among the first to feel the effects of the measures taken by the National Assembly shortly after the fall of the Bastille. On 13 February 1790, the National Assembly passed a decree which suppressed the regular clergy; current members were given a choice between continuing some form of communal life or secularizing.[11] Most of the men, including Dom Gourdin, opted for the latter. Sicard ascribed this apparent willingness to vacate the cloister to the manifestation of the degeneration and interaction with secular society which characterized the orders before the Revolution. Vovelle's thesis seems to fit well with such an evaluation; these men eagerly embraced life outside the monasteries in 1790 because the spirit of secularization had already penetrated the abbey walls decades before.

This assumption, however, oversimplifies the experiences of these men. An appreciation and assessment of the condition of the individuals in the regular clergy during the late eighteenth century requires a controlled, narrow, and thorough inspection of one order in one region. Few historians have attempted such a study. Those who have—Bernard Plongeron, who researched religious orders in Paris, and Claude Muller, who collected data on Alsatian Benedictines—have rejected the notion that the Revolution provided the final push which brought down the monastic walls, already crumbling from the rot of decadence, lack of discipline, and discontent with the communal lifestyle.[12] Rather, as even Aulard's cursory work on the regular clergy seemed to suggest, the religious orders may have faced challenges both internally and externally, but the communal vitality and the scholarly and charitable activities in which some religious houses still engaged neither precipitated nor necessitated the 13 February 1790 suppression decree.[13]

Limiting its focus, this study will first assess the Benedictines of the Congregation of Saint-Maur in upper Normandy (which includes the two departments of Seine-Inférieure, presently Seine-Maritime, and Eure) before the Revolution. The eighteenth century did witness increasing interaction between these monks and the world beyond their cloister walls. This work aims to examine if these secular associations inspired disenchantment with the monastic lifestyle and influenced these men to welcome the suppression of their Congregation as the opportunity to completely discard any attachments to their former, unsatisfying religious vocations. This study takes the innovative approach of tracing the lives of these monks *after* 1790 to ascertain whether their occupations and actions after

12. Plongeron, *Les Réguliers de Paris,* 69; Muller, *Les Bénédictins.*
13. Plongeron, *Les Réguliers de Paris,* 69; Aulard, ed., *La Révolution française,* 12–13

the suppression of their Congregation betrayed a discontent with their former religious identities.

One of the reasons historians have not explored the topic of the regular clergy during the Revolution is the lack of available sources due to their destruction during the French Revolution and the World Wars. Fortunately, most of the documents on upper Normandy's numerous Maurist abbeys have been preserved, thanks in part to Dom Gourdin who became the librarian for the department of Seine-Inférieure. Also, the archives of upper Normandy received relatively little damage during World War II, compared to those of lower Normandy. Furthermore, since upper Normandy had such a substantial Maurist population, the monasteries from this region figured prominently in the works of the Congregation's historians, such as the eighteenth-century writers Dom Edmond Martène and Dom René Prosper Tassin.[14]

The biggest challenge of this study was following the monks and their experiences after the National Assembly suppressed the orders. None of the individuals examined in this work left memoirs and the references to them in the recollections and correspondences of their contemporaries were infrequent. In the 1960s however, the *Revue Mabillon*, a Belgian Benedictine journal named for the most famous monk of the Congregation of Saint-Maur, published the names, personal information, and even archival citations of all the members of the Congregation in 1790.[15] This data, based on the list compiled by the Congregation's last general superior in 1790 and presently in the *Archives nationales*, provided the groundwork to trace these individuals in the documents of the national, departmental, and municipal governments.[16] Such sources have rarely been used for the study of the regular clergy after its suppression. Without this invaluable list of names to serve as a guide, it would be almost impossible to trace monks in the government documents which only sporadically record *ci-devant religieux* or *ex-Bénédictin de la Congrégation de Saint-Maur* next to the names of these men. Thus, a prepared list of names, supplemented by Emile Sévestre's published lists of the clergy in upper Normandy during the Revolution and the reign of Napoleon, opened new avenues of resources. Pension records indicated how long these men lived in the vicinity of their abbeys after 1790, while the cartons on the constitutional church and the *police des cultes* provided information on the careers of those who swore the oath to the Civil Constitution of the Clergy and practiced their sacerdotal duties from 1790 onward.[17]

---

14. Martène, *Histoire de la Congrégation,* I–IX; Tassin, *Histoire littéraire*

15. "Les Religieux de la Congrégation," 45–72, 101–68, 157–219, 219–50, 253–91.

16. AN, D XIX, 10, no. 147. Based on this information, a list of the monks who lived in the Maurist houses of upper Normandy in 1790 is available in Appendix A and those who moved to that region after 1790 can be found in Appendix D. For this study, the Archives nationales document has provided the spelling of monks' names, unless otherwise indicated. Modern spelling has been used for place names.

17. Sévestre, *L'Enquête gouvernementale;* Sévestre, *Le Personnel de l'église.*

18. Bellenger, "'Superstitious enemies,'" 153, 158.

Based on research from national and regional archives, this examination of the experiences of the Norman Maurists in the eighteenth century and their increased connections with secular society does *not* reveal an insidious dissatisfaction with their religious vocations which resulted in the absolute abandonment of those vocations after the 13 February 1790 decree of suppression. Thus, this study supports neither Vovelle's theory of a secularizing century before the Revolution nor the notion of Sicard and others that monastic degeneration precipitated the National Assembly's suppression legislation. As the initial zeal for monastic reform and scholarly achievement, which earned the Congregation of Saint-Maur its legendary renown, began to moderate, the Congregation, like all religious orders in the eighteenth century, faced internal and external challenges as described in Chapter 1. In Chapter 2, the presence of young men in the order and the continuation of their academic pursuits reflected the Congregation's persistent vitality and its ability to weather conflicts. The interaction of monks with the temporal world during this period often resulted from their research, as they sought comparison and intellectual exchange with their fellow academics. In this way, they made integral contributions to Enlightenment scholarship.[18] Furthermore, *Enlightenment piety*—as defined by Aston, the growing interest in charitable works among the laity—also brought the religious into contact with their secular neighbors, and monks and laity often cooperated on alimentary projects as exemplified by the freemasons and the Maurists in the town of Fécamp.[19]

Chapter 3 highlights the active role which the members of the Congregation played in the preliminary assemblies for the calling of the Estates-General in 1789 and in the composition of the *cahiers de doléances* for their Estate. Although the Norman Maurist who sat in the National Assembly did not speak out in opposition to the proposed suppression of the religious orders, his fellow monks did voice their disapproval of the project. The declarations which they made to their local municipal officials after the passing of the suppression decree highlight the attachment of these Maurists to their religious state. Many stated that they would leave only because circumstances required it. Had the Revolutionary policies on religion resulted from a condition which had taken root in the previous decades, then most of these monks would have failed to maintain any connection with their previous religious identities after vacating their cloisters. Yet, this was certainly not the case for the Maurists in the Benedictine-saturated region of upper Normandy.

Chapter 4 describes how some ex-monks preserved their religious identities in varying degrees by choosing to live in or near their former abbeys or taking jobs particularly suited to the Maurist's love of learning. That other former monks maintained their religious vocations in a very direct way and fostered their bonds with the laity as parish priests in the constitutional church is detailed in Chapters 5 and 6. Whichever path these men chose, Chapters 7 and 8 illustrate that

19.   Aston, *Religion and Revolution,* 55–56.

even the threats of imprisonment, deportation, and death during the Revolution's de-Christianization phase and during the final years of the Directory could not dissuade them from persevering in their ecclesiastical vocations. Those who did submit to the government's attacks on the core of their religious identities—the priesthood—attempted to rehabilitate their ministry during the Directory, and after Bonaparte ended the controversy over the Civil Constitution of the Clergy by signing the Concordat with Pope Pius VII. Thus, a focused and thorough investigation of the experiences of an understudied subset of the clergy demonstrates the vitality which religious orders such as the Congregation of Saint-Maur enjoyed before the French Revolution and the unique, and at times, heroic ways in which former monks maintained connections to their religious vocations after the National Assembly forced them from their cloisters.

Figure 1

MAURIST MONASTERIES
IN THE DEPARTMENT OF EURE

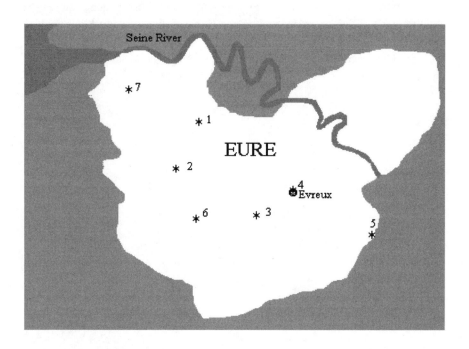

1. Notre-Dame du Bec
2. Notre-Dame de Bernay
3. Saint-Pierre et Saint-Paul de Châtillon-lès-Conches
4. Saint-Taurin d'Évreux
5. Notre-Dame d'Ivry
6. Notre-Dame de Lyre
7. Saint-Pierre de Préaux

Figure 2
MAURIST MONASTERIES
IN THE DEPARTMENT OF SEINE-INFÉRIEURE

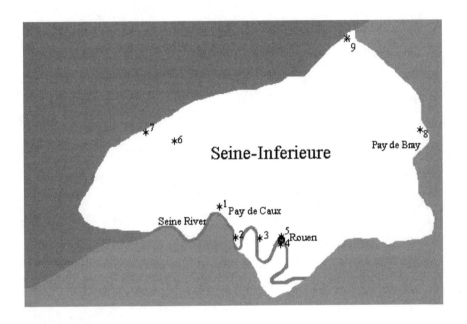

1. Saint-Wandrille de Fontenelle
2. Saint-Pierre de Jumièges
3. Saint-Georges de Boscherville
4. Notre-Dame de Bonne-Nouvelle de Rouen
5. Saint-Ouen de Rouen
6. Notre-Dame de Valmont
7. Sainte-Trinité de Fécamp
8. Saint-Pierre d'Auchy d'Aumale
9. Saint-Michel de Tréport

CHAPTER I

BENEDICTINE REFORM AND THE FOUNDATION OF THE CONGREGATION OF SAINT-MAUR

The late seventeenth-century Maurist historian Dom Edmond Martène described the Benedictine Order in France as in a state of total dilapidation before the introduction of the reform movement of the Congregation of Saint-Maur, "Nearly all the monasteries were in the worst relaxation. God was not served in them. Many religious had never read their rule; there were even some who did not know to what order they belonged."[1] While Martène may have exaggerated somewhat, the Congregation of Saint-Maur did become the most influential and esteemed branch of the Benedictines in France during the seventeenth and eighteenth centuries. Its reform platform, the likes of which France had not seen since the Cluniacs in the tenth century or the Cistercians in the twelfth century, claimed to promote strict enforcement of the Rule of Saint Benedict. At the same time, the Congregation adapted the Rule to create a strong, centralized leadership for the order which overcame the limitations and defects of the Gallican practice of commendatory abbots and prevented the depopulation of its houses. The Maurists fulfilled Saint Benedict's first command for *ora* by requiring both communal and private prayer; they performed their *labora* in the realm of academia by producing seminal works in the fields of history, science, philosophy, and theology. In upper Normandy, they restored monastic discipline to some of France's most ancient establishments, rebuilding edifices and turning decaying structures into vibrant, grandiose communities of worship.

Demands for reform of the monastic orders resounded throughout the Tridentine Church during the late sixteenth and early seventeenth centuries. The first successful effort to reinvigorate the Benedictine order in Western Europe originated with a program arranged by the commendatory abbot of the abbey of Saint-Vanne in Lorraine. Insisting on stricter adherence to the Rule of Saint Benedict regarding the canonical hours, fasting and hard work, Dom Didier de la Cour

---

1. Martène, *Histoire de la Congrégation,* I, 6; Simon "Réforme de Saint-Maur," 251.

1

received papal sanction in 1604 to promulgate his disciplinary stimulus plan to other Benedictine establishments. It spread rapidly throughout the order's houses of Champagne and Alsace; all who adopted this reform became part of the Congregation of Saint-Vanne, under the authority of the abbot of the order's motherhouse in Lorraine. Spurred on by this success, Didier de La Cour conceived a project to extend the Vannist system to monasteries in all parts of France. King Louis XIII, however, refused to allow French monasteries to pledge obedience to a motherhouse in the Holy Roman Empire. (Lorraine did not become a province of France until 1766.) [2] For the king to endorse a reform movement within his borders, it had to encompass French houses exclusively, with the nucleus located within his realm.

Determined to see the discipline of St. Benedict's Rule enforced in the French monasteries with the same fervor as at his abbey of Saint-Vanne, Dom Didier de La Cour cooperated with the prior of the college of Cluny in Paris in adjusting the system to meet the demands of the king. In 1618, delegates from various French Benedictine establishments met at the abbey of Blancs-Manteaux in Paris. They agreed to follow the platform of Didier de la Cour but only extend it to houses within France and locate the motherhouse at Saint-Germain-des-Près in Paris. To further underscore the Gallican nature of this reform movement, the delegates to this first general chapter placed this reform movement under the patronage of Saint-Maur, a disciple of Saint Benedict who, according to legend, had introduced the Rule of Saint Benedict into France.[3] The king granted his approval of the Congregation of Saint-Maur in 1619.[4] Pope Gregory XV issued a papal bull of establishment on 17 March 1621; reconfirmation of the Maurist reform arrived from Rome in 1628. Three years later, the general chapter unanimously elected Dom Grégoire Tarisse as superior general of the order and commissioned him to draw up the official constitutions for the new Congregation. After much debate the final draft received the approbation of the general chapter in 1645.[5]

The Maurist goal was to restore strict adherence to the Rule of Saint Benedict in the houses which embraced the Congregation. However, similar to the Cluniac movement of the tenth century, the constitutions of Saint-Maur included some adjustments to the Rule. St. Benedict had stipulated a decentralized governance with each monastery managed by an abbot and only loosely connected to other establishments. The Cluny reformers however had recognized that a centralized leadership aided in the prevention of abuse and relaxation. Therefore, they placed priors at the heads of each house; each prior then reported to the abbot of

2. Cousin, *Précis d'histoire,* 426.
3. Simon, *"Réforme de Saint-Maur,"* 585; Cousin, *Précis d'histoire,* 426; Baudot, *Normandie bénédictine* (Pacy-sur-Eure, 1979), 71.
4. Martène, *Histoire de la Congrégation,* I, 59–60; Beaunier, *Recueil historique,* 90; Baudot, *Normandie bénédictine,* 71; Cousin, *Précis d'histoire,* 426.
5. Martène, *Histoire de la Congrégation,* I, 95–97, 224; Lemoine, *Le Monde de religieux,* 29; Beaunier, *Recueil historique,* 95; Simon, *"Réforme de Saint-Maur,"* 585.

Cluny who governed the whole order. The Maurist constitutions sought to emulate Cluny's hierarchical structure by appointing priors to oversee the day-to-day functioning of individual monasteries while the superior general served as the executive power of the entire Congregation. The final authority, though, rested with the Congregation's general chapter. Convened every three years on the fourth Friday after Easter, the order's representative body, the general chapter, included the superior general, his two assistants, the provincial visitors, and the deputies from each of the houses. The delegates to the general chapter passed legislation, elected new superior generals, selected new priors to govern the individual communities, and designated visitors for the six Maurist provinces of France.[6] The visitors—another Cluniac innovation—had the twofold task of inspecting the abbeys in their assigned areas and convening provincial diets on the years between the meetings of the general chapters. Although more complex than Saint Benedict's regulations, this organization was designed to protect against corruption and contribute to monastic health and growth.[7]

The constitutions of the Congregation did make other innovations to the Rule, particularly regarding the vow of monastic stability. In the past, this vow required the monk to live his life in one monastery and to safeguard its well-being as long as it remained in existence. Members of the Congregation of Saint-Maur on the other hand swore stability to the entire Congregation which meant that the general chapter could move individuals from house to house within the order. While this seemed in direct violation of the Rule of Saint Benedict, it did in fact aid in the survival and perpetuation of the reform movement. To facilitate the better education of monks, one or two houses in each province served as training centers for novices, ensuring that all future monks received an equal and satisfactory training before receiving their monastic assignments. Furthermore, since the order shifted men from one community to another, no Maurist house ever suffered from depopulation, a problem that plagued many other religious orders in the eighteenth century.[8]

In terms of monastic discipline, the reform of Saint-Maur did follow the letter of the Rule with the Benedictine duality of *ora et labora*. Every monk spent one hour each day in personal meditation in addition to the communal divine office and the Mass. The movement also encouraged monks to practice acts of mortification, denying themselves not only meat but even fish. For *labora*, Maurists

6. Beaunier, *Recueil historique,* 95; Cousin, *Précis d'histoire,* 427; Simon, *"Réforme de Saint-maur,"* 587.

7. Lemoine, *Le Monde de religieux,* 30; Cousin, *Précis d'histoire,* 427. The superior general could hold this office indefinitely while the positions of visitor and prior were only renewable once.

8. Mathan, *"Deux abbayes voisines,"* 312; Lemoine, *Le Monde de religieux,* 32, 400; Simon, *"Réforme de Saint-Maur,"* 589; Cousin, *Précis d'histoire,* 428. Monks rarely transferred to houses outside the Maurist province in which they had made their professions. The case of Dom Guillaume Picheré serves as an exception; the general chapter sent him from the Burgundy province to the Norman abbey of Fécamp in order to take over the abbey's illustrious music program ["Des minutes du greffe de hôtel de ville de Fécamp," AN, F19 6113; Montier, "Les Moines de Fécamp," III, 205].

engaged in labor of the mind and distinguished themselves, throughout France and abroad, for their intellectual endeavors. Men such as Dom Jean Mabillon and Dom Bernard de Montfaucon became some of the most celebrated scholars of their age.[9]

The zeal for reform of the Congregation's members proved so persuasive and the Maurist constitutions so appealing that not long after its establishment, the Congregation had become the largest branch of the Benedictine Order in France. It incorporated such famous houses as the royal necropolis Saint-Denis and Saint-Benoît-sur-Loire in its ranks.[10] In upper Normandy, which had one of the heaviest concentration of Maurists in the entire nation, nearly all of the Benedictine monasteries that survived until the French Revolution adopted the Congregation's reform. The ancient abbey of Saint-Pierre-de-Jumièges acted as the vanguard by first embracing the Vannists in 1604; however, in November 1608 the *Parlement* of Normandy forbade all establishments within its jurisdiction from adopting a foreign reform movement. In 1616, Jumièges became one of the first abbeys in all of France to rally to the new Gallican form of Benedictine renewal and even sent a representative to the Congregation's general chapter in 1618.[11] At the same time, the commendatory abbot of Saint-Pierre-de-Préaux demanded that Maurists colonize his abbey and reinfuse it with fervor for the cenobitic life. After witnessing the success which the Congregation had in houses such as Jumièges, other commendatory abbots, over the next century and a half, invited the members of the Congregation to do likewise for their holdings in upper Normandy. By 1760, when the Benedictine house of Notre-Dame-de-Valmont became the last in the region to join the ranks of the reformed, the Maurist province of Normandy, the largest of the Congregation's six divisions, contained thirty-one monasteries.[12]

---

9. Tassin, *Histoire littéraire*, 205–69; 585–616; de Viguerie, *"Les Abbayes mauristes,"* 215; Baudot, *Normandie bénédictine*, 71; Simon, *"Réforme de Saint-Maur,"* 611; Cousin, *Précis d'histoire*, 428; Lemoine, *Le Monde de religieux*, 32. Some ascetic practices bordered on the extreme such as the story of a monk who allowed himself to nearly hemorrhage to death rather than break the regulation of silence during the night.

10. Beaunier, *Recueil historique*, 91–92. Cardinal de Richelieu even proposed, unsuccessfully, combining all the other branches of the Benedictine order with the Congregation of Saint-Maur. The Chezal-Benoît branch of Benedictines did merge with the Maurists in 1636.

11. Martène, *Histoire de la Congrégation*, I, 43. One of the oldest monasteries in northern France, Jumièges was founded in the seventh century. The Benedictine community, which once counted 900 monks, thrived under the Merovingians and Carolingians until the Vikings burned it and dispersed its population in the ninth century. Although rebuilt in the tenth and eleventh centuries, Jumièges' buildings suffered from dilapidation and its monks from relaxation of the Rule during the Hundred Years War and the Wars of Religion. To remedy the situation, the commendatory abbots introduced the Benedictine reform of Chezal-Benoît in 1515, the Congregation of Saint-Vanne in 1616, and finally the Maurists in 1618. Nearly the entire monastery complex was dismantled during the French Revolution, but the skeleton of the church still remained as one of the finest examples of Norman architecture and as a symbol of upper Normandy [*Répertoire des abbayes et prieurés de Seine-Maritime*, 79].

12. de Viguerie, *"Les Abbayes mauristes,"* 210–11; Simon, *"Réforme de Saint-Maur,"* 585; Baudot, *Normandie bénédictine*, 71. First mentioned in 833, Saint-Pierre-de-Préaux may have been destroyed by the Vikings before monks from Saint-Wandrille recolonized it in the eleventh century. It was demolished after its closure in 1791 [Charles, de La Conté, and C. Lannette, *Répertoire des abbayes*, 46].

In Normandy, as in the rest of France, the adoption of the Maurist reform did not always proceed uncontested. When Maurist colonists settled in the Norman houses, some of the indigenous monks, labeled the Ancients, refused to accept a stricter interpretation of the Rule and the elimination of their relaxed lifestyle. Some of the old members even expressed open hostility toward the newcomers. At the famous abbey of Notre-Dame-du-Bec, the Ancients forced the members of the Congregation to live in the most decrepit buildings.[13] At Valmont the opposition grew so acrimonious that the Maurists had to wait until the death of the last Ancient in 1753 before they could fully place the abbey under the Congregation's leadership.[14] Even Jumièges' transition from Vannist to Maurist did not progress without malice, but the disharmony here as elsewhere finally ended in an accord between the reformers and the unreformed. Rather than force the Ancients of Jumièges to comply with the new regime, the Maurists agreed to allow them to remain in their community with their own lodging and their own prior. While the Congregation had control over the monastery's offices and communal worship, the Ancients could join their counterparts in the choir if they so desired.[15]

In rare instances, some Norman establishments welcomed Maurist discipline with much ceremony and apparent willingness on the part of the current occupants. François de Péricard, bishop of Évreux, celebrated a pontifical Mass on Quinquagesima Sunday, 1642, for the formal installation of the Congregation in the abbey of Saint-Taurin at Évreux.[16] The monks of the Seine valley abbey, Saint-Wandrille-de-Fontenelle, voluntarily adopted the Congregation in 1636 after vain attempts to reform themselves without outside intervention. The Ancients of the

---

13. Martène, *Histoire de la Congrégation,* I, 191–93; Besnard, *Monographie de l'église,* 26; de Viguerie, "Les Abbayes mauristes," 210–11. Notre-Dame-de-Bec was founded in the eleventh century by the Norman knight Herluin, and under the leadership of Lanfranc of Pavia and Saint Anselm, it became one of the most renowned centers of learning in Northern Europe. The abbey buildings began to fall into disrepair in the sixteenth century, and the inhabitants became lax in their practice of the communal life. The Congregation of Saint-Maur, introduced in 1626–27, restored monastic discipline and undertook the reconstruction of the edifices. After the suppression of the abbey during the French Revolution, it became a horse depot for the army, and in 1802, Napoleon Bonaparte made it the headquarters of the fourteenth cohort of the Legion of Honor. In 1948, the French government allowed the Benedictines of the Congregation of Mont Olivet to return the abbey to its original function [Martène, *Histoire de la Congrégation,* I, 190, IV, 108–9; Charles, de La Conté, and Lannette, *Répertoire des abbayes,* 21; La Varende, *L'Abbaye du Bec-Hellouin,* 28].

14. Martin, *Notes pour servir à l'histoire,* 9; de Viguerie, "Les Abbayes mauristes," 211.

15. de Viguerie, "Les Abbayes mauristes," 211; Simon, "Réforme de Saint-Maur," 590.

16. Simon, "Réforme de Saint-Maur," 594. Named after the first bishop of Évreux, the abbey of Saint-Taurin suffered damage several times throughout its history, but it managed to survive each attack until the introduction of the Maurists in 1642. The church was converted into a saltpeter factory during the French Revolution and afterwards a parish church. [Charles, de La Conté, and Lannette, *Répertoire des abbayes,* 33–34].

17. Simon, "Réforme de Saint-Maur," 593; de Viguerie, "Les Abbayes mauristes," 210. Saint-Wandrille-de-Fontenelle was founded around 650 by its namesake Wandrille (major-domo to Dagobert I) who became a priest. The degradation which the abbey suffered during the fifteenth and sixteenth centuries convinced its inhabitants to willingly adopt the Maurist reform in 1636. After the Revolution, the church was demolished and the abbey buildings became the private residence of an English lord until Benedictine monks reinhabited it in 1898 [*Répertoire des abbayes,* 139–40].

abbey made a procession to neighboring Jumièges, gathered fifteen Maurists from that house and led them back to Saint-Wandrille where they solemnly entrusted the governance of their house to the invited colonizers.[17]

Implementation of the Congregation's constitution, especially in the realms of leadership and dedication to the ideal of *ora et labora*, promoted the reinvigoration of the Benedictine establishments of upper Normandy. The Maurist system of government in particular tried to prevent the worst effects of the commendatory system, one of the chief causes of decay in other religious houses from the sixteenth to the eighteenth centuries. During the Avignon captivity, popes began appointing bishops as abbots *in commendam* of powerful and wealthy monasteries. Prelates actively sought these appointments as means of raising revenue. The Concordat of 1516 transferred to King Francis I of France the right to appoint not only France's bishops, but also commendatory abbots. These absentee leaders received the benefice from their offices but did not have to live at the monasteries and serve the monks in the role of spiritual fathers as Saint Benedict had envisioned.[18] The income of a house with such an abbot was divided into three—not always equal—parts: the commendatory received the first part of the abbey's revenues, another part paid for building repairs and charity, and the monks used the remaining amount for their own needs.[19] This uneven distribution drove some houses into financial ruin. Nevertheless, by 1789, about eighty percent of the monasteries of all orders operated *in commendam*.[20]

By placing the prior at the head of an individual monastery and naming a superior general as the head of all, the Congregation of Saint-Maur adapted to the commendatory system and managed to prevent the obstacles which this practice often occasioned. In essence, the Maurist constitution rendered the abbot unnecessary for the functioning of the monastery, and in fact seemed to encourage his absenteeism. By the eighteenth century, the majority of the Maurist institutions of upper Normandy (with apparent indifference) allowed the king to dole them out as he willed. Revenues from smaller, less prosperous abbeys, such as Saint-Georges-de-Boscherville, went to clergy of lower rank, Claude de Cheylar, in this case.[21] Nominations for famous houses, on the other hand, went only to a top-ranking member of the upper clergy. Such a distinction was considered a mark

---

18. Sicard, *Le Clergé,* I, 276; Simon, "Réforme de Saint-Maur," 252–53.

19. Lekai, "Cistercian Monasteries and the French Episcopate," 73; Kessler, "The Suppression of the Benedictine Order, 3.

20. Simon, "Réforme de Saint-Maur," 252; Kessler, "The Suppression of the Benedictine Order," 4.

21. Besnard, *Monographie de l'église,* 30. William the Conqueror's grand chamberlain, Raoul de Tancarville, established the abbey of Saint-Georges-de-Boscherville as a sign of his devotion to Saint George. Although patronized by the kings and queens of England, it never achieved as much fame as its Seine valley neighbors, Jumièges and Saint-Wandrille. After the ravages of the Hundred Years War in the fourteenth and fifteenth centuries and the Protestants in the sixteenth century, the Maurists reconstructed its buildings upon their arrival in 1660. The church was saved from destruction during the Revolution thanks to the local townspeople who insisted on using it as their parish church [*Répertoire des abbayes,* 131–32].

of the king's favor, as the Comptroller General Étienne-Charles de Loménie de Brienne must have perceived his appointment by Louis XVI to the commend of Saint-Ouen-de-Rouen, one of the wealthiest abbeys in the realm.[22]

In a few instances, commendatory abbots played active roles in spreading the Maurist movement. Jacques Le Noël du Perron, the chaplain of the queen of England in 1642, and Monseigneur de Lort de Serignan-Valvras, the bishop of Mâcon in 1754, encouraged their commend abbeys of Saint-Taurin and Valmont to welcome the reform.[23] Most commendatory abbots, however, took little interest in their positions. Martial de Loménie de Brienne, nephew of the king's financial minister, only visited Jumièges once, for his abbatial installation ceremony, although he received an annual income of 80,000 livres from the benefice. De Cheylar preferred his Parisian salon to Saint-Georges-de-Boscherville and left it up to the priors and the leaders of the Congregation to enforce discipline and promote academic achievements in the monastery.[24] When the commendatories did meddle in abbey business, particularly regarding financial matters, they usually drew the ire of the inhabitants. The monks of Valmont even brought legal proceedings against their abbot in 1785.[25] There were of course the rare exceptions, commendatories who took a genuine interest in the benefices assigned to them. Cardinal Dominique de la Rochefoucauld, the archbishop of Rouen, personally traveled to Fécamp for his solemn installation as the beneficiary of the abbey of Sainte-Trinité and visited the port town again to aid the monks in their charitable distributions to the poor.[26] For the most part though, commendatory abbots preferred to ignore monastic affairs, and the Maurists seemed to foster this apathy.[27]

The Congregation had sought to return monastic inhabitants to the command for *ora* found in the Rule of Saint Benedict, and as the largest of the

---

22. de la Bunodière, *Derniers jours de l'abbaye de Saint-Ouen de Rouen,* 6; Deries, "La Vie d'unbibliothécaire," 209. Another Merovingian establishment dating from 535, the abbey of Saint-Ouen took its name from one of the first bishops of Rouen. The Maurists arrived in 1660 and reconstructed some of the abbey's buildings which then became the *hôtel de ville* of Rouen during the Revolution [*Répertoire des abbayes,* 108].

23. Martin, *Notes pour servir à l'histoire,* 9; Simon, "Réforme de Saint-Maur," 594.

24. Jouen, *Jumièges: Histoire et légendes,* 75; Savalle, Les Deniers moines, 14; Besnard, *Monographie de l'église,* 30.

25. Montier, "Les Moines de Fécamp," 176.

26. Martin, *Histoire de Fécamp,* II, 87; Bellamy, Bénédictins et Annonçiades, 17. One of Normandy's most illustrious abbeys, Sainte-Trinité-de-Fécamp was first established as a convent for nuns in the seventh century. After the Vikings sacked it and massacred its inhabitants, a group of canons reinhabited it in 938 and then the Benedictine monks moved in around 1000. The abbey became famous as a school for Gregorian chant and as a pilgrimage site due to its relic of the Precious Blood. It fell into disrepair during the Hundred Years War, and the Huguenots vandalized it during the Wars of Religion. The Maurists, introduced in 1642, restored it to its original splendor and prestige, but their continued production of its famous liqueur "Benedictine," gave the abbey its most enduring legacy. During the French Revolution, the church became the parish church of Sainte-Trinité. As for the liqueur, the manuscript containing the recipe was lost during the Revolution but rediscovered by an entrepreneur named Alexandre Le Grand who resumed production during the second half of the nineteenth century [Répertoire des abbayes, 55–56].

27. Loth, *Histoire du Cardinal,* 30. Dom Robert Lemoine claimed that abuses of the commendatory system were rarely cited in the eighteenth century [Lemoine, *Le Monde de religieux,* 386].

Congregation's provinces, Normandy witnessed a flourishing of cenobitic spirituality in the years following the introduction of the reform. First and foremost, this meant scrupulously following the canonical hours, even rising in the middle of the night despite the winter's cold. Jumièges' priors did allow their monks a few moments by the fire after the 2:00 A.M. matins, but at the same time, they inflicted harsh punishments on choir no-shows or on those who chanted off-key. This Norman abbey gained such a reputation for the piety of its dwellers that the Maurist historian Dom René Prosper Tassin hailed one of its priors, Dom Claude Martin, as "one of the holiest religious and the greatest superior, not only of the Congregation of Saint-Maur, but perhaps of the whole order of Saint Benedict at that time."[28]

The Norman Maurists poured their energy into their scholarly *labora*, but they also labored physically for the restoration of their abbey buildings.[29] The dilapidated state in which the first colonizers found these ancient establishments prompted them to undertake extensive building projects to restore the churches to their original splendor. They also erected new structures in the baroque and neoclassical styles of which Saint-Ouen's abbatial edifices serve as the best example.[30] When the Maurists finally arrived at Valmont, they infused new blood into the abbey, and within six years they had nearly rebuilt its structures from ruin.[31] Saint-Michel-de-Tréport's denizens even carried out their renovation at the expense of their own well-being, at times surviving on week-old potage in order to secure enough building funds.[32] The monks of Sainte-Trinité succeeded in turning their Fécamp community into a pilgrimage center in the medieval tradition. Possessing drops of the Precious Blood of Christ, they converted their entire abbey into a reliquary of Eucharistic devotion with magnificent artwork, furniture, vestments and a golden monstrance in order to display their sanguinary relic beneath a white marble baldachin.[33]

The Maurist reform in Normandy, as in the rest of France, restored discipline to the Benedictine life for an illustrious century and a half. During this time, the Maurists distinguished themselves for their scholarship and dedication to the Rule of Saint Benedict. However, during the eighteenth century the Congregation could not escape the insidious torpidity which had plagued the unreformed orders for centuries. Lack of discipline, allegations of financial and administrative

---

28. Tassin, *Histoire littéraire,* 163; Savalle, *Les Deniers moines,* 14; de Viguerie, "Les Abbayes mauristes," 215.

29. See Chapter 2 for the scholastic achievements of Norman Maurists.

30. Boivin-Champeaux, *Notice pour servir à l'histoire,* 230–31; de Viguerie, "Les Abbayes mauristes," 213; Baudot, *Normandie bénédictine,* 93.

31. Martin, *Notes pour servir à l'histoire,* 7, 9, 21.

32. de Viguerie, "Les Abbayes mauristes," 212. Seeking to emulate his father (Duke Richard I of Normandy, who founded Mont-Saint-Michel), Count Robert d'Eu founded the abbey of Saint-Michel-de-Tréport; however, this endowment did not achieve the fame of Mont-Saint-Michel. It prospered during the thirteenth century and was revitalized by the Maurists in the seventeenth century but was destroyed after 1791 [*Répertoire des abbayes,* 148].

33. Bellamy, "La Vie religieuse," 45; de Viguerie, "Les Abbayes mauristes," 215.

mismanagement, the presence of individuals without a true monastic calling, and increasing sympathy for the Jansenist movement afflicted the Congregation from within its own ranks and gave the impression that even the Maurists had gone soft. The order also suffered attacks from the outside as the *philosophes* in the secular realm assailed the very concept of communal life. The *Commission des Réguliers*, established by the king to suggest measures for reforming the entire body of the regular clergy, took particular interest in the Congregation of Saint-Maur. The *Commission*'s chief motivator, Loménie de Brienne, and the Maurist leadership tried to restore the order to their primitive reform in the decade before the French Revolution.

One of the chief sources of criticism of eighteenth-century monasticism stemmed from the same issue that the original Maurists had sought to remedy, relaxation of the Rule. After 150 years of fervor and austerity in the spirit of Saint Benedict, the Norman houses of the Congregation began to palliate the most self-mortifying aspects of monastic life. At Jumièges, dispensations could excuse the monks from compulsory matins or Mass attendance.[34] The refectory, like the choir, also witnessed amelioration of the Rule's rigors. Since monks could not eat any meat except fish, Jumièges' procurer, who had the task of obtaining the necessary food and supplies for the abbey, traveled every week to Dieppe for the choicest seafood. The keeper of the monastery's cellar on the other hand journeyed to Burgundy once a year to purchase the wine supply for his fellow brothers.[35] The men at Saint-George-de-Boscherville enjoyed their coffee, tea, liqueurs, chocolates and tobacco in violation of the Rule's dietary restrictions.[36] According to Saint Benedict, leaving the monastery required the permission of the superior, but the monks of Jumièges seemed to enter and leave the gates at will, taking walks along the Seine and playing board games at a nearby farmhouse.[37]

In upper Normandy complaints about monastic immorality seemed scarce in the eighteenth century; the only apparent case—of dubious credibility—involved Dom Antoine Alexandre Joseph de Saulty who had to leave Jumièges and move to Saint-Étienne in Caen because he allegedly had taken a fancy to a young village girl.[38] Much more commonplace, on the other hand, were accusations of

---

34. Sicard, Le Clergé, I, 308–9; Lemoine, *Le Monde de religieux,* 35; Savalle, Les Derniers moines, 15.

35. Savalle, *Les Derniers moines,* 17.

36. Ibid.; de Viguerie, "Les Abbayes mauristes," 219; Lemarchand, "Les Monastères de Haute-Normandie," 23.

37. Savalle, *Les Derniers moines,* 15; Deshayes, *Histoire de l'abbaye royal,* 161.

38. Savalle, *Les Derniers moines,* 27. Savalle does not give any sources for his salacious tale about de Saulty. While documents and primary accounts verify some of his other information, nothing appears to exist which can confirm such indiscretion by any of the monks at Jumièges. All other secondary works which repeat this story quote Savalle. This author perhaps misunderstood the Maurist concept of stability and assumed that de Saulty's dislocation resulted from some transgression. Dom de Saulty did return to Jumièges after the suppression of the religious orders in 1790, and later abdicated his priesthood there. Although he became the mayor of Jumièges during the reign of Napoleon, he never married ["Les Religieux de la Congrégation," 56, no. 226 (Oct-Dec 1966): 123].

mismanagement and faulty record keeping such as Dom Antoine François Dechy leveled against his procurer predecessor at Saint-Wandrille. Incompetent steward-ship occasioned by the prior of Valmont, Dom Jean Collibeaux, had caused such deterioration in that abbey's financial and administrative affairs that he lost his position in 1788.[39] The orderly balance sheets of his replacement, Dom Placide Joseph Monthois, received high praise from the municipal administration in 1790, but the monastery still had to float 2,700 livres in loans in 1788 and 1789.[40] De-nunciations of tyranny against the "deceitful prior" of Jumièges, Dom Pierre Ar-mand Bride, flowed liberally from the acrid, frequently employed pen of Dom Toussaint Outin.[41] Further scathing criticism of Dom Bride's priorship by Dom Charles Matthieu Allix seemed to betray an underlying distrust of superiors in general and a breakdown of central authority. As the debates over the fate of mo-nasticism in France raged in the National Assembly in 1790, Dom Allix wrote to the legislative body charging his prior with attempting to remove or conceal the most precious objects of the monastery. According to the complainant, Dom Bride intended to take these treasures with him if the Assembly decreed the termination of the Congregation.[42]

In the realm of finances, the revenues of nearly all Norman Maurist es-tablishments seemed to more than double in the eighteenth century. Fécamp, the wealthiest abbey in the province of Normandy, saw its annual income from feudal dues elevated to 140,000 livres, engendering the expression, "From every direc-tion that the wind blows, the abbey of Fécamp collects rents."[43] The agricultural improvements of the eighteenth century and the blossoming of Norman industry benefited smaller houses as well. Saint-Georges-de-Boscherville, often overshad-owed by its illustrious neighbors Saint-Wandrille and Jumièges, quadrupled its earning from 10,000 livres (c. 1700) to 40,000 livres (in 1790).[44] Yet, despite all these indications of economic expansion, how individual establishments managed their good fortune meant the difference between solvency and destitution.

With the exception of the poor administration of Valmont during Dom

---

39. Frère H. L., "Dom Antoine Fidèle Dechy: Le Dernier cellérier de Saint-Wandrille avant la Révolution," ASWF (1980), 11; Montier, "Les Moines de Fécamp," 176–78.

40. Directory of the department of Seine-Inférieure to the directory of the district of Cany, 1 February 1791, ADSM, L 2593; Martin, *Notes pour servir à l'histoire,* 36–37, 49.

41. Dom Toussaint Outin to the National Assembly, 22 June 1790, AN, D XIX 59, liasse 268; Montier, "Les Moines de Fécamp," 281, f. 135. Dom Outin also denounced the Congregation's top leadership which he described as the "cruelly despotic regime . . . of our officials, abominable, egotistical, without religious principles, without social sense."

42. Dom Matthieu Charles Allix to the president of the National Assembly, 20 November 1789, AN, D XIX 14, liasse 206, 2nd.

43. Bellamy, *Bénédictins et Annonçiades,* 17; Cousin, *Précis d'histoire,* 472; Lemarchand, "Les Monastères de Haute-Normandie," 15–16; de Viguerie, "Les Abbayes mauristes," 291. Guy Lemarchand provides a more detailed assessment of monastic revenues during the eighteenth century, taking into account inflation. He attributes monastic debt to the deficit-spending spirit of the ancien regime which perceived increased revenues as license for even greater expenditures, especially on the luxuries which contributed to monastic decadence [Lemarchand, "Les Monastères de Haute-Normandie," 26].

44. Besnard, *Monographie de l'église,* 30.

Collibeaux's priorship, smaller communities appeared particularly scrupulous in maintaining their financial stability. The rural and sparsely populated Notre-Dame-de-Lyre seemed to prosper under the priorship of Dom Pierre Hommeril who boasted that he found the abbey in debt 76,000 livres and in one year left it producing an annual profit of 15,000 livres.[45] Perhaps a rather exaggerated claim, but in 1790, the directory of the district of Breteuil declared that the abbey's finances did just barely break even.[46]

In the capable hands of Dom Alexis Davoust, Saint-Ouen remained the exception for urban establishments, showing a profit in spite of lavish building reconstructions and the luxuries tolerated by a relaxation of the Rule.[47] Other Norman abbeys with vast feudal holdings and extensive sources of income could still end up in the red due to incompetent fiscal management. The procurer and wine-cellar keeper had procured the Burgundy wine and chocolate luxuries for the monks of Jumièges at the expense of the monastery's financial solvency. Although it had experienced a doubling of revenues during the eighteenth century, on the eve of the suppression, the abbey had to sell the lead from the roof of the Norman Romanesque church in order to satisfy its most pressing debts.[48]

As if lack of respect for the order's leadership and budgetary insufficiencies did not lower monastic morale enough, ancien régime families sometimes viewed the monasteries as expedient havens for undesirables. Relatives of a young man with a mental illness, undetectable after only a brief acquaintance, might confide him to the ranks of the regular clergy. If he made his profession before the disorder fully manifested itself, he would become the responsibility of the religious community. Such familial unburdening could constitute a real challenge, especially for less populous establishments such as Saint-Martin-d'Auchy-les-Aumales—where Dom François Outin's mental instability and behavior became so violent and disruptive that the rest of the community forced him to live under lock and key in a house of the Cordeliers.[49] The government also used abbeys as detention centers for insubordinate clergy. By order of the king, Dom Jean Jacques Evrard, a monk at Saint-Ouen, was incarcerated in the Bastille for four

---

45. Dom Pierre Hommeril to M. Pouret Roquerie, [n. d.], AN, D XIX 63, liasse 331, 2nd–6th.

46. Guéry, *Histoire de l'abbaye*, 315. Established in 1045, Notre-Dame-de-Lyre remained a prosperous and wealthy abbey throughout its history. The Maurists who arrived there in 1646 restored nearly all the abbey's buildings. Part of the church collapsed due to neglect in An VI (1797–98); the rest of the complex was sold and demolished [Charles, de La Conté, and Lannette, *Répertoire des abbayes*, 53].

47. de la Bunodière, *Derniers jours de l'abbaye de Saint-Ouen,* 9.

48. AN, F19 6112; ADSM, 9 H 33; Savalle, *Les Derniers moines,* 11–12; Jouen, *Jumièges: Histoire et légendes,* 77–78. For more on Jumièges' financial problems, see Dubuc, "Les Difficultés financières," I, 115–22;

49. ADSM, L 2267. The monastery of Saint-Martin-d'Auchy-les-Aumales was founded in the eleventh century by the comte d'Aumale, but the siege of Philippe Augustus, the Hundred Years War and the Wars of Religion left it nearly destroyed and abandoned. The Maurists, arriving at the beginning of the eighteenth century, managed to reconstruct all the buildings just in time for the Revolution to destroy them again [Martène, *Histoire de la Congrégation,* VIII, 53–55; *Répertoire des abbayes,* 11].

months, and, upon his release on 11 November 1786, a *lettre de cachet* ordered him to live under house arrest at Bec. For the rest of the inhabitants, the imposed presence of a former inmate could not have contributed favorably to their spiritual edification.[50]

Scandalized and revolted by the same strife, poor management and lax discipline which the Congregation had sought to remedy one hundred years previously, Maurists in the eighteenth century began to demand a renewal of the rigor which had characterized those germinal years of their reform. In searching for the means to return monasticism to its primitive austerity, however, some monks fell under the spell of Jansenism. Its egalitarianism appealed to those religious who criticized the order's leadership and who wanted to give ordinary professed monks a greater voice in determining the Congregation's policies. As early as 1651, the General Chapter of the Congregation of Saint-Maur issued a condemnation of the heresy anticipating the pope's first condemnation in 1653. Yet, the movement continued to make inroads even in Maurist houses such as Saint-Ouen.[51] The bull *Unigenitus*, which anathematized Jansenism in 1713, split the Maurists into the *appellants*, those who opposed *Unigenitus*, and the *acceptants*, those who accepted the bull. The battle over the superior generalship between the factions nearly rent the Congregation in two. Although Normandy did not experience the stage of the most acrimonious battles, the flurries of denunciations against their *acceptant* prior earned three Jumièges brothers *lettres de cachet* exiling them to other houses. Other, more vociferous *appelant* monks even received prison sentences. The bitterness of the divisions between the two camps had so defamed the Maurists that Clement XI considered dissolving the Congregation altogether. After thirty years of upheaval, some mitigation of the Jansenist crisis finally came in 1736 when an overwhelming majority of the general chapter gave its assent to *Unigenitus*.[52] After that, the hierarchy of the Congregation sought to restore stricter enforcement of the Rule while some of the rank and file monks exhibited the remnants of lingering Jansenist sympathies by clamoring for more democratic procedures governing the election of superiors.[53]

In the secular world, criticism of all religious orders reached new levels of intensity with the scathing lampoons of the *philosophes*. Enlightenment savants like Voltaire, went well beyond demanding the rectification of abuses. They decried the very concept of monasticism as an archaic and tyrannical institution:

50. ADE, 95 L 1, dos. Premier Cahier; 95 L 1, dos. 1790–An III; Baudot, *Normandie bénédictine,* 77.

51. Lemoine, *Le Monde de religieux*, 34; de la Bunodière, *Derniers jours de l'abbaye de Saint-Ouen,* 41–42. For the historiographical debate concerning the impact of Jansenism on the Congregation of Saint-Maur, see Kessler, "The Suppression of the Benedictine Order," 6–7.

52. Martène, *Histoire de la Congrégation,* IX, 31–33; Beaunier, *Recueil historique,* 98; Cousin, *Précis d'histoire,* 450–51; Van Kley, *The Religious Origins,* 88, 306; de Viguerie, "Les Abbayes mauristes," 216–17.

53. Lemoine, *Le Monde de religieux*, 35, 386. 54. Voltaire, Dictionnaire, 891; Cousin, Précis d'histoire, 472, 474; de la Bunodière, Derniers jours de l'abbaye de Saint-Ouen, 41.

"The greater part [of the monks] are slaves enchained under a master to whom they bow; they speak to him on their knees, they call him *monseigneur* . . . and still in this abasement they secretly long for the grandeur of their despot."[54] Among the general population, however, the regulars still enjoyed a level of acclaim, and while some among the laity did advocate a purification of the religious orders, very few demanded complete eradication.[55]

At the annual General Assembly of the Clergy of France in 1765, one of the representatives reminded the attendees that improvements in the state of the regulars ought to constitute one of the Assembly's chief responsibilities. In response to this advice, and probably hoping to avoid another catastrophe like the expulsion of the Jesuits the previous year, the clergy voted to establish a commission of inquiry with the power to investigate and address the turmoil which afflicted the French orders.[56] That same year, a complaint addressed to King Louis XV by the Maurists of Saint-Germain-des-Près against their longtime rival, Blancs-Manteaux, brought the issue of monastic reform to the royal attention, and the king decided to intervene.[57] At the 1766 gathering of the clergy, Louis XV announced his endorsement of the commission on the regular clergy and afforded its recommendations the authority of law. The *Commission des Réguliers* comprised ten members: five bishops and five laymen. Members of the regular clergy, those most affected by the *Commission*'s measures, were conspicuously absent. The archbishop of Reims, Charles de La Roche-Aymon, presided, but the real puppet master was the young prelate who had first alerted the General Assembly to this critical situation: Loménie de Brienne, the archbishop of Toulouse.[58]

A protégé of Louis XV's chief minister (Étienne François de Stainville, duc de Choiseul), Brienne persuaded the Royal Council to issue decrees ordering the heads of all male orders to provide the *Commission* with the rules and constitutions which governed their communities. Along with this information and that supplied by the bishops regarding the houses in their diocese, the *Commission*

---

54. Voltaire, *Dictionnaire*, 891; Cousin, *Précis d'histoire*, 472, 474; de la Bunodière, *Derniers jours de l'abbaye de Saint-Ouen*, 41.

55. Lekai, "The Cistercian Order and the 'Commission,'" 186.

56. Ibid., 185.

57. Rousseau, *Moines bénédictins martyrs*, 6; Lemoine, *Le Monde de religieux*, 35; Sicard, *Le Clergé*, I, 308; Cousin, *Précis d'histoire*, 451. There appears to be some debate whether the monks of Saint-Germain-des-Près merely wished for the king's involvement in their petty clash with Blancs-Manteaux or whether they wanted their monarch to take the initiative in promoting a monastic revival. Abbé Sicard uses this incident to support his general assumption that the regular clergy of the eighteenth century had "completely degenerated." Dom Robert Lemoine seems to support Sicard, but Patrice Cousin and François Rousseau argue that the religious of Saint-Germain legitimately desired royal intervention in the hopes of resurrecting greater adherence to the Rule of Saint Benedict.

58. Lemoine, *Le Monde de religieux*, 383–85; Lekai, "The Cisterican Order and the 'Commission,'" 185; Lekai, "Cistercian Monasteries and the French Episcopate," 67. For two opposing views of Loménie de Brienne and his attitude toward the religious orders, see Lekai, "The Cistercian Order and the 'Commission,'" and Montier, *Martial de Loménie*.

59. Lemoine, *Le Monde de religieux*, 386–87.

began to formulate improvements for both the regular clergy as a whole and for individual orders.[59] After six years, Brienne tried to promulgate the *Commission*'s suggestions with his Edict of 1774, but Pope Clement XIV refused to acknowledge its authority.[60] Louis XV commissioned his foreign minister, Armand Desiré du Plessis, duc d'Aiguillon, to obtain papal sanction of the Edict, but the deaths of both the king and the pope ended this mission. When faced with the impossibility of enforcing the Edict, the archbishop of Toulouse chose to withdraw it.[61]

When Louis XVI inquired after the efficacy of the *Commission*, de La Roche-Aymon responded that its proposals had not met with unbridled outbursts of approval by anyone in France. Based on this assessment, the new monarch slowly withdrew his royal support. Left exposed to the opposition of secular and regular clergy and the *Parlement* of Paris, the *Commission* began to dissolve. Although in theory it still functioned until 1790 under the revised title of *Bureau des Réguliers*, it no longer had the force it had once enjoyed after it lost its leadership with the resignation of Brienne in 1784.[62]

Brienne's Edict of 1774 did not meet with success, but some of the *Commission*'s suggestions were implemented, namely the stringent guidelines for the age of monastic profession and the minimum number of monks required at each house. These measures did have lasting effects on the regular clergy of France. According to the decrees of the Council of Trent, fifteen-year-olds could enter the monastery as novices, but only those who had reached the age of sixteen could make a solemn religious profession. The *Commission* raised the age requirement for monastic vows to twenty-one and for the novitiate to eighteen. At the same time, young men at least fifteen years of age could live at the abbey as "scholars" in order to begin their education.[63] With respect to the number of inhabitants, Brienne believed that each community needed at least nine in order to effectively practice the communal life. By suppressing houses whose membership did not meet this requirement, the archbishop claimed to eliminate financial waste by obliterating the appropriation of large revenues by nearly vacant abbeys. At the same time, this measure aimed to rejuvenate the spirit of conventuality. The population of houses closed by the Edict of 1768 joined the larger establishments of their order.[64]

The *Commission des Réguliers* suppressed over 450 religious communities from various orders. Those houses allowed to remain often did notice a drop in membership. Some among the laity perceived the *Commission*'s work as not one of rejuvenation but of gradual dissolution of the regular clergy. Consequently, they hesitated to send their sons into the ranks of what they saw as dying organizations.[65] Brienne may have assumed that his measures would alleviate the

---

60. Ibid., 391; Lekai, "The Cistercian Order and the 'Commission,'" 186. Brienne's Commission faltered from its very inception, partly due to its disregard for the prerogatives of the pope and its elevation of those of the French prelates.

61. Lemoine, *Le Monde de religieux*, 388.

62. Ibid., 393; Lekai, "The Cistercian Order and the 'Commission,'" 206.

63. Lemoine, *Le Monde de religieux*, 388–89, 399.

64. Ibid., 389–90; Lekai, "The Cistercian Order and the 'Commission,'" 185.

internal turmoil which troubled the Congregation of Saint-Maur in the eighteenth century. The Maurists, for their part, were initially in favor of the *Commission*'s work because it would eliminate institutions which had outlived their usefulness. On the other hand, Brienne's terms had a unifying effect for the Maurists as they put petty differences aside in order to condemn, as one body, any measures which threatened the existence of their monasteries. The Congregation of Saint-Maur did suffer the closure of some of its communities and, according to some figures, experienced a population drop of about ten percent.[66] In upper Normandy, Brienne's operations did not have a devastating effect on the religious orders in general or on the Congregation in particular.[67] All of the Maurist establishments remained open and operating until 1790 in spite of the fact that the membership of Notre-Dame d'Ivry and Notre-Dame-de-Bernay dropped below the requisite minimum of nine. This perhaps attests as much to the solidity of the Norman houses as it does to the *Commission*'s inability to enforce its regulations after the resignation of Brienne.[68]

The outward unity which the Maurists displayed in attempting to prevent the closure of some of their establishments proved short-lived. Once the threat subsided, tensions again flared between superiors and subordinates. At the 1781 provincial assembly of Normandy, a letter from the Congregation's leadership demanded the deposition of the priors of Bernay and Ivry. According to the judgment of the motherhouse of Saint-Germain-des-Près, these monks did not follow the constitutions in the elections of their officers; therefore, they should be replaced with individuals committed to voting regularity. This provoked outrage and uproar among the assembly, and the deputies issued a formal protest of what they perceived as managerial despotism.[69]

---

65. Lemoine, *Le Monde de religieux,* 390, 395; Lekai, "The Cistercian Order and the 'Commission,'" 185–86. Loth reported that the population of male religious dropped from 26,674 in 1766 to 16,236 in 1790, nearly a forty percent decrease [Loth, *Histoire du Cardinal,* 38].

66. Rousseau, *Moines bénédictins martyrs,* 8. Authors disagree on the exact number of Maurist monasteries closed by the Commission, but between twenty and twenty-five seems a good estimate. See Cousin, *Précis d'histoire,* 451; Kessler, "The Suppression of the Benedictine Order," 14; Lemoine, *Le Monde de religieux,* 399; Baudot, *Normandie bénédictine,* 78. Regarding the use of monastic population statistics in eighteenth-century France, see Lekai, "Cistercian Monasteries and the French Episcopate," 66–67; and Lekai, "French Cistercians and the Revolution," 87. Although his articles focus on Cistercian establishments, the issues which he raises apply to all religious orders.

67. Of all the religious houses in the diocese of Rouen (in the city of Rouen alone, there were at least sixty), the Commission closed only nine [Lemarchand, "Les Monastères de Haute-Normandie," 21; Fournée, "Abbayes prieurés et couvents généralités," 29].

68. de Viguerie, "Les Abbayes mauristes," 219. In 1790, the abbey of Notre-Dame d'Ivry housed only two monks and Notre-Dame-de-Bernay five [Baudot, *Normandie bénédictine,* 79]. A retainer of William the Conqueror built Notre-Dame d'Ivry. Despite the introduction of the Maurists in 1669, the abbey remained underpopulated and poorly financed throughout the seventeenth and eighteenth centuries. It became a cotton factory during the Revolution until a fire damaged it in 1809 [*La Révolution en Haute-Normandie,* 164–65; Charles, de La Conté, and Lannette, *Répertoire des abbayes,* 36]. Notre-Dame-de-Bernay was founded in 1013 by the wife of Richard II, Duke of Normandy and sacked during the Wars of Religion. The Maurists who took possession of the abbey in 1628 restored its buildings and monastic life. During the Revolution, the church was converted into a grain bin. That saved this unique piece of Norman Romanesque architecture from destruction [Charles, de La Conté, and Lannette, *Répertoire des abbayes,* 24].

This issue—which divided the Congregation between the provincial establishments and the Parisian superiors—escalated into a national drama when the representatives from the provinces found themselves barred from attending the General Chapter of 1781.[70] Louis XVI tried to put a stop to the bickering by ordering the Maurists to convene an extraordinary general chapter in 1783 at Saint-Denis. Although this special meeting elected new superiors for the order and priors for individual houses, it did not have the conciliatory effect which the king had intended. Rather, it resulted in a schism between those who acknowledged the authority of the officials elected at Saint-Denis and those who rejected them as unconstitutional. The latter claimed that the king had no right to call a general chapter; and therefore, all proceedings conducted at such an illegitimate gathering were null and void.[71]

In this case, the cure proved worse than the illness. The upheaval caused by the king's demand for this extraordinary general chapter provided more fuel for the conflict. Dissent reached every Maurist province, especially Normandy. Much of the opposition to Dom Bride's priorship at Jumièges stemmed from his election at Saint-Denis. He replaced Dom Louis-Hippolyte Daspres whose pamphlet denouncing the convocation of the chapter as an example of extralegal, royal encroachment earned him a trip to the Bastille.[72] The prior of Préaux, Dom Jean Antoine Chahau, showed his reluctance to turn over the reins of his abbey to the newly elected Dom Jean-Pierre-Marie Le Vasseur despite the military escort which accompanied the latter.[73] Dom Hommeril threatened to file a suit with the *Parlement* of Rouen against his fellow monks at Notre-Dame-de-Lyre for the abuse which he received when they selected him to act as the assistant to their Saint-Denis-chosen prior.[74]

Yet, in the remaining decade of the Congregation's existence, signs of improvement began to emerge. Despite the vehement opposition to the extraordinary chapter, the election of Dom Ambroise Augustin Chevreux as superior general in 1783 eventually reestablished some unity. His fair and adept management placated the belligerents and allowed the leadership of the Congregation to concentrate on revitalizing discipline. The General Chapter of 1787 began to enforce

69. Montier, "Les Moines de Fécamp," 170.

70. Ibid., 171–72.

71. "Registre des actes capitulaires de l'abbaye de Jumièges, depuis 1745 au 20 février 1790," p. 116v–122r, ADSM, 9 H 37; Porée, ed., "Lettres de quelques bénédictins," 175.

72. "Registre des actes capitulaires de l'abbaye de Jumièges," p. 116v, 122r–122v, ADSM, 9 H 37; H. Leroy, "Dom Jean-François Daspres: Prieur de Saint-Wandrille et pensionnaire du Roi à la Bastille," ASWF (1986), 105; Montier, "Les Moines de Fécamp," 171.

73. Dom Jean-Pierre Marie Le Vasseur to unknown, 1 June 1785, Porée, ed., "Lettres de quelques bénédictins," 177.

74. Dom Pierre Hommeril to unknown, 8 May 1785, Porée, ed., "Lettres de quelques bénéditins," 176.

75. "Registre des actes capitulaires de l'abbaye de Saint Wandrille, 6 juillet 1745 au 24 avril 1790," p. 140r–143r, ADSM, 16 H 39; Dom Pierre François Boudier to Étienne-Charles de Loménie de Brienne, 15 September 1787, Lamare, *Mémorial de Philippe Lamare,* 226–33; Plongeron, *Les Réguliers de Paris,* 152; Loth, *Les Conventionnels,* 357; Rousseau, *Moines bénédictins martyrs,* 15.

the Rule once again, requiring strict adherence to communal recitation of the canonical hours including the 2:00 AM matins.[75] Although the Congregation which had piloted a Benedictine reform suffered from laxity, financial embarrassment, and superior-subordinate conflicts, the monks of Saint-Maur appeared poised to renew their monastic discipline on the eve of the Revolution.

CHAPTER 2

THE MAURISTS IN UPPER NORMANDY DURING THE EIGHTEENTH CENTURY

THE DAMAGE TO THE CONGREGATION OF SAINT-MAUR by external assaults and internal strife did put a grave strain on the ranks of the cloister; however, historians have disagreed on the impact of that vexation. Nineteenth-century ecclesiastical authors appeared the most critical of their eighteenth-century counterparts, assuming that monastic decadence and neglect of the Rule caused the eventual suppression of the regular clergy during the Revolution. Despite his obvious partiality for the clergy and utter contempt for the Revolution's principles, Abbé Sicard claimed that all religious orders had fallen too far from grace to hope for redemption: "the monastic tree no longer had the vitality which had allowed it throughout history to be infused with new youth by powerful grafts. The sap seemed dry."[1] The Norman historian Abbé Julien Loth applied Sicard's conclusion to Saint-Wandrille asserting that it had lost "its primitive fervor."[2] On the other hand, some twentieth-century historians have painted more favorable portraits of the monks before the Revolution.[3] In a debate between M. de la Bunodière and Abbé Loth at the *Académie des Sciences, Belles-lettres et Arts* in Rouen, the former directly challenged the Abbé's assertion of monastic degeneration by demonstrating the respect which the Norman Benedictines still commanded during the second half of the eighteenth century.[4] Marcel Baudot concurred with Bernanrd Plongeron and de la Bunodière in concluding that some mildew may have festered in the corners of the Congregation, but overall the abbeys still contained men of great virtue.[5]

Research on the Maurists of upper Normandy in the eighteenth century seems to indicate that regional and national disputes may at times have disrupted

---

1. Sicard, Le Clergé, I, 276–308.
2. Loth, Les Conventionnels, 357. For a similar opinion regarding the Maurist houses in upper Normandy, see Pigout, La Révolution en Seine-Maritime, 133.
3. Plongeron, Les Réguliers de Paris, 69; Bellenger, "'Superstitious enemies,'" 154.
4. de la Bunodière, Derniers jours de l'abbaye de Saint-Ouen, 41.
5. de Viguerie, "Les Abbayes mauristes," 210, 220; Baudot, Normandie Bénédictine, 78.

the full appreciation of the communal experience, but the houses of the Congregation continued to function as vibrant communities of piety and scholarship. The standards set by the *Commission des Réguliers* for age of profession and minimum number of inhabitants, as well as the other challenges of the Age of Enlightenment, did take their toll on the population of Norman houses. The two largest establishments, Fécamp and Bec, dropped from forty monks each in 1730 to less than thirty each in 1790. Of those, however, about one third had made their monastic profession after the promulgation of the Edict of 1768. This same proportion applied to all of the Congregation's abbeys throughout upper Normandy, a traditionally fertile region of Maurist recruitment.[6] The list supplied to the National Assembly by the last superior general of the order in 1790 divided all the Maurists into three categories according to age: 1) under fifty years old, 2) between fifty and seventy years old, and 3) over seventy years old. This data reveals that at least fifty percent of the monks in upper Normandy at the time of the Revolution were under the age of fifty and therefore had lived in communal life for thirty years or less.[7] The work of the *Commission* may have deterred some parents from sending their sons to the cloister, but the Congregation in upper Normandy did not suffer from a lack of infusion of new blood.[8]

For some families, the opportunity for education and social mobility which the Congregation presented may have overcome other misgivings. Since the Rule of Saint Benedict demanded that all monks treat each other with equality and fraternity, all segments of society were represented behind the abbey walls. Analysis of available information about the social backgrounds of Maurists reveals that the children of bourgeois or professional parents dominated the Norman ranks. Members of the Second Estate, particularly nobility of the sword, counted few of its progeny in the order, and unlike the situation among the secular high clergy, this minority did not hold a monopoly on the Congregation's positions of authority or special distinctions.[9] Scholarly merit and leadership potential, rather than birth, seemed to determine which monks received such honors and responsibilities. Dom Alexis Davout, the son of a baker from Étampes, rose through the

---

6. AN, F19 6113, D XIX 10, liasse 147; ADE, 116 L 2, 57 L 13; de Viguerie, "Les Abbayes mauristes," 214–15. Regarding the total number of Maurists in France in 1790, figures have differed from Marcel Baudot's estimate of 600 to about 2,000 as stated by Dom Lemoine [Baudot, Normandie bénédictine, 77; Lemoine, Le Monde de religieux, 390]. Dom Yves Chaussey provides the most realistic figure. Based on the two lists compiled by the superior general, he put the number of Maurist choir monks, commis stabilisés, and frère convers at 1,699 [Chaussy, ed., Matricula Monachorum, 45].

7. AN, D XIX, 10, no. 147.

8. Lemoine, Le Monde de religieux, 390.

9. ADSM, L 1202, L 1205, L 1206, L 1209, L 1211, L 1212, L 1214, L 1327; ADE, H 106, 57 L 24, 57 L 62; ASWF (1967), 103, (1950), 74, (1980), 21, 105; Guéry, Deux bénédictins normands, 1; Pigout, Bolbec, 43; Tougard, La Révolution à Yvetot, vol.1, 182; Savalle, Les Derniers moines, 26; de la Bunodière, Derniers jours de l'abbaye de Saint-Ouen, 14; Montier, "Les Moines de Fécamp," 204, 162, 165, 173, 188. Baptismal certificates, which monks sometimes had to turn over to the local administration after the closure of their monasteries in 1790, provide a wealth of information on the social backgrounds of these men.

ranks of the order to become the prior of the prosperous Saint-Ouen and even earned the esteem of his fellow clerics—who elected him as their representative to the Estates-General in 1789.[10]

One of the chief indications that the Congregation as a whole, and Norman Maurists in particular, had not deteriorated into complete stagnation in the eighteenth century was the perpetuation of the tradition of superior scholarship for which these Benedictines had enjoyed a revered reputation for nearly two centuries. The Congregation's religious and military academies—numbering about thirty—trained the regular and secular clergy as well as France's military officers. Saint-Germain-des-Près had become a scholastic nucleus, and priors from each Maurist house dispatched their brightest novices to the motherhouse to collaborate with other monks on the various projects.[11] The production of monumental tomes on history, theology, philosophy, and diplomatics had given the Congregation of Saint-Maur such acclaim that, by the end of the eighteenth century, *travailler à la bénédictine* became an idiom for undertaking an arduous intellectual task. Even the anti-monastic Voltaire grudgingly admitted the contribution of the Maurists by using this phrase in his writings.[12]

Some historians have asserted that the establishment of the *Commission des Réguliers* in 1766 and the upheaval which the Congregation experienced in the second half of the eighteenth century brought Maurist literary activity to an end.[13] However, the tradition of learning continued within the cloister as the superiors recognized that "the desire and application of study is the safeguard of good order in the monasteries."[14] In an effort to renew the Maurist commitment to academia, a circular letter from Saint-Germain-des-Près in 1767 admonished the inhabitants of its daughter houses that "periods of idleness and dissipation have never created savants or religious" and urged them to contribute works to the Congregation's new *Bureau de littérature*.[15]

The Maurists in upper Normandy endeavored resolutely to maintain their scholarly reputation despite the challenges of the eighteenth century. Many promising stars of the French intelligentsia, such as the future author of *Manon Lescaut*,

---

10. ADSM, L 1212; Horcholle, "Anecdotes de ce qui s'est passé dans la ville de Rouen depuis l'établissement des états généraux dont l'ouverture s'est faite à Versailles le 4 mai 1789," in Chaline and Hurpin, ed., Vivre en Normandie, I, 327; Lemoine, Le Monde de religieux, 386.

11. Dom François Philippe Gourdin to Dom Grappin, [n. d.], Dantier, ed., Rapports sur la correspondance, 184; Aston, Religion and Revolution, 21, 85; Denis, "Les Bénédictins de la Congrégation," 295; Cousin, Précis d'histoire, 430–31, 451; Sicard, Le Clergé, I, 305–6; de Viguerie, "Les Abbayes mauristes, 209.

12. Gourdin to Grappin, [n. d.], Dantier, ed., Rapports sur la correspondance, 184; Cousin, Précis d'histoire, 429.

13. Baudot, Normandie bénédictine, 78; Cousin, Précis d'histoire, 450. Rousseau did not assert that the Maurist reservoir of savants dried up in the latter half of the eighteenth century, but he did claim that the monks ceased to collaborate with one another on their works [Rousseau, Moines bénédictins martyrs, 4].

14. Circular letter of Dom Pierre François Boudier, 17 January 1768, Dantier, ed., Rapports sur la correspondance, 127.

15. Ibid., 127–28.

Abbé Antoine-François Prévost, still began their monastic careers by professing their vows at the abbey of Jumièges, the novitiate of the Norman province.[16] The monastic libraries of Saint-Wandrille, Notre-Dame-de-Bonne-Nouvelle, and Fécamp served as theological and philosophical centers where newly professed religious could pursue in-depth study.[17] The careers of individual Norman monks illustrate the fruits of such training and dispel the notion that "idleness and dissipation" had supplanted Maurist erudition on the eve of the French Revolution. Men such as Dom Olivier Dupont and Dom Guillaume Dominique Letellier occupied posts as professors of rhetoric and theology while the *Parlement* of Paris granted Dom François Henry Legrand a certificate of law.[18] Dom Charles Antoine Blanchard corresponded on matters of Classical literature, history, and strategy with one of his former military students, Charles-Gaspard de Toustain-Richebourg, who had become the commissioner of the États de Bretagne in 1772.[19]

Throughout the seventeenth and early eighteenth centuries, the Congregation had gained a reputation for its dedication to history. As soon as the Maurists took possession of a house, they began a detailed account of the abbey's past, consulting both ancient manuscripts and local folklore. They had become so celebrated for work on this subject that the General Assembly of the Clergy in 1710 bestowed on the Saint-Ouen brother, Dom Denys de Sainte-Marthe, the monumental commission of overseeing the compilation of the *Gallia Christiana*, a history of all the dioceses of France.[20]

The number of historical works produced by Maurists did dwindle in the second half of the eighteenth century, but this does not indicate that the Congregation had abandoned its dedication to scholarship.[21] While the philosophic luminaries Voltaire and Baron Paul-Henri d'Holback lampooned the authority of the Church and championed the supremacy of science and reason over superstitious religion, Norman Maurists joined with the rest of their order and others of the Catholic Enlightenment to demonstrate the compatibility between rational learning and religion. Although living behind the cloistered walls of their abbeys, these

---

16. Jouen, Jumièges: Histoire et légendes, 77; Savalle, Les Derniers moines, 13. The abbey only lost its distinction on the eve of the Revolution when financial constraints forced it to cease its training functions. The novitiate was then transferred to the abbey of Bec.

17. Bourienne-Savoye, "Les Fecampois," 81; Guéry, Histoire de l'abbaye, 323; Bellamy, "La Vie religieuse," 81; de Viguerie, "Les Abbayes mauristes," 216. With the prompting of Saint Anselm of Bec, Matilda—the wife of William the Conqueror—established the priory of Notre-Dame-de-Bonne-Nouvelle on the left bank of the Seine River in the city of Rouen. Although the monastery was destroyed during the Hundred Years War, the Maurists finally succeeded in reestablishing it in 1626. The church became a parish church after the Revolution, but it was eventually destroyed in 1848 [Répertoire des abbayes, 112].

18. Tougard, La Révolution à Yvetot, vol. 2, 8; Denis, "Les Bénédictins de la Congrégation," 300; Montier, "Les Moines de Fécamp," 134.

19. Dom Charles Antoine Blanchard to Charles-Gaspard de Toustain-Richebourg, 21 November 1772, Porée, ed., "Lettres de quelques bénédictins," 171–73.

20. Tassin, Histoire littéraire, 448–49; Cousin, Précis d'histoire, 429, 431; Deries, "La Vie d'un bibliothécaire," 209.

21. Cousin, Précis d'histoire, 450–51.

monks still remained products of their age. In response to the tastes of the Age of Reason, the Norman Maurists put aside their elaborate narratives on an abbey's foundation by the long-haired Merovingians or its sudden sack by the Vikings for treatises on electricity, mechanics, and government.

Their research in fields prized by the *philosophes* brought the Maurists into close contact with contemporary lay scholars. This interaction sometimes required the monk-savants to journey beyond the abbey walls, an apparent violation of Saint Benedict's Rule which ordered cenobites to retreat from worldly society. On the other hand, Dom Mabillon had set the precedent for Maurist participation in the realm of the secular intelligentsia with his treatise on diplomatics and the lay acclaim it received. Similarly, the eighteenth-century monks of Saint-Maur occasionally mingled with secular society for scholarly exchange on topics of interest to the Enlightenment mind.

Dom Jean Antoine de Maurey of Fécamp forged ties with secular scholars by becoming a member of the *Académie des Sciences, Belles-Lettres et Arts de Rouen*, one of the many societies of amateur scientists which emerged in the late eighteenth century as the premier forums of scientific and literary advancements. Dom de Maurey, who excelled at mechanical engineering, presented numerous papers to the *Académie* both on his various inventions for farm machinery and naval instruments and on the need for a technical school in upper Normandy. His achievements with seafaring equipment earned him recognition from the Congregation, and as an illustration of its commitment to scholarship in the sciences as well as the liberal arts, the General Chapter of 1788 voted Dom de Maurey a grant to pay for the costs of pursuing his research.[22]

The career of Dom François Philippe Gourdin in particular exemplifies the Maurist's interaction with fellow scholars during the Enlightenment. Born the son of an artist, Goudin made his profession at Jumièges in 1761 and was appointed a professor of rhetoric at the military college of Beaumont-en-Auge. During his residence there, he published a treatise on his scientific observations of the then enigmatic phenomenon of electricity as well as his designs for a buoyancy machine similar to a hot air balloon.[23] These earned him a premium place among the scientific savants of Normandy; and upon his transfer to Saint-Ouen in 1778, he was inducted into the *Académie de Rouen* at the Associate level. The relationship between the religious and the lay members of the *Académie* for the most part appeared to be that of mutual respect. The monks of Saint-Ouen opened their extensive library to the academicians while the members of the

22. Gourdin to Grappin, 16 March 1786, Dantier, ed., Rapports sur la correspondance, 184; Montier, "Les Moines de Fécamp," 205, 209; Tougard, La Révolution à Yvetot, vol.1, 141. For more on the Catholic Enlightenment in general, see Aston, Religion and Revolution, 81–99.

23. Deries, "La Vie d'un bibliothécaire," 210, 212, 216; Rousseau, Moines bénédictins martyrs, 3–4. His fascination with electricity led him into the eighteenth-century mystical movement of Mesmerism on which he presented a paper at the Académie.

learned society showed their regard for Dom Gourdin by electing him as the secretary for the *Section des Belles-Lettres*.[24]

The prolific writings of this true Renaissance man included a proposal presented to the *Académie* on an education system for rural and working-class children which received the approval of the provincial assembly of the Norman Maurists in 1781. At about the same time, Dom Gourdin began delving into political science. In his publication *Les Moeurs considerées relativement à l'État*, he defended the supremacy of a monarchy over a republic.[25] Dom Gourdin also combined the rational philosophy of the Enlightenment with the Maurist tradition of scholarship in his monumental theological tome, *De la prescription en matière de foi et de discipline*.[26] In the then century-old tradition of Maurist historical narratives, he published a three volume *Histoire de la Picardie*, his birthplace, and exchanged critiques and prehistoric artifacts with Dom Grappin. Dom Gourdin's literary career continued until 1789 when he published one of his most well-known works, *Traité de Traduction*, a guide for Latin translation and grammar.[27]

Despite his monastic profession, Dom Gourdin remained a man of his age. He participated in the secular society of the *Académie* and read the works of his Enlightenment contemporaries (he made reference to Voltaire's grudging recognition of Maurist scholarship in a letter to Dom Grappin).[28] Perhaps the works of Rousseau prompted him to reverse his position on government in 1788 when he declared, in contradiction of his earlier defense of monarchies, "The government of nature is the republic."[29] The librarian also kept close contacts with lay intellectuals such as Jean-Paul Marat, who at that time practiced medicine for the army corps of the king's brother, the Comte d'Artois. This unexpected friendship proved professionally advantageous for the future editor of *L'Ami de peuple*. Marat was initiated into the *Académie de Rouen* upon the recommendation of Dom Gourdin although their correspondence cooled on the eve of the Revolution.[30] Dom Gourdin serves as an excellent example of a monk-savant who became involved with the philosophical movements of the eighteenth century and established ties with his lay—and even anticlerical—peers. However, his reaction to the suppression of

24. Deries, "La Vie d'un bibliothécaire," 210, 213. One apparent defect in the relationship between the Maurists and the Académie was the latter's statutes regulating admission; religious could only enter its ranks as Associés and not as full members. However, Dom Gourdin's election as secretary and the active participation by both Dom Gourdin and Dom de Maurey in the Académie's proceedings testify that their associate status did not deprive them of the privileges of full membership [Montier, "Les Moines de Fécamp," 206; Deries, "La Vie d'un bibliothécaire," 211].
25. Deries, "La Vie d'un bibliothécaire," 213–15.
26. Ibid., 216.
27. Gourdin to Grappin, 10 March 1788, Dantier, ed., Rapports sur la correspondance, 185; Gourdin to Grappin, [n. d.], Ibid., 184; Deries, "La Vie d'un bibliothécaire," 215.
28. Gourdin to Grappin, [n. d.], Dantier, ed., Rapports sur la correspondance, 184; Deries, "La Vie d'un bibliothécaire," 212, 217.
29. As cited in Deries, "La Vie d'un bibliothécaire," 214.
30. Ibid., 212; de la Bunodière, Derniers jours de l'abbaye de Saint-Ouen, 15.

the religious orders during the Revolution demonstrated that this interaction with secular society had not had a detrimental effect on his monastic commitment.

The maintenance of the centuries-old tradition of monastic hospitality and generosity also forged bonds between the monks and the less privileged of secular society. When a food shortage in the winter of 1788–1789 brought famine to most of France and sent wheat prices skyrocketing, the Norman monks opened the doors of their abbeys to their needy neighbors. For the inhabitants of Préaux, this meant donating eight bushels of grain per week throughout November and December to the nearby town of Pont-Audemer. The doubling of the cost of bread in 1789 spurred the monks of Saint-Pierre et Saint-Paul de Châtillon-lès-Conches to bake 143 bushels of wheat into loaves for the lay poor of the local town.[31]

In the late 1780s, the Maurists at Fécamp redoubled their generous doles to 1,000 livres of bread per day, preventing an outbreak of urban unrest which had accompanied an unfruitful harvest twenty years earlier.[32] The monks of Jumièges knew well the acuteness of rural poverty in the eighteenth century. For all the controversy which Dom Bride's installation had caused, during the 1789 season of privation, the prior himself set the example for his fellow monks by giving daily provisions of soup and clothing and weekly alms to approximately one hundred people. The indigent sick received medical examinations by the monastery's doctor, lodging in the infirmary, and treatment at the expense of the abbey. The abbey of Jumièges had acquired the title Jumièges the Almsgiver, but never did it justify the appellation more than on the very eve of its suppression.[33]

Within the clergy of upper Normandy, evidence did exist of cooperation between regulars and seculars—traditionally at odds with one another. Although few Maurists in upper Normandy actually served as secular curés and vicars before the Revolution, they did welcome the involvement of parish priests in the abbey's events such as the profession of vows. The Jumièges monks in particular seem to have enjoyed an excellent rapport with local seculars. The prior entertained the local clerics at dinner every week and distributed presents of wine to them on holidays. Often, the novices of that abbey chose the curé of Jumièges, instead of relatives, to function as one of the two secular witnesses required for all Maurist professions.[34]

---

31. Cousin, Précis d'histoire, 472; Besnard, Monographie de l'église, 31; Boivin-Champeaux, Notice pour servir à l'histoire, 242–43; Savalle, Les Derniers moines, 8, f. 2; La Révolution à Yvetot et dans (unpaginated). Founded in 1035, Saint-Pierre et Saint-Paul de Châtillon-lès-Conches was almost destroyed when the English set fire to it during the Hundred Years War. The Maurists who colonized it in 1630 succeeded in reconstructing the buildings; however, the church was demolished after 1791 and the rest of the complex converted into a hospital [Charles, de La Conté, and Lannette, Répertoire des abbayes, 30].
32. Genouillac, Histoire de l'abbaye, 169; Martin, Histoire de Fécamp, II, 90, 94; Bourienne-Savoye, "Les Fecampois," 81; Bellamy, Bénédictins et Annonçiades, 17; Dupuy, "Ordre et désordre," 458–60; Bellamy, "La Vie religieuse," 45.
33. Deshayes, Histoire de l'abbaye royal, 162; Jouen, Jumièges: Histoire et légendes, 77.
34. ADSM, L 1211; Savalle, Les Derniers moines, 16–17.

Some Maurists formed liaisons with the laity by participating in civic affairs. As the Congregation's representative to the *Parlement* of Rouen, Dom François Robert Delénable, of the less populous Rouen house Notre-Dame-de-Bonne-Nouvelle, established contacts with some of the most prominent lawyers and politicians in Normandy.[35] Rural abbeys such as Saint-Wandrille were often the largest landowners and the economic mainstay of the area. Therefore, when the village of Saint-Wandrille became incorporated in 1790, it chose as its first mayor the monastery's forty-four-year-old prior, Dom Alexandre Jean Ruault.[36]

As the central focus of the seaside port of Fécamp, the abbey opened its doors to civic activities.[37] The year before the calling of the Estates-General, the prior of Sainte-Trinité, Dom Jacques Alexis Lemaire served in the municipal government. The following year, the electoral assembly met at the monastery to draw up the *cahiers* for the Third Estate. After the election of municipal officers according to the National Assembly's new regulations in February of 1790, Dom Lemaire not only blessed them and ordered the singing of a Te Deum in their honor, but he even put the abbey's buildings at the disposal of the municipal administration.[38]

Maurists in Normandy also participated in secular society by joining local lodges of the Grand-Orient de France, the French freemason affiliation. This participation may seem to indicate defiance of the Catholic Church's position on freemasonry in the eighteenth century. Pope Clement XII issued the bull *In Eminenti Apostolatus Specula* in 1738 which condemned the secret brotherhood and forbade Catholics from associating with its members and rituals under penalty of excommunication. Thirteen years later, Pope Benedict XIV repeated this prohibition; however, the *Parlements* of France did not register these bulls. Since the Gallican Church refused to promulgate any papal pronouncements without letters patent from the king and the approval of the *Parlements*, the anathematization of freemasonry was never recognized in France.[39] Many historians have identified lodge participation as a sign of the degeneration of monastic life in the eighteenth century.[40] Perhaps, though, these Maurists viewed masonic membership as another way to forge ties with local lay society, as these groups often included the elite of the Norman Third Estate.[41] As a member of the Rouen lodge *Les Bons-Amis*,

---

35. AN, F19 6113; Lohier, "Dom Étienne Mauger," 348.

36. "Procés Verbal des effets de l'abbaye de Saint-Wandrille dressés par les officiers municipaux dudit lieu," AN, F19 6113; Premier registre des délibérations du conseil municipal de Saint-Wandrille, as cited in ASWF (1950), 51, f. 2.

37. Bourienne-Savoye, "Les Fecampois," 81; Bellamy, Bénédictins et Annonçiades, 16.

38. Gourdon de Genouillac, Histoire de l'abbaye de Fécamp, 169; Bellamy, Bénédictins et Annonçiades, 22; Martin, Histoire de Fécamp, II, 88; Bourienne-Savoye, "Les Fecampois," 81–83; Bellamy, "La Vie religieuse," 47.

39. Jean-Paul Lefebvre-Filleau, Moines Francs-Maçons du pays de Caux (Nanterre, 1991), 35–37, 40, 44; Kessler, "The Suppression of the Benedictine Order," 11.

40. See for example Eric Saunier, ed., Encyclopédie de la Franc-maçonnerie (Paris, 2000), 75. For an opposing viewpoint, see Cooney, "Très Chers Frères, 173–83.

41. Saunier, ed., Encyclopédie, 151; Camou and Maillard, La Loge de la Triple Unité, 26.

Dom Jacques François Travers, of Saint-Ouen, fraternized with the president of the *Parlement* of Normandy as well as international personalities such as Benjamin Franklin.[42]

Whether attracted by the opportunity to interact with prominent laity or by the similarities between freemasonry and the cenobitic life—both emphasized the virtues of brotherhood and charity—monastic participation in masonic meetings spread throughout upper Normandy. The Maurist practice of transferring men from one house to another facilitated the spread of the secret society among the Congregation's establishment. Dom René Guillaume Alexandre Coquil deslongchamps, initiated at Rouen while living at Saint-Ouen in 1782, relocated to the rural, lodgeless locale of Saint-Wandrille. He must have convinced some of his fellow religious of the benefits of masonry because, four years after his own reception into the secret brotherhood, he led six other Maurists and four laymen (two nobles and two bourgeois) in the foundation of *L'Union Cauchoise* at the nearby town of Caudebec.[43] In 1784, another provincial masonic seed germinated in the monastic soil of Notre-Dame-de-Bernay. The fellowship between religious and lay masons at the town's lodge, *L'Amis de la Vertu,* may have even acquired new recruits for the communal life. The friendship between two of the founding masters, a haberdasher named Robert René d'Huldebert and the Maurist Dom Marc Antoine de Courdemanche, may have persuaded the bourgeois that his nineteen-year-old son should pursue a religious vocation. In 1787, Pierre René Robert d'Huldebert professed his solemn vows at the Bernay abbey.[44]

The Maurists at Fécamp showed the greatest enthusiasm for freemasonry by establishing the most famous and well-documented lodge with Benedictine membership in upper Normandy. On 23 September 1778, several of the town's most prominent citizens along with monks and musicians from the monastery assembled at Sainte-Trinité for the formal installation of the new masonic lodge, *La Triple Unité.*[45] Within two years, the lodge had acquired thirteen new members including four more Benedictines. Perhaps it owed its popularity to the close association which *La Triple Unité* formed with the Grand Master of the Grand-Orient

---

42. "Tableau des FF...," 27ème jour du 12ème mois de l'an de la vraie lumière 5785 (27 Décembre 1785), and "Tableau des FF...," 27ème jour du 12ème mois de l'an de la vraie lumière 5787 (27 Décembre 1787), BN, Baylot FM2 582.

43. "Extrait du registre des délibérations de la L... de L'Ardente Amitié," 2ème jour du 3ème mois de l'an de la vraie lumière 5784 (2 May 1784), BN, FM2 382; "Tableau des FF...," [n. d.], BN, FM2 205; F. de Loucelles, Histoire générale de la Franc-maçonnerie, 121. Monks played such an important role at this lodge that after the suppression of the religious orders in 1790, L'Union Cauchoise had to terminate its operations [Frère Folloppe to Grand-Orient, 2ème jour du 8ème mois de l'an de la vraie lumière 5790 (2 Octobre 1790), BN, FM2 205].

44. "Tableau de la Loge Saint Jean sous le titre d'istinctif [sic] des Amis de la Vertu," 30ème jour du 9ème mois de l'an de vraie lumière 5784 (30 November 1784), BN, FM2 163; "Registre des actes capitulaires de l'abbaye de Jumièges," p. 113r, ADSM, 9 H 37; de Loucelles, Histoire générale de la Franc-maçonnerie, 50.

45. "Rapport des deputés installateurs," 23ème jour du 7ème mois de l'an de la vraie lumière 5778 (23 Septembre 1778), BN, FM2 233II; "Obligation," 23ème jour du 7ème mois de l'an de la vraie lumière 5778 (23 Septembre 1778), BN, FM2 233II.

only one year after its foundation. On 15 July 1779, Louis Philippe Joseph, duc d'Orléans, the Grand Master, traveled to Fécamp to inspect his hussar regiment stationed at the port. When the masonic members heard of his arrival, they invited him to visit their lodge so that they could pay him their respects. Five Benedictines and seven lay masons took their petition to the duke. Two days later, the masonic brothers of *La Triple Unité* welcomed the Duc d'Orléans to their abbey lodge; and to further prove their devotion, they solicited from their Grand Master a portrait of him to decorate their lodge. The duc d'Orléans did not forget this request. Two years later, in honor of the reception and installation of his portrait, the monks celebrated a High Mass in the abbey church, and the monastery's musicians performed sacred, masonic music which they had composed especially for this event. After the Mass, the members of the Rouen lodge *La Céleste Amitié* joined their Fécamp protégés in a masonic banquet after which the Benedictine orator of *La Triple Unité*, Dom Jean Charles Derouvroy urged his brother masons to reiterate their attachment to their Grand Master. "Let us address to the Grand Architect of the Universe the most sincere wishes for the preservation of a master whose dear souvenir today decorates this temple and will always be in our hearts."[46] The portrait remained in the abbey and figured on the inventory of the monastery's goods which the town compiled in 1790.[47]

Since the precepts of the secret brotherhood required that a member not "avert his face from suffering humanity," the lay masons assisted their religious brothers in their distributions of bread to the poor and aid for the sick. Thus, as interest in Enlightenment piety, which focused on the performance of charitable deeds rather than ascetic practices, became more popular among the bourgeois and noble laity in the latter half of the eighteenth century, freemasonry's humanitarian projects provided a way for monks to interact with these segments of the population.[48] By their participation in masonic activities, the monks forged close bonds with the lay members of *La Triple Unité*, and the dedication which they had shown for the less fortunate of Fécamp earned the respect and admiration of their lodge brothers. When the first years of the Revolution threatened their existence, the monks who had joined the Grand-Orient perhaps hoped that their affiliation with distinguished Norman masons (including the cousin of the king) would prove advantageous. In their lay Fécamp masonic brothers, they did in fact

46. "Registre des délibérations de la Triple Unité," 23ème jour de 2ème mois de l'an de la vraie lumière 5781 (23 April 1781)," BN, FM2 233II.

47. "Des minutes du greffe de hôtel de ville de Fécamp," AN, F19 6113.

48. "Discours prononcé par la F... de Pierre," 11ème jour de 3ème de l'an de la vraie lumière 5785 (11 May 1785), BN, FM2 163; La Triple Unité to Grand-Orient, 3ème jour de 10ème mois de l'an de la vraie lumière 5782, BN, FM2 233II; Camou and Maillard, La Loge de la Triple Unité, 29; Aston, Religion and Revolution, 54–55; Bourienne-Savoye, "Les Fecampois," 81. Despite scanty documentation, some sources suggest that the other lodges with religious members wanted to perform charitable work as well. A letter to the Grand-Orient by L'Union Cauchoise masons expresses their desire to assist in a national hospital project, but the rural brothers lacked sufficient funds [L'Union Cauchoise to the Grand-Orient, 18ème jour du 4ème mois de l'an de la vraie lumière 5787 (18 June 1787), BN, FM2 205].

find earnest advocates within secular society. Throughout 1790, the lay masons on the town's council petitioned the National Assembly for the preservation of the abbey.[49]

The discord from within the Congregation of Saint-Maur and threats from without may have jeopardized the very existence of the order, but the upper Norman Maurists of the late eighteenth century proved their mettle. Novices continued to populate the houses up to 1789, and their training still required rigorous scholarship. Although the monks of Saint-Maur may have turned away from the historical works of their predecessors, their writings on science, government, and philosophy illustrated their ability to adapt to the issues and sensibilities of their age. The exchange of ideas which accompanied this research, as well as their activities with charities, civic government, and secular sociability, brought them into contact with the world beyond their cloister. But this interaction did not as a whole dampen their zeal for their monastic vocations. The monks of Saint-Maur showed in their words and actions following the National Assembly's decree ordering the dissolution of their order, that, contrary to the claims of previous historians, if they chose to leave their abbeys, it was for *other* reasons, often beyond their control.

---

49. Lefebvre-Filleau, Moines Francs-Maçons, 150; Camou and Maillard, La Loge de la Triple Unité, 20.

CHAPTER 3

THE SUPPRESSION OF
THE CONGREGATION

ALTHOUGH MEMBERS OF THE MONASTIC CLERGY, the men of the Congregation of
Saint-Maur had actively participated in the secular society of eighteenth-century
France. When Louis XVI called for the election of deputies to the Estates-General
and the compilation of *cahiers de doléance*, the monks once again found themselves interacting with the world beyond the cloister walls. But, the outside world
seethed with discontent, and this time, when the monks ventured into the secular
realm, they found themselves swept up in the whirlwind of revolution.

Despite repeated attempts and propositions for reform, the nation of
France in 1789 faced financial ruin, political collapse, and social unrest. The
French economy had grown throughout the eighteenth century, and while the
standard of living for most people rose, so did prices, and not in proportion to
wages. A population boom in the early part of the century meant plenty of labor
which kept wages down. Industries suffered a severe blow when France signed a
free trade agreement with its longtime rival Great Britain. French textile manu-
factures could not compete with the cheap goods produced using the latest tech-
nologies of the Industrial Revolution taking place across the Channel. As a result,
the economy of France dove into depression in 1787. The prices of manufactured
goods fell, but the bad harvests of 1787–89 drove the price of grain skyward. By
1789, farmers had little yield from the bad crops, city artisans could not afford the
price of bread, and industrialists had gone out of business.

The economic crisis exacerbated the political and social problems which
France faced. French society still retained its medieval demarcations and trap-
pings despite their irrelevancy. Of the three estates, the clergy made up the First,
the nobility the Second, and everyone else the Third. The clergy enjoyed the privileges of landownership but paid no taxes to the state. The *philosophes* and critics
of religion found much to disparage about the clerical state of France, from the
morality of its members to its very utility in society.

The Second Estate still asserted their feudal prerogatives and kept a lock on government and military positions. They still insisted that their peasants pay the feudal dues and rents in addition to paying taxes to the state. While a few nobles made efforts to promote reform of the social order, the majority vigorously opposed any attempts to alter the economic and social structure of France.

The Third Estate included everyone else from rich bourgeois to poor street beggars. Needless to say, the interests and desires of the members of the Third were hardly uniform. The bourgeois, who paid the largest share of the taxes, wanted greater participation in the government and an end to noble privilege. The city artisans clamored for lower food prices and more steady employment while the peasants, burdened with feudal dues and state taxes, still remained rather attached to the king as a father figure.

Into this brew of potential unrest ascended King Louis XVI in 1774. A gentle family man, pious and conscientious, he showed genuine concern for his people but lacked the charisma, decisiveness, and interest in state affairs to effect real change. Every reform attempt which he or his ministers undertook met with obstruction from the nobility, at times the Church, and on occasion even the Queen.

In 1787, the state faced bankruptcy, and the recent poor harvest and the disastrous trade treaty meant less tax revenue. The clergy and nobility demanded that Louis call the Estates-General to attempt to solve the financial crisis. The king finally relented and announced in August 1788 that the Estates-General would convene in May 1789, the first meeting in nearly two centuries. This institution of medieval origin was a consultative body composed of representatives of the three estates. Upon the summons of the king, the representatives met in the respective estates and discussed the pressing issues of the realm. Like Parliament, its English counterpart, the Estates-General originally dealt in particular with matters of taxation and finance.

As a component of the First Estate, the regular clergy were expected to vote for their electors and delegates as well as assist in the composition of their Estate's *cahiers de doléance*. The king's decree of 24 January 1789, which overruled the previous laws governing the elections of the First Estate, severely restricted their input, however. By the new protocol, each curé could vote individually for the representatives to the electoral assemblies, but an entire monastery could cast only one ballot. Furthermore, while the number of secular clergy living in a particular region determined its number of deputies to the electoral assemblies, the same formula did not apply to the religious orders. Instead, each house received only one deputy, regardless of the community's population.[1] As a result, the monks did not receive representation in proportion to their population within the First Estate.

Although information on the Norman First Estate remains incomplete, the documentation which does exist seems to indicate that the Maurists still

---

1. Lekai, "French Cistercians and the Revolution," 92; Martin, *Notes pour servir à l'histoire,* 40.

received significant representation despite these disadvantageous changes in procedure. In some *bailliages*, monks participated in every step of the preparations
for the Estates-General: the naming of electors to the electoral assemblies, the
composition of the *cahiers*, and the election of representatives to the national
body.[2] The electoral assembly for the *bailliage* of Caux, held in March 1789 at
Caudebec, included Doms Monthois, Ruault, Allix, and Lemaire—each repre-
senting the region's largest abbeys: Valmont, Saint-Wandrille, Jumièges, and Fécamp.[3] In addition to these men, other Maurists attended and cooperated in the
assembly's sessions as well in spite of the king's one-deputy-per-abbey policy.
When the Third Estate of Caux requested two members from the First to administer the required oath for the electoral assembly, the clergy chose Dom Charles Du-
jardin from Valmont—although himself not a delegate to the proceedings—and a
curé to satisfy this obligation.[4]

Maurists of upper Normandy also played crucial roles in the assembly
debates and the compositions of the *cahiers de doléance* for Caux's First Estate.
In an attempt to circumvent the king's voting restrictions, the procurer of Fécamp, Dom Jacques Joseph Louis Charles Quennouel, urged the members of the
bailliage assembly to allow a religious who possessed a benefice one vote for
the election of deputies to the Estates-General. His arguments did not ensure the
measure's passage despite the heavy concentration of monks in this *bailliage*. He
made the same appeal, albeit with the same lack of success, at the electoral assembly of the First Estate in Rouen in April 1789.[5] The *cahiers* from the First Estate
of Caux did not demand the preservation of the regular clergy, but with Doms
Lemaire and Ruault—the priors of Fécamp and Saint-Wandrille—sitting on the
five-man committee that compiled them, they issued no criticism of the monastic
orders either. In fact, the grievances made no mention of the regular clergy at all.
The First Estate *cahiers* for Caux seemed more concerned with requesting consul-
tation of the Estates-General in matters of taxation and reaffirming the traditional
jurisdiction of the Church, although the Maurist contingent may have contributed
to the demand for a better education system for the laity.[6]

After compiling the *cahiers* from the individual communities, the representatives at the *bailliage* electoral assemblies proceeded to elect their representatives to the Estates-General. Despite the heavy concentration of monks in the

---

2. Vernier, *La Seine-Inférieure*, xxv–xxvi. The *généralité* of Rouen was divided into four bailliages: Rouen, Caux, Chaumont-en-Vexin, and Évreux. Each of these was then subdivided into smaller
bailliages.

3. AN, F19 6113; Loth, *Histoire du Cardinal*, 127; Martin, *Notes pour servir à l'histoire*, 40–41;
Tougard, *La Révolution à Yvetot*, vol.1, 182; Bellamy, *Bénédictins et Annonçiades*, 18.

4. "Procès verbaux des séances des trois ordres du bailliage de Caux, mars 1789 apparenant à M.
Elise Valin," p. 7r–7v, BMR, Ms g 181.

5. Ibid., p. 3v–7r, BMR, Ms g 181; Loth, *Histoire du Cardinal*, 153–54; Montier, "Les Moines de
Fécamp," 188–89.

6. "Procès verbaux des séances des trois ordres du bailliage de Caux," p. 4v, BMR, Ms g 181;
Bellamy, *Bénédictins et Annonçiades*, 18; Pigout, *La Révolution en Seine-Maritime*, 96; Tougard,
La Révolution à Yvetot, vol.1, 183.

7. "Procès verbaux des séances des trois ordres du bailliage de Caux," p. 11r–12r, BMR, Ms g 181.

area, the First Estate of the Caux *bailliage* selected two curés and a vicar general as their voice in Estates-General.[7] In fact, of all the electoral assemblies in upper Normandy, only the First Estate of the *bailliage* of Rouen displayed its respect for the Maurists by choosing the prior of Saint-Ouen, Dom Davoust, as one of its four deputies. The only Norman religious of any order to take a seat at Versailles on 5 May 1789, he was also one of only twenty-three delegates, out of 296, from the regular clergy of France at the Estates-General.[8]

While the First Estate of upper Normandy composed its lists of grievances and selected its deputies for Versailles, the Third Estate assembled its *cahiers* from the individual towns and villages. Regarding the regular clergy, the majority of the *cahiers* from this region remained silent, and those which did mention this branch of the clerical body seemed influenced by the familiarity and interaction between the religious and local laity who wrote the grievances. Municipalities in which Maurists had played vital roles in religious and civic life tended to register no complaints against the religious orders. For example, fostering good relations with prominent laity appeared to bear fruit for the monks of Fécamp. The delegates of Fécamp's Third Estate, several of whom were freemason brothers with monks from Sainte-Trinité, met in the nave of the abbey church and issued no statement, negative or otherwise, about any of the town's religious communities.[9]

On the other hand, areas with a less pronounced Maurist presence tended to be more critical of the Congregation and religious orders in general, especially in the realm of finance. In demanding the abolition of feudal dues and privileges, the forty landowners and farmers who composed the *cahiers* for the village of Beaussault raised an objection over the *dîme*, a tithe paid either to the Church or a holder of a benefice. In the case of Beaussault, the people protested, not the payment of this tithe, but that they paid more *dîme* money to a Maurist in Dauphiné, whom they had never met, than to their own curé just because the Benedictine had the good fortune to enjoy a high-income benefice in their area.[10] The village of Bosc-Bordel as well registered its discontent at paying half of its *dîme* to the religious of Saint-Ouen who had, until recently, rendered no services or funds to the town in return, despite the need for a new bell tower for the parish church.[11]

---

8. ADSM, L 1212; Horcholle, "Anecdotes de ce qui s'est passé dans la ville de Rouen depuis l'établissement des états généraux dont l'ouverture s'est faite à Versailles le 4 mai 1789," in Chaline and Hurpin, ed., *Vivre en Normandie,* II, 327; Brette, *Les Constituants,* 215; Lemoine, *Le Monde de religieux,* 386; de la Bunodière, *Derniers jours de l'abbaye de Saint-Ouen,* 10–11; Lekai, "French Cistercians and the Revolution," 92. The twenty-three delegates that represented the regular clergy included both professed religious and commendatory abbots.

9. Bourienne-Savoye and Desjardins-Menegalli, *Marins, moines, citoyens,* 15; Bellamy, *Bénédictins et Annonçiades,* 21; Bourienne-Savoye, "Les Fecampois," 81; Bellamy, "La Vie religieuse," 47.

10. "Cahier des représentations, plaintes, doléances et remontrances que nous soussignés propriétaires fermiers et habitants de la paroisse de Beaussaut bailliage de Neufchâtel en Normandie faisons pour être inséré dans le cahier général du bailliage du Neufchatel," as cited in Le Parquier, ed., *Cahiers de doléances,* 30–31; "Cahier [of Bezancourt]," as cited in Ibid., 42; Dupy, "Ordre et désordre," 461.

11. "Doléances, plaintes et remontrances des habitants de la paroisse de Bosbordel," Le Parquier, ed., *Cahiers de doléances,* 53.

Three-fourths of the *dîme* from the coastal town of Saint-Valery-en-Caux was allotted for the Congregation's monastery at Aumale, about eight kilometers away. The municipality's *doléances* did not denounce the collection of this sum for the regular clergy, but it did raise the issue of equal taxation for all estates, "Why did the Benedictines of the abbey of Aumale . . . not pay the *taille* [a land tax from which the nobility and clergy were exempt] when they have the amount of it in the *dîme* alone?"[12] The *bailliage* of Cany which contained no Maurist establishment in its jurisdiction suggested the more radical measure of nationalizing the lands of the religious orders to alleviate the national debt.[13]

A few towns in close proximity to houses which contained only a few inhabitants who had not fostered relations with the local laity also tended to reproach the regular clergy and even to demand its partial or total elimination. As a means of enhancing the quality of communal life in France, Val-de-la-Haye-Quincampoix proposed the closure of underpopulated houses like its Maurist neighbor of Aumale, the transfer of its inhabitants to larger abbeys of their orders and the payment of a salary to the regulars in place of feudal revenues.[14] The seventy dwellers of Serqueux, also near Aumale, went even further and suggested that suppressing the religious orders altogether would bring the most benefit to the nation. The revenue from the sale of their property could pay off the national debt and fund alimentary institutions.[15] In general, however, few *cahiers* from upper Normandy even addressed the issue of the regular clergy, but those that did seemed influenced by the amount of interaction that existed between the religious and the local laity.[16]

As Dom Davoust left Rouen on 28 April 1789 for the Estates-General, he could not have known that he had just traded the beautiful tranquility of his medieval cloister for the revolutionary fury which would permanently alter his life, as well as the lives of all French clergy. Four days later, he and the other

---

12. "Cahier [of Saint-Valery]," as cited in Ibid., 267.

13. Tougard, *La Révolution à Yvetot*, vol.1, 142–43; "Cahier de plaintes, doléances et mandat que donnent, etc. [of Dancourt]," Le Parquier, ed., *Cahiers de doléances*, 95; "Cahier de doléance laintes et remontrances [of Serqueux]," Ibid., 278–79; Dubuc, "Bibliothèques et œuvres d'art," 141.

14. "Cahier [of Val-de-la-Haye-Quincampoix]," as cited in Le Parquier, ed., *Cahiers de dolances*, 298. See Appendices F and G for the salary amounts of constitutional curés and vicars.

15. "Cahier de doléances plaintes et remontrances [of Serqueux]," as cited in Le Parquier, ed., *Cahiers de doléances*, 277–79; Dubuc, "Bibliothèques et œuvres d'art," 142.

16. Exactly how many of the cahiers nationwide mentioned partial or total suppression of the religious orders is unknown, but the number may have been low. Louis J. Lekai cites A. Denys-Buirette's sampling of 3,743 cahiers in which only 77 (or 2 percent) shared the sentiments expressed by those of Serqueux, while a sizable portion of the rest of the sample actually spoke in favor of the regular clergy [Lekai, "French Cistericans and the Revolution," 90]. Despite Sicard's criticisms of the regular clergy, he concedes that very few cahiers expressed open hostility toward the regular clergy [Sicard, *Le Clergé*, I, 279]. Baudot on the other hand asserts that many cahiers did manifest ambivalence towards the religious. This attitude later influenced the National Assembly to dissolve their orders [Baudot, *Normandie bénédictine*, 79]. Aulard took the middle-of-the-road position; he noticed little consensus of opinion regarding the religious orders [Aulard, ed., *La Révolution française*, 12]. Timothy Tackett examined the Third Estate's 202 cahiers which were presented to the Estates-General and found that only eight of these demanded the abolition of the regulars [Tackett, *Religion, Revolution, and Regional Culture*, 13, Table 1].

representatives of the First Estate gathered in the Hall of Mirrors at Versailles where Louis XVI personally greeted every deputy. On 4 May 1789, Davout joined the solemnities marking the official opening of the Estates-General. The day began at Notre Dame in Paris with the intoning of the *Veni Creator* in the presence of the king and all the deputies. Perhaps the chant in the medieval structure reminded Davout of his own Gothic monastery and his brother monks back in Rouen. From the great cathedral, the procession of the estates led out to the Church of Saint Louis at Versailles. First, the clergy, Dom Davoust among them, processed through the streets, followed by the royal family, the Second Estates and the somberly dressed representatives of the Third Estate. Once assembled in the Church, the attendees heard Mass and concluded with a Te Deum. The king who had fallen asleep during the sermon, awoke in time for the hymn. The king and most of the deputies seemed pleased with the days' events; the Estates-General was off to an auspicious beginning.

The first meeting of the Estates-General the following day dampened the high spirits. Representatives of all three estates assembled in the *Salle des Menus Plaisirs* to hear opening speeches by the king, his keeper of the seal, and Jacques Necker, the Director-General of Finance. Those deputies who wanted the Estates-General to lead to social and economic reform believed that Necker shared their vision. But, his ridiculously long speech about budget numbers and tax statistics bored and disappointed the delegates. Some had hoped that Necker would change the meeting regulations for the Estates-General—that he would announce that all estates would meet together and conduct business as one body. His speech, though, made only vague references to protocol; the estates would still meet separately as they had done in the last Estates-General of 1614.

After Necker's oration, the deputies of the First and Second Estates adjourned to their separate meeting halls to register the credentials of each delegate. The members of the Third Estate refused to budge. They demanded that all deputies meet together and register their credentials together. They also called for vote by head instead of by estate. Their intransigence lasted for the rest of May and into June. Meanwhile, the Third Estate issued an invitation to the clergy, particularly the representatives of the parish priests, to join them. On 10 June, a few curés took seats among the Third Estate in the *Salle des Menus Plaisirs*. Other clergy and even some nobles defected in the coming days. Finally, on 19 June, the majority of the First Estate voted to join the Third. Dom Davoust formed part of the clerical deputation which announced to the delegates in the *Salle des Menus Plaisirs* to expect the addition of the rest of the clerical deputies to its members. The day after the entire defection of the First Estate, the delegates found the original meeting hall locked. They assembled instead in an empty tennis court and declared to remain united until they had ratified a constitution for France. Reluctantly, the king finally ordered the remaining members of the Second Estate to join with the rest as a legislative body, renamed the National Assembly. [17]

---

17. Thibault and Coster, *Les Séances des députés du clergé,* 83, f. 3.

Beyond Versailles, mobs of Parisian workers, upset by the high price of bread and incited by radicals, stormed the Bastille, an ancient fortress for political prisoners and symbol of royal tyranny. With the threat of civil unrest in the capital and fear spreading to the countryside, the members of the National Assembly picked up the pace of their reforms, including work on a constitution for France and the Declaration of the Rights of Man and the Citizen. Unfortunately, Dom Davoust left no record of his experience in the Estates-General and its turbulent transformation into the National Assembly. Accounts of other eyewitnesses describe an atmosphere of hostility towards the religious which permeated the secular clergy and, with the union of the estates, found reinforcement in the anticlericalism of some members of the Third Estate.[18] With the deck already stacked against the regulars in terms of representation, Dom Davoust and his fellow monks must have had little hope that the policies of the National Assembly would encourage the preservation of the religious orders. The first blow against the monastic establishments struck on the night of 4 August 1789. In a display of emotional outpouring and patriotic frenzy, the noble delegates resigned all feudal dues and rights. Ratifying this noblesse generosity, the National Assembly decreed the abolition of all such feudal remnants throughout France. For the clergy as a whole, although they too relinquished their feudal rights on the same night, this meant that they would no longer receive the income from the *tithe* or the *dîme*. For the religious orders, this legislation meant financial crisis; in addition to losing the *tithe* and the *dîme*, as feudal landholders they also lost the income from their dues and rents.

With the decree of 4 August, which deprived the clergy of much of its income, the National Assembly stood poised to exercise the same control over the Church in France which the kings had once held. After Benjamin-Éléonor-Louis Frotier, Marquis de La Coste, proposed the total suppression of the religious orders on 8 August, the National Assembly sought suggestions from its Ecclesiastical Committee regarding the fate of the regular clergy.[19]

On 23 September, the Ecclesiastical Committee's spokesman, Jean-Baptiste Treilhard, mounted the rostrum to address the National Assembly. This lawyer from the *Parlement* of Paris had served as a representative of the Third Estate of Paris to the Estates-General in 1789. As one of the more prominent, lay members of the Ecclesiastical Committee, he advocated subordination of the Church to the state, but his proposals in the National Assembly indicated that he favored the reform of the clerical orders rather than their elimination. His proposal on that autumn day demonstrated this position. Rather than demand the total abolition of all orders, he suggested a procedure for consolidating smaller houses with larger

---

18. Beugnot, *Mémoires,* I, 109; Aulard, ed., *La Révolution française,* 13.

19. Aulard, ed., *La Révolution française,* 13; Loth, Histoire du Cardinal, 191; Aston, *Religion and Revolution,* 129. The Ecclesiastical Committee had been established before the convocation of the Estates-General to draw up proposals for the reform of the clerical order.

20. Dom François Robert Delénable to the president of the National Assembly, 4 October 1789, AN, D XIX 14, liasse 206, 21ème; Assemblée nationale constituante, *Journal des débats,* 1–2; J.-R. Suratteau, "Jean-Baptiste Treilhard," in Soboul, ed., *Dictionnaire historique,* 1044–46; Aston, *Religion and Revolution,* 141, 147.

ones, similar to Loménie de Brienne's Edict of 1768.[20] Almost immediately, petitions from the religious and the laity alike flooded the Committee's office. For Dom François Laurent Bardel, the Maurist librarian of Fécamp's abbey Sainte-Trinité, Treilhard's scheme came as welcome news. The monk praised the National Assembly for "having effaced the traces of servitude which disfigured the surface of France" and begged it to do an even greater service for the nation by suppressing the religious orders altogether. He claimed to speak only for himself, but his allegation that "already these generous [religious] victims are ready to sacrifice themselves for the security of all" seemed to indicate that others at his monastery or in his Congregation shared his sentiments.[21]

Despite his claim, Dom Bardel's plea did not reflect the general opinion of his Maurist brothers. On the contrary, Treilhard's proposal and rumors that some Maurists publicly supported it sounded the alarm in the houses of the Congregation and spurred their pens into action. In a missive directed to the president of the National Assembly, the monks of Jumièges condemned any attempt at redistributing religious populations as "prejudicial to their tranquility, more likely to cause discord and dissension to reign." The brothers of the Seine valley abbey adamantly insisted on the preservation of all regular houses, but if the National Assembly could not content itself with leaving the religious alone, then they preferred secularization to any reform platform which would affect the internal organization or regulation of their Congregation.[22] In another petition to the Assembly, three monks from Valmont reminded the national representatives that the Congregation of Saint-Maur could still provide valuable services for education and religion, but only by maintaining the status quo. If the Assembly, however, insisted on tampering with the regulars, then they concurred with their *confrères* at Jumièges, "Permit us to live as Benedictines in the form and manner in which we have lived until now, or set us free. . . . In the name of this liberty to which you raise a temple . . . do not allow us to be the only ones deprived of it."[23]

Letters from other Norman Maurists reverberated with the preservation theme. The brothers from the obscure, rural community of Tréport joined with those of the Rouen house Saint-Ouen to add their names to lists of those religious who requested the continuation of the Congregation.[24] From the other, less famous Rouen establishment, Bonne-Nouvelle, came an indirect condemnation of Dom Davoust's efficacy as a monastic representative to the national legislature:

21. "Adresse respectueuse à l'Assemblée nationale par Dom Bardel très jeune religieux bénédictin de la Congrégation de Saint-Maur," [n. d.], AN, D XIX 14, liasse 207, 32ème.

22. Doms Allix, Thomas Antoine Jean Despinose, Charles de Qu'ane [*sic*], Jean Pierre Guesdon, Gaspard Léon Gobard, Georges Eloy Vallary Montéage, Antoine Joseph Broncquart, and two absent to the president of the National Assembly, 7 October 1789, AN, D XXIX 42.

23. Doms Placide Joseph Monthois, Jean Dominique Richer, and Philippe Antoine Joseph eigniot to the president and deputies of the National Assembly, [n. d.], AN, D XIX 14, liasse 205, 15ème.

24. Jacques Joseph Rivart, Henry Chesnon, Jean Martin Cartié [*sic*], Augustin Joseph Bonnard, and Denis Delaplace to [National Assembly], [n. d.], AN, D XIX 14, liasse 208, 21ème; Delénable to the president of the National Assembly, 4 October 1789, AN, D XIX 14, liasse 206, 21ème.

"We had hoped that those of our *confrères* who have the honor to sit among you, *Nosseigneurs*, would protect this congregation from the misfortune with which it is threatened, while coming up with a proper means of developing its patriotism and of serving more usefully the Church and the state."[25] The laity too defended the utility of the regular clergy. The townspeople of Fécamp, showing their esteem for their local Benedictines, issued a statement to the legislature in Paris affirming the vital role which their Maurist house played in the distribution of alms and the administration of charity in their municipality. Apparently, the citizens of Fécamp did not share Dom Bardel's opinions about his abbey or its denizens.[26]

Norman Maurists in favor of maintaining their Congregation in its original state offered to provide immediate proof of their willingness to serve the nation. In petitions to the National Assembly, they proffered all of the Congregation's lands to pay off the national debt in exchange for maintaining the orders.[27] The National Assembly eagerly accepted this offer, but without a promise of preservation. On 2 November, the convincing arguments of Charles Maurice de Talleyrand-Périgord, the bishop of Autun, carried the day as a vote of 510 to 346 secured the nationalization of all church property. This last act paved the way for the total elimination of the regulars since this decree and the abolition of the *dîme* on the night of 4 August deprived the religious of any means of supporting themselves financially. The deputies realized that the issues of Church property and the regular orders went hand in hand. Five days before the nationalization of ecclesiastical lands, the National Assembly had suspended all solemn, religious vows and prohibited the contracting of any such vows in the future until the representatives of the nation had passed definitive legislation on the future of the

---

25. Doms Delénable, Jacques Nicolas Delarue, Jean-Baptiste Billard, Thomas Bautier, André Blanchet, and Jean Charles Joseph Aubin to [National Assembly], [n. d.], AN, D XIX 14, liasse 206, 22ème. The religious who defended the continuation of their order based on its contributions to education and scholarship represented an example of monastic decline to Sicard. He believed that had they truly felt committed to their religious vocations, they would have used this calling as their argument [Sicard, *Le Clergé*, I, 310]. Perhaps the Norman Maurists put forward the utility argument because they knew it would have the most appeal to the Enlightenment-saturated society of late eighteenth-century France.

26. Monthois, Richer and Meigniot to the president and deputies of the National Assembly, [n. d.], AN, D XIX 14, liasse 205, 15ème; Rivart, Chesnon, Cartié [*sic*], Bonnard, and Delaplace to [National Assembly], [n. d.], AN, D XIX 14, liasse 208, 21ème; Delénable, Delarue, Billard, Bautier, Blanchet, and Aubin to [National Assembly], [n. d.], AN, D XIX 14, liasse 206, 22ème; Delénable to the president of the National Assembly, 4 October 1789, AN, D XIX 14, liasse 206, 21ème; Bellamy, Bénédictins et Annonçiades, 21.

27. Monthois, Richer, and Meigniot to the president and deputies of the National Assembly, [n. d.], AN, D XIX 14, liasse 205, 15ème; Rivart, Chesnon, Cartié [sic], Bonnard, and Delaplace to [National Assembly], [n. d.], AN, D XIX 14, liasse 208, 21ème; Delénable, Delarue, Billard, Bautier, Blanchet, and Aubin to [National Assembly], [n. d.], AN, D XIX 14, liasse 206, 22ème; Delénable to the president of the National Assembly, 4 October 1789, AN, D XIX 14, liasse 206, 21ème; Allix, Despinose, de Qu'ane [*sic*], Guesdon, Gobard, Montéage, Broncquart, and two absent to the president of the National Assembly, 7 October 1789, AN, D XXIX 42. Kessler claimed that the abbey of Bec also offered to hand over its property to the nation, but such a statement does not appear in the same *Archives nationales* carton with the other petitions [Kessler, "The Suppression of the Benedictine Order," 23].

religious orders. Since Maurists took solemn vows, this legislation prevented any novices from becoming fully professed monks.[28]

On 17 December Treilhard offered another attempt at reforming the French regulars. As before, he did not advocàte their complete suppression. He did though paint a vivid picture of lax discipline and lack of ascetic rigor both of which had led to a loss of prestige for the residents of the cloisters. In order to rectify this unfortunate situation, which even some monks themselves had admitted in their petitions, Treilhard proposed that the Assembly allow any religious who so desired to secularize. At the same time the government should protect those who wished to remain committed to their vows and furnish them with the means of regenerating their establishments.[29]

Again, the legislative body hesitated, and Treilhard's speech and proposed decree remained without discussion for two months. Finally, on 5 February 1790, the National Assembly prohibited any order from having more than one house per municipality. For example, the Maurists could no longer operate both Saint-Ouen and Bonne-Nouvelle in the city of Rouen. This new pronouncement rekindled the issue of monastic suppression, and one week later, the debate over the fate of the religious orders began in earnest.[30]

Surprisingly, as the battle for suppression or retention waged in the Assembly, very few of the representatives of the regulars spoke in their own defense. Dom Jean-Pierre Le Breton, a deputy from Vannes and the only Maurist to say anything during the debate, merely restated the topic of discussion and offered no argument—convincing or otherwise—for or against the preservation of the regular clergy. While men all around them shouted diatribes at their brothers and lampooned their way of life, Dom Davoust kept silent.[31]

In defending the utility of the orders, the *cahier* did indicate that the legislators

In an extraordinary show of support for the regular clergy, their traditional rivals, some of France's bishops did present impassioned appeals for the preservation of the religious orders. On 11 February 1790, the first day of the debate over suppression, at the first signs of hostility toward the monastic houses, François de Bonal, the bishop of Clermont-Ferrand and the president of the Ecclesiastical Committee, mounted the speaker's platform. After affirming his responsibility to execute the will of his electorate, he proceeded to recite for the deputies the proscription of his *cahier* from the First Estate of Clermont,

> The religious orders of both sexes being able to be of such use to the
> Church and to the State, and to contribute effectively still, as they have

28. Assemblée nationale constituante, *Collection complète,* I, 12–14, 41; Rousseau, Moines *bénédictins martyrs,* 19. Solemn vows, contracted between the individual and God, remain binding for the duration of the existence of the swearer or the religious order in which he/she professes. Simple vows made between a person and the Church are usually temporary [Fournée, "Abbayes, prieurés et couvents," 28; Duchet-Suchaux and Duchet-Suchaux, *Les Ordres Religieux,* 291–92].

29. Treilhard, *Rapport fait au nom du comité ecclésiastique,* 1–11; Delénable, Delarue, Billard, Bautier, Blanchet, and Aubin to [National Assembly], [n. d.], AN, D XIX 14, liasse 206, 22ème.

30. Assemblée nationale constituante, *Collection complète,* I, 111–12; Martin, *Notes pour servir à l'histoire,* 62.

done in the past, to the glory and prosperity of one and the other, we deputies invoke the powerful protection of the Estates-General, not only so that these orders will not be suppressed, but so that they will recapture their former splendor.[32]

should adopt measures "to reestablish among them monastic discipline and to foster in their cloisters subordination and conformity to their holy rules." Toward this end, Bonal endorsed Treilhard's December proposal to allow those discontented with their vocation to leave the communal life, although, as the president of the Ecclesiastical Committee, he had initially expressed his disapprobation for this plan and had claimed that Treilhard did not speak for the Committee. The escalating demands for suppression must have changed the prelate's mind.[33]

Bonal also addressed the social utility of the monastic orders and rationalized their existence on the spiritual benefits gained for society from the prayers which these cenobites offered on its behalf.[34] Other deputies called to mind more secular advantages which the orders provided for the Church and the State. The marquis de La Coste, who had appeared eager to mandate the end of the regulars, did concede to spare the orders which administered to the unfortunate.[35] On the issue of education, the Congregation of Saint-Maur, which had distinguished itself for its secular and religious scholarship, was singled out as worthy of conservation. After depicting the Maurist motherhouse, Saint-Germain-des-Prés, as an indispensable center of learning, Abbé Henri Grégoire concluded that "it would be impossible and dangerous to suppress entirely the ecclesiastical establishments." Jean-Pierre Roger, a judge from Comminges, like de La Coste, supported the elimination of most orders but with an amendment "to save only the Congregation of Saint-Maur, because it has real merit for the State by its virtues and by its love for letters."[36] Thus, Maurist interaction with secular society in the academic realm had earned the respect even of those who advocated the destruction of the other religious orders.

---

31. Aulard, ed., *La Révolution française,* 66–67. A few representatives of other religious orders did add to the debate. Before Treilhard's report in December, Dom Christophe-Antoine Gerle, the prior of the Chartreuse monastery of Port-Sainte-Marie, had set before the Assembly his own proposal for the retention of religious houses as well as the institution of reforms [*Discours de Dom Gerle, prieur de la Chartreuse du Port-Sainte-Marie, député de Riom, visiteur de son ordre,* AN, AD XVIII, 35. An abridged version of Dom Gerle's speech can be found in *Moniteur,* 14 December 1789.] Reform, rather than destruction, found an expected advocate in Jean-Félix de Cayla de La Garde, the superior general of the Lazarists. In response to comments that corruption in the monastic ranks necessitated suppression, he likened this logic to chopping down trees just to get the fruit. He deplored any notions of collective culpability for the failings of a few [*Moniteur,* 14 February 1790; Aulard, ed., *La Révolution française,* 87, f. 2].

32. AN, AD XVIII, 35.

33. Ibid., 35. Bonal's cahier might not serve as a true gauge of the will of the clergy of Clermont-Ferrand since he himself oversaw the cahier's composition, inserting those issues which he deemed important and omitting any opposing views. See Mage, "Public Spirit and Public Opinion in Auvergne." For other problems with using the cahiers as barometers of the sentiments of all Frenchmen, see Hyslop, *A Guide to the General Cahiers of 1789;* Lekai, "French Cistercians and the Revolution," 86–118.

34. AN, AD XVIII, 74.

35. *Moniteur,* 13 February 1790.

36. Ibid., 14 February 1790; *Journal de Paris,* 15 February 1790; Le Hodey de Saultchevreuil, *Journal des États,* VIII, 339

Unlike Henry VIII who cited degeneration and turpitude as his justification for suppressing the religious houses of England, the proponents of suppression in the National Assembly did not dredge up the issue of cloistral corruption. Instead, they focused on the Enlightenment metric of social utility and rejected suggestions that monasticism had any value for the Church or the Nation. To Bonal's assertion that the religious served society by dedicating themselves to praying on its behalf, Pierre Louis Rœderer rejoined with a quasi-Protestant commentary about each man and woman praying for himself or herself, without the need for intermediaries. Expanding this principle of self-sufficiency from the individual to the national level, Rœderer also attacked de La Coste's arguments concerning monastic charity and assigned to the State the duty of providing for its needy citizens.[37] Although no one specifically responded to Grégoire and Roger's praise of the Congregation of Saint-Maur, the arguments in favor of monastic education and scholarship fared no better in the hostile arena of the National Assembly. The Chartres native, Jérôme Pétion de Villeneuve, posited that men who voluntarily renounced individual freedom in order to live in community should not educate the nation's future citizens.[38]

Since the religious appeared to have no usefulness for the nation, some deputies even asserted that society would benefit from the total elimination of the regular clergy. For an example of this, Pétion directed the eyes of the Assembly across the Channel. "If England flourishes, it owes it in part to the abolition of the religious."[39] In a clever and irreverent series of rhetorical questions, the Bordeaux lawyer, Joseph-Dominique Garat, described how various social groups and functions would profit from forcing this body of men to reenter secular society, "Will religion gain by the suppression of the religious? It will gain some ministers: the elimination of the regular priests will be an advantage for the secular priests. . . . Will the poor gain? To doubt it insults our morality . . . by the laws which you will decree on alimentary aid, the fate of the poor will be less precarious."[40] A deputy of the nobility of Clermont-en-Beauvaisis, Louis-Alexandre de La Rochefoucauld-Liancourt, even claimed that "the public opinion of France . . . for a long time . . . has requested the suppression of the religious orders," and that the religious themselves would offer thanksgiving to the august deputies for having rent their chains.[41]

---

37. *Moniteur,* 14 February 1790; Lekai, "French Cistercians and the Revolution," 91.

38. *Moniteur,* 14 February 1790.

39. Ibid., 14 February 1790.

40. Ibid., 15 February 1790; *Journal de Paris,* 16 February 1790. The impetuosity and impiousness of Garat's arguments so scandalized the bishop of Nancy that the prelate feared for the fate of Catholicism in France. On 13 February 1790, the bishop with a thundering voice like Moses cried out in the midst of the Assembly, "Declare, Frenchmen, that the Catholic, apostolic, and Roman religion is the national religion." His motion was shouted down and the deputies returned to the debate over the religious orders [Le Hodey de Saultchevreuil, *Journal des États généraux,* VIII, 342; *Journal de Paris,* 16 February 1790; M. Dorigny, "Joseph-Dominique Garat," Soboul, ed., *Dictionnaire historique,* 488].

41. *Moniteur,* 14 February, 1790; Journal de Paris, 15 February 1790. Given the percentage of the cahiers of all estates which shared Louis-Alexandre de La Rochefoucauld-Liancourt's sentiments

In his speech, the bishop of Clermont-Ferrand had tried to allay concerns that monastic vows were incompatible with the natural right to liberty afforded to all in the Rights of Man and the Citizen. While each person enjoyed freedom as an inalienable right, he/she had the right to voluntarily sacrifice that freedom to enter the service of God.[42] This preemptive strike did not satisfy Garat as he mounted the tribune—amid heckles and murmurs—and denounced the vows of communal life: "The religious establishments were the most scandalous violation of them [Rights of Man] . . . I swear that never have I conceived what kind of a God could take away from man the goods and liberty which he has given him."[43]

Antoine-Pierre-Joseph-Marie Barnave, a self-proclaimed champion of the pitiable men and women imprisoned in the medieval darkness of the cloisters, believed that the suppression of the religious orders and the nationalization of Church property would "consummate the Revolution." This Protestant parliamentarian from Grenoble saved his most inflammatory rhetoric for the solemn vows. He perceived them as mandating the swearer to renounce his civil life, even though monks like Dom Ruault, the first mayor of the town of Saint-Wandrille, proved the fallacy of this judgment. Barnave could not conceive why anyone would voluntarily give up his civil duties, and hence, to him the monastic profession represented a perpetuation of the tyranny of the ancien régime. Despite jeers and challenges from some clerical representatives, Barnave's concise speech left no room for attempts at reform or regeneration of the regular clergy: "The religious orders are incompatible with social order and public welfare." And, like Cato denouncing Carthage, he concluded with, "You must destroy them without restriction."[44]

On the last day of the debates, thunderous applause accompanied Abbé François-Xavier-Marc-Antoine de Montesquiou-Fezensac to the speaker's podium. Although he had opposed all previous clerical legislation, both advocates and opponents of monastic suppression demonstrated their high esteem for Montesquiou-Fezensac as he delineated a potential middle-ground decree. His proposal strongly resembled the advice given by Treilhard in December—not surprising, as the Abbé had also served on the Ecclesiastical Committee. He acknowledged that the government had the right to refuse to recognize solemn vows, but since vows were a sacred contract between the individual and God, the law did not have the power to sever existing bonds. Therefore, he concluded that the deputies ought to enact legislation to allow those who wished to relinquish the common life to leave with the permission of their superiors, "who alone can break their contract with the Eternal One." By the same token, those who persevered in their religious commitment must remain free to continue their lifestyle. In order to facilitate this,

---

and the petitions of Norman monks reaffirming their monastic commitment, his allegation of speaking for "the public opinion of France" appears rather exaggerated.

42. AN, AD XVIII, 35.

43. *Moniteur,* 14 February 1790 and 15 February 1790; *Journal de Paris,* 16 February 1790.

44. *Moniteur,* 15 February 1790; *Journal de Paris,* 15 February 1790; Aston, *Religion and Revolution,* 135.

he suggested that each department group such individuals into a "common house" and close all the others. Both clerical and lay deputies responded to Montesquiou's scheme with enthusiasm and approbation as it seemed to maximize the profit and convenience for the State while conserving some religious houses. On the other hand, this forced amalgamation failed to take into consideration the sentiments of the monks it would affect. In fact, it ignored the petitions of Norman Maurists who had taken up their precatory pens for fear of just such a program.[45]

Montesquiou's proposal for the first article of a decree on the religious orders reflected his theory that the government had the right to refuse recognition of monastic vows but made no mention of elimination, "The National Assembly declares that the law no longer recognizes the solemn vows of one or the other sex." Shortly after the abbé reclaimed his seat among the deputies, Barnave, who still wanted to advance his earlier demand for the total abolition of all orders, issued his own wording for the first article. In contradiction to Montesquiou's speech, Barnave's draft affirmed the legislature's right to refuse recognition and to abolish, "The National Assembly decrees, as a constitutional article, that the religious orders and congregations are and remain forever suppressed in France, without the possibility of being established in the future."[46] In the end, Article One of the final decree which the National Assembly passed on 13 February 1790 combined the versions of Montesquiou and Barnave and incorporated Mirabeau's suggestion: "The constitutional law of the kingdom no longer recognizes the solemn monastic vows of persons of one or the other sex: declares, as a result, that the regular orders and congregations in which one makes such vows, are and will remain suppressed in France, without the possibility of reestablishing them in the future."[47]

The second and third articles indicated the options for those affected by the suppression. Those who wished to leave their monasteries and secularize had the blessing of the National Assembly and the promise of a pension to hearten them in their decision. Mandating only one house per department—regardless of monastic rule—for those who refused to abandon the communal life, Article Two revealed the legislators' prejudice for those who would opt for seculariza-

---

45. *Moniteur,* 15 February 1790; *Journal de Paris,* 16 February 1790. The commendatory abbot of the Cistercian abbey of Beaulieu, Abbé François-Xavier-Marc-Antoine Montesquiou-Fezensac served as agent general of the clergy of France in 1785. As a representative of the Parisian clergy, he opposed all of the religious reforms proposed in the National Assembly, but he did so in such a circuitous fashion that Honoré Gabriel Riqueti, comte de Mirabeau nicknamed him "the bewitching little serpent." Regarding the religious orders, he did appeal for retention of the female religious establishments even though his suggestion mentioned that the government would not recognize "solemn vows of one and the other sex" [Jean Tulard, "François-Xavier-Marc-Antoine Montesquiou-Fezensac," in Tulard, ed., *Dictionnaire Napoléon,* II, 339].

46. *Moniteur,* 15 February 1790. In front of the Assembly, Mirabeau, the most unlikely character to scrupulously concern himself with connubial morality, asked that Montesquiou amend the phrasing of his draft to stipulate that this decree would affect only solemn, monastic vows. He did not want the general public to think that the government no longer recognized solemn, marriage vows either.

47. Assemblée nationale constituante, *Collection complète,* I, 198. The king issued the letters patent a week later ["Lettres patentes du rei, sur un décret de l'Assemblée nationale, du 13 février, qui prohibent, en France, les vœux monastiques de l'un et l'autre sexes; donnée à Paris, le 19 février 1790," ADE, 56 Edt 5 P 1]. See Appendix B for the entire text of the suppression law.

tion. Orders involved in education or charity work would temporarily remain in operation according to Article Three. Thus, the final legislation overstepped Treilhard's December suggestions but at the same time was not as inclusive or conclusive as Barnave and his supporters had desired.

The Maurist reputation for scholarship which Grégoire and Roger had mentioned did not earn for the Congregation as a whole the application of Article Three's exception.[48] On an individual basis, only the abbey at Fécamp benefited from this clause in upper Normandy. Almost immediately after the suppression decree passed, the town's mayor and newly formed municipal administration—which included some of the freemason brothers of the monks—drafted a petition to the National Assembly to allow the monks to remain at Sainte-Trinité and continue their alimentary distributions:

> If the suppression of the abbey of Benedictines of Fécamp takes place, this city will see a decrease in it resources. There are many poor aided by the daily and public alms of the religious of this abbey; in the recent calamities, their head has even increased the alms of bread and clothing, and employed such care for the relief of the unfortunate families, that the city of Fécamp fortunately does not feel the effects of the troubles which have afflicted other areas.[49]

On 20 May 1790, the municipal administration deputized Louis Albert Quévanne, a member of the monastic masonic lodge *La Triple Unité*, to hand over to the government in Paris another letter warning of the social and economic deterioration which the town would suffer if the abbey had to close its doors.[50] The National Assembly relented, and a law passed in October 1790 reaffirmed Article Three's stipulation that all ecclesiastics involved in health care or education could remain at their houses unless they had received permission to leave from the local government. This measure allowed the Benedictines to continue temporarily their charity at Sainte-Trinité.[51]

One month after the suppression decree, the National Assembly ordered the municipal officials to inspect the abbeys in their vicinities and draw up detailed records of all the furnishings, revenues, and possessions. At the same time, they were to inquire of each monk whether he wished to secularize or join with other communal holdouts in the department's house of union. Once this was accomplished, the officials would forward the records of these decisions to the national government. The monks would still remain at their houses under the authority of their superiors until the assembly set more specific guidelines on the distribution of ecclesiastical pensions and the houses of union.

48. Assemblée nationale constituante, *Collection complète,* I, 198–99.

49. Municipal administration of Fécamp to the National Assembly, Archives municipales de Fécamp, as cited in Martin, *Histoire de Fécamp,* II, 101–3; Bellamy, Bénédictins et Annonçiades, 23.

50. Bellamy, *Bénédictins et Annonçiades,* 23; Lefebvre-Filleau, Moines Francs-Maçons, 114–16.

51. "Loi concernant les religieux, les religieuses et les chanoinesses seculiéres et réguliéres, donnée Saint-Cloud le 14 octobre 1790," p. 12, ADE, 57 L 1; Municipal administration of Fécamp to the National Assembly, AN, DXIX 54; Lefebvre-Filleau, *Moines Francs-Maçons,* 114–16.

Those who chose to shed their cowls prematurely would forfeit their monetary remunerations.[52] However, in some circumstances, monks who left before the proper authorization later successfully petitioned for their pensions. Dom Michel Nicolas Banse addressed a woeful letter to the mayor and municipal officers of Jumièges describing how abuse from the prior and his Maurist brothers had forced him to flee from the monastery before the town's inventory. The municipal government referred the case to the Ecclesiastical Committee which appeared more than willing to grant Dom Banse's request. It is probable that, since Dom Banse's account of hierarchical tyranny confirmed Garat's claims about the superiors of the religious orders, this helped the former monk gain a favorable response to his petition.[53]

For upper Normandy, the inventories began in April and continued until the end of May. On occasion, this initial encroachment by the local government on the cloistral realm led to confrontation and mutual inculpation between the monks and the municipal officials. In the Seine valley, Dom Allix complained that only the directory of the district of Caudebec had the authority to inspect his monastery of Jumièges, not the municipal government. While seconding this protest, Dom Toussaint Outin could not resist the urge to append his own accusation about conflicts of interest. As creditors or renters of the abbey, he argued, the local officials had a vested interest in the monastery's financial situation; a visit by the more impartial district directory would serve as a better means of securing fair treatment for the monks. Doms Allix and Outin's protests fell on deaf ears as Jumièges' mayor, Varanguien, and the municipal corps performed their task on 3 May. This did not stop the recalcitrant brother from further expressing opposition throughout the operation.[54]

Conflicts also accompanied the inventory at the abbey of Lyre. Here, as in other parts of France, the news of the nationalization of monastic property and the suppression of the religious orders gave looters an excuse to ransack abbeys, taking whatever they liked of the monks' moveable goods. Although such incidents rarely occurred in upper Normandy, someone did steal a significant number of Lyre's precious objects on the night of 16–17 May, only two days after the municipal administrators had paid their visit. The thief must have been familiar with the abbey precincts since he knew exactly where to look for the treasury. The townspeople immediately accused the monks themselves, and, denouncing them as the devil's own, the mayor placed the abbey under lockdown with guards stationed at all the entrances and around the walls. No one could enter or leave

52. "Lettres patentes du roi, sur un décret de l'Assemblée nationale, concernant les religieux; données à Paris le 26 mars 1790," p. 2–3, ADE, 56 Edt 5 P 1; "Loi concernant les religieux," p. 9, ADE, 57 L 1; Assemblée nationale constituante, Collection complète, I, 153.

53. ADSM, L 6195; "Délibérations de la municipalité de Jumièges," 15 May 1790, ADSM, L 6195; Ecclesiastical Committee to municipality of Jumièges [n. d.], ADSM, L 6195; AN, F[19] 611[3].

54. AN, F[19] 611[3]. According to Savalle, the inventory at Jumièges proceeded more peacefully, commencing with the prior inviting the townsmen to share a glass of wine with him [Savalle, Les Derniers moines, 21].

the grounds without permission.[55] During a month-long house arrest, the robber remained at large, but investigators did manage to recover some of the purloined gold and silver plate. Although the local administration gradually lifted the restrictions, suspicion of the monks still lingered. Therefore, after abiding in an atmosphere permeated by mistrust, it came as little surprise that all of the monks of Lyre shared Prior Hommeril's lament, "O National Assembly, allow me to enjoy this precious liberty which you promised me," and left the abbey.[56]

With regard to the conduct of the monks and the municipal officials during the inventories, the turmoil at Lyre and Jumièges did not represent the norm for Maurist houses in upper Normandy. More often, the inhabitants of the monasteries enjoyed the type of respect which the municipal administration of Fécamp showed toward the monks of Sainte-Trinité. When they took the tally of the monastic goods on 4 April 1790, the local officials found friends, relatives, masonic brothers, or former feudal lords within the cloistered walls, and so they did not execute the National Assembly's law with tactless obduracy.[57] In the cases of Fécamp and Saint-Wandrille, some members of the administration even included a few brown robes. The introduction of Saint-Wandrille's inventory delicately indicated that all the municipal officials performed the inspection "with the exception of the mayor, who being the prior of the abbey of the said place . . . can neither preside nor assist us in the functions which we are going to fulfill."[58]

After escorting their visitors through their cloistral interior—opening every cabinet and counting each chalice and alb—the ineluctable moment had come for the monks. Faced with the prospect that the French government no longer recognized their way of life, each had to declare for himself whether he would remain in the cloister or embrace secular society. In the Assembly's debates over suppression, La Rochefoucauld-Liancourt had asserted that when presented with the choice, the religious would unflinchingly select the freedom of secular citizenship over the "tyranny" of the monastic lifestyle.[59] In reality, however, the financial and moral complications involved rendered the choice hardly obvious for most of these men.

In terms of finances, the law of 13 February provided each secularizing monk with a pension in lieu of his entitlement to revenues from the abbey's nationalized property. The amount of this remuneration, however, was not stipulated until 25 February 1790 when letters patent by the king qualified it according to

55. Duval du Mesnil to president of the National Assembly, 19 May 1790, AN, D XXIX 46; Hommeril to Pouret Roquerie, 21 May 1790, AN, D XIX 63, liasse 331; Hommeril to Pouet Roquerie, 26 May 1790, AN, D XIX 63, liasse 331; Guéry, *Histoire de l'abbaye,* 294.

56. Hommeril to Pouret Roquerie, 26 May 1790, AN, D XIX 63, liasse 331; Hommeril to Pouret Roquerie, 30 May [1790], AN, D XIX 63, liasse 331; Hommeril to Pouret Roquerie, 7 June 1790, AN, D XIX 63, liasse 331; Hommeril to Pouret Roquerie, 16 June 1790, AN, D XIX 63, liasse 331; Guéry, *Histoire de l'abbaye,* 306.

57. "État des inventaires des maisons ecclésiastiques et religieuses envoyés au comité ecclésiastique de l'Assemblée nationale," AN, F19 6113; Bourienne-Savoye, "Les Fécampois," 81; Sicard, *Le Clergé,* I, 288; Savalle, *Les Derniers moines,* 20, 42.

58. "Procès Verbal des effets de l'abbaye de Saint-Wandrille," AN, F19 6113; Bourienne-Savoye, "Les Fecampois," 81–83; Bellamy, *Bénédictins et Annonçiades,* 22; 88; Bellamy, "La Vie relgieuse," 4.

59. *Moniteur,* 14 February, 1790; *Journal de Paris,* 15 February 1790.

age and monastic status. The oldest choir monks would receive 1,200 livres and the youngest 800 livres per annum.[60] Besides the financial dilemma, the choice between secularizing or remaining presented the monks with a moral quandary. According to canon law, a solemn vow no longer bound the swearer when the conditions upon which it depended or the purpose for which it was sworn ceased to exist.[61] Maurists swore vows of stability to the Congregation of Saint-Maur on the condition that the order would continue. The government's decree permanently suppressing the regular orders meant that the condition upon which the Maurists took their vows no longer existed. This nullification of the vows particularly applied to the Maurists, perhaps even more than to any other religious order.

Unlike Cistercians, Carmelites, Dominicans, and others, the Congregation of Saint-Maur, a uniquely Gallican branch of the Benedictines, only existed within the borders of France. Thus, French Maurists could not simply leave the country and join religious establishments of their order elsewhere, as the French Jesuits had done after their expulsion from France a few decades earlier. Some Maurists opted to reside in other Benedictine communities outside of the Congregation, but canon law did not require this. Therefore, a Benedictine who chose to secularize in no way became a turncoat to his vocation. To further ease troubled consciences, the solicitous commendatory abbot of Fécamp, Cardinal de La Rochefoucauld, obtained from Pope Pius VI a papal bull officially relieving all religious of their solemn vows on 31 March 1790. In a letter to Dom Chevreux, the superior general of the Congregation, the cardinal authorized Chevreux to promulgate the Holy Father's pronouncement throughout the Maurist establishments. At the same time, the cardinal urged those who chose secularization to continue their service to the Church as secular ministers. Dom Chevreux's letter to his French Benedictines reiterated this exhortation, "Whatever part each of us takes, these dispositions merit from us the greatest recognition, and especially require that in any position we never cease to be zealous and fervent ministers of the Church, as well as good and virtuous citizens respectfully submitted to the nation, to the law, and to the king."[62]

When questioned about their decision by the local authorities, between seventy and eighty monks, out of more than 150 present in upper Normandy in 1790, declared that they would definitely vacate the cloister. Among these, most did not leave willingly—including Dom Bardel, whose petition to the National Assembly in October 1789 seemed to betray his dissatisfaction with the monastic lifestyle. Only two appeared eager to vacate their cells. Dom Georges Eloy

---

60. "Lettres patentes du roi," p. 2, ADE, 56 Edt 5 P 1; Assemblée nationale constituante, *Collection complète*, I, 115. See Appendix E for pension amounts.

61. Lemoine, *Le Monde de religieux*, 3–7; Duchet-Suchaux and Duchet-Suchaux, *Les Ordres religieux*, 291–92.

62. Cardinal de La Rochefoucauld to Dom Ambroise Augustin Chevreux, 6 May 1790, Chevreux to the abbeys in his obedience, [n. d.], as cited in Loth, *Histoire du Cardinal*, 257–59; Kessler, "The Suppression of the Benedictine Order," 43; Montier, "Les Moines de Fécamp," 137; Lohier, "L'Inventaire," 180–81; Lekai, "French Cistercians and the Revolution," 89.

Vallary Montéage, who had previously signed the plea for preservation with his fellow Jumièges brothers, must have changed his mind. His declaration indicated that he welcomed the chance "to accept with a good heart the offer which the National Assembly affords him to break his chains so that he can enjoy honestly his liberty."[63] From the other Seine valley abbey, Saint-Wandrille, Dom François Capperon even shared his enthusiasm for the suppression decree in a letter to the National Assembly's Committee of Legislation.[64]

These two hardly represented the majority however. Most monks who explained their decisions to secularize still affirmed their attachment to their religious calling. Dom Étienne Alexis Trémauville told the municipal officials of Évreux that "it is with the greatest sorrow that he sees himself forced to declare that under all reports it is impossible for him to continue the common life."[65] The thirty-third degree freemason Dom Charles Jean Bonvoust also protested his devotion to his ascetic lifestyle although he chose to leave the abbey, "I am inviolably attached to my state and full of respect for the engagements which I have freely contracted."[66] The deputy to the Estates-General, Dom Davoust, claimed that he had no intention of abandoning a religious vocation altogether even though he could no longer pursue it in a monastery, "I have taken the resolution to leave while remaining always faithful to the essential obligations of my [religious] state."[67]

While some secularizing Maurists still professed their love for the communal life, others used their declarations as forums for criticizing the government. Dom Jacques Antoine Michel Pichonner, a forty-two-year-old monk from the abbey of Préaux, leveled his attack against the new regime for failing to recognize the legality of preexisting vows and commitments: "According to the sacred pact which he contracted in good faith, he had a just right to expect to live and die in that state which he had voluntarily and solemnly embraced." Another Préaux monk, Dom Chahau, left little doubt of his disapproval of the new regime's treatment of the regular clergy: "He submits only by force to the decree of the assembly which robs him of the state which he has freely embraced under the protection and guarantee of the civil and ecclesiastical laws."[68] Dom Philippe Antoine Joseph Meigniot, the only inhabitant of Valmont who chose to immediately reenter secular society, stated his intentions with a sarcastic lampoon at the National Assembly: "He declared to want to enjoy the liberty to leave which the august

63. ADSM, 1327. Bernard Plongeron agreed that the declarations to leave were not indicative of the degenerated state of monasticism in the late eighteenth century [Plongeron, *Les Réguliers de Paris,* 310]. See Appendix C for the declarations of individual monks.

64. Plongeron, *Les Réguliers de Paris,* 385–86.

65. AN, F^{19} 611^3; "Tableau dressé conformément à l'article quatre du titre 1 de la loi du 14 octobre 1790 sur décret concernant les religieux contenant les noms, age, date de profession et déclaration faites par les religieux bénédictins, cordeliers, jacobins, et capucins," ADE, 116 L 2; Bellamy, "La Vie religieuses," 51–52.

66. AN, F^{19} 611^3; Dom Charles Jean Bonvoust to de Parnajon, Commissioner of the district of Montivilliers, 4 December 1790, as cited in Montier, "L'Abbaye de la Sainte-Trinité," I, 327, f. 25.

67. AN, F^{19} 611^3; ADSM, L 1200; de la Bunodière, *Derniers jours de l'abbaye de Saint-Ouen,* 11.

68. ADE, 57 L 24.

representatives of the nation have accorded him, that he sees with pain that the services rendered for the state by such a body as his are counted for nothing."[69]

None of these monks listed dissatisfaction with their regular lifestyle or lack of a true monastic calling as determinants in their decisions to leave their cloisters. Thus, the interaction with secular society before the Revolution did not seem to prejudice them against their monastic commitment. Rather, other factors appeared to have prompted them to terminate their cloister careers. Some religious interpreted this decision as a choice between fidelity to the Congregation and loyalty to *la patrie*: "First of all, I want to maintain my vows; this is my first duty. . . . On the other hand, I am a citizen and devoted to the general well-being. . . . I desire with all my heart to fulfill the duties which these two qualities impose upon me."[70] Those who perceived their decision in these terms usually chose secularization in order to demonstrate their devotion to the new regime. Dom Olivier Joseph Cadet did not join with his fellow brothers of Préaux in denouncing the government, but his declaration recorded that "he will submit to the decrees of the National Assembly although they keep him from the state which he freely embraced."[71]

Several monks cited the ambiguous nature of the houses of union as their reason for preferring to secularize. At Saint-Wandrille on 28 April 1791, after the municipal officials had inspected the abbey, they recorded the declaration of the prior, Dom Ruault as, "not knowing the house which will be assigned to him or the regime which he would be obliged to follow, he has decided to leave." With identical declarations, the rest of his brothers present at the time followed suit, except for Dom Louis François Lebrun. He amended his statement with the qualification that he would go to a house of union if the one chosen suited his proclivity for scholarly pursuits.[72] Some of the Maurists who declared that they wanted to leave their monasteries gave similar addenda, either "to reenter a house of his order at any time," or as the monks of Rouen's Bonne-Nouvelle added, "to return to my order if ever the National Assembly judges it proper to reestablish it."[73] Indeed, for Dom Jean Louis Dubuisson of Saint-Ouen the government owed it to the Maurists to preserve the order: "While contracting with the Congregation of Saint-Maur under the protection of the laws of the state, I have contracted with the state; I demand from the state the execution of its engagements with me, as I persist in the execution of mine."[74] Thus, those who chose to terminate their monastic lifestyle did not do so because their religious vocation failed to appeal to them but because they felt circumstances prevented them from living a genuine, Maurist experience.

69. AN, F19 6113.

70. "Des minutes du greffe de hôtel de ville de Fécamp," AN, F19 6113; Bellamy, "La Vie religieuse," 52.

71. ADE, 57 L 24.

72. AN, F^{19}611^3; "Extrait du procés verbal dressé par les officiers municipale de la paroisse de Saint-Wandrille de la presente année," ADSM, L 1327; Lohier, *Dom Louis-François Le Brun,* 12; Lohier, "L'Inventaire," 157, 177.

73. ADE, 57 L 24; "Extrait des registres des déclarations des religieux quittant l'état monatiques," ADSM, L 1200.

74. AN, F^{19} 611^3.

Among the monks who wished to continue the common life, less than twenty declared in the spring of 1790 that they would do so unconditionally and would willingly reside in whatever establishment the department would designate as the house of union.[75] The remaining men confessed their desire to stay in the cloister but only under certain conditions. Most of these individuals—who resided in the prominent and rather populous Maurist houses of Jumièges, Notre-Dame-du-Bec, Saint-Ouen, and Fécamp—expressed their intention to maintain their monastic lifestyle if the abbey of their current residence stayed open. A few pleas for preservation also came from less illustrious establishments such as Pré-aux and Bonne-Nouvelle. Five of the six men residing at the small but ornate abbey of Valmont tried desperately to keep their doors open. They attempted to convince the local administration that their complex was extensive enough to accommodate fifteen or sixteen monks and thus serve as Seine-Inférieure's house of union. If their plan did not meet with success, the five declared that they would leave rather than live in any house other than Valmont.[76]

Just as lack of knowledge regarding the houses of union had prompted some to decide to leave, this issue also occasioned a number of monks to add conditions to their decisions to stay. Still others could not judge one way or the other in the spring of 1790.[77] With the petition of the laity for the preservation of the abbey still unanswered by the National Assembly, nearly all of the monks of Sainte-Trinité delayed their declarations. Perhaps they held out the hope of qualifying for the exemption of Article Three and prolonging their poor relief.[78] The National Assembly's October decree permitted the temporary continuation of these distributions, but in December 1790 the district directory appointed a special commissioner to determine what the inhabitants intended to do in the inevitable event that their monastery permanently shut its doors.

After receiving a letter from the commissioner, the monks gathered for their last official capitulary meeting. As one body, they composed a unified response and affirmed their commitment to their monastic vows.[79] At that time, seven stated that they would persist in their monastic lifestyle unconditionally,

75. At Notre-Dame-de-Lyre, Dom Jean-Baptiste Labigne expressed the desire to continue his monastic life unconditionally on 4 January 1790, but five days later, he repudiated this declaration in favor of leaving the abbey and living at Bernay with his family [Guéry, *Histoire de l'abbaye,* 306].

76. AN, F[19] 611[3]. The sixth inhabitant of Valmont, Dom Meigniot, declared his intention to secularize.

77. About seventeen Maurists from other establishments also remained indecisive in the spring of 1790 [AN, D XIX 13, dos. 181; AN, F[19] 611[3]].

78. AN, D XIX 13, dos. 181; Guéry, *Deux bénédictins normands,* 2; Bellamy, "La Vie religieuse," 48; Montier, "L'Abbaye de la Sainte-Trinité," 85, Appendix B. Dom Jacques-Pierre Fontaine d'Épreville was the only monk who gave a definitive answer on 8 May 1790; since his poor health would not allow him to travel to another location, he resided at Fécamp until his death, nine months later. Doms Pierre-Alexis Cartault, Jacques-Augustin Pataillier, and Jean-Marie Herment were too sick to state their intentions. Dom Jean Collibeaux refused to appear before the municipal officers [AN, DXIX 13, dos. 181].

79. Montier, "Les Moines de Fécamp," 275, f. 49; Bellamy, *Bénédictins et Annonçiades,* 23–24, 77; Bourienne-Savoye and Desjardins-Menegalli, *Marins, moines, citoyens,* 36; Chaussy,

and four of their fellow brothers agreed to remain behind the cloister walls as long as Sainte-Trinité continued its charitable operations. All refused to join the department's house of union, although by that time an establishment of their Congregation had been selected. The very concept of men from various monastic rules living together and trying to maintain some shred of conventual life repulsed them. "I do not call the *état monastique* a confused heap of individuals thrown together by fate without rules and without pastors," challenged Dom Collibeaux in his statement to the district's special commissioner. "To me, these are not the rules, statutes and exercises of the Congregation of Saint-Maur; it is under its laws alone that I want to continue to live."[80] Rather than "submit to the illusory conditions [and] to the humiliating formalities imposed on those who want to remain in the cloister and . . . to live in a state which the dominant opinion seems to prescribe," Dom Collibeaux and five other Fécamp monks decided to leave even before Sainte-Trinité had shut its doors.[81]

Throughout France, municipal and district officials condensed the statements of the religious into the categories "desires to remain" or "desires to leave." In its summation of the declarations, the special commission of the Montivilliers district accomplished such brevity by listing all the monks of Fécamp as desiring to secularize despite their actual statements.[82] Reliance solely on this simplified report as a gauge of monastic sentiment fails to capture the complexity of the decisions which these men faced. The municipal assembly of Fécamp must have realized this; in January 1791 it ordered the monks to appear at the *hôtel de ville* to record a third and final declaration. Once again, the religious expressed their regret over the suppression of their Congregation and their disgust over the "unmonastic" conditions of the houses of union. This time, only five remained firm in their decision to continue the common life without conditions. Those who refused to leave stayed at the abbey until its final closure in July 1791.[83]

Maurists had become integral members of eighteenth-century society both in the temporal and spiritual realms. In the preparations for the Estates-General of 1789, they actively took part in the deliberations of their estate and sought

"Les Derniers moines," II, 256; Bellamy, "La Vie religieuse," 47–48.

80. Dom Collibeaux to de Parnajon, commissioner of the district of Montivilliers, 8 August 1790, as cited in Montier, "Les Moines de Fécamp," 178–79; Bellamy, *Bénédictins et Annonçiades*, 82–85; Montier, "Les Moines de Fécamp," 155–210.

81. Dom Pierre Desmares to de Parnajon, commissioner of the district of Montivilliers, [n. d.], as cited in Montier, "Les Moines de Fécamp," 167; Montier, "Les Moines de Fécamp," 139, 151, 185–86; Bellamy, *Bénédictins et Annonçiades,* 84. By the time the monks presented their declarations to the special commissioner, the two siblings, Dom André Jerôme Joseph Nicolle and Dom Jean-Baptiste Noël Nicolle, had already left Sainte-Trinité. They appointed Dom Louis Ambroise Blandin to convey to the commissioner their declaration to abandon the common life and live with their family [Bellamy, *Bénédictins et Annonçiades*, 81; Montier, "Les Moines de Fécamp, 156–58].

82. Montier, "Les Moines de Fécamp," 136.

83. Doms Charles Noël Sarazin, Noël Le Riche, Guillaume Picheré, Léonard Nicolas Lepicard, and Louis Julien to the directory of the department of Seine-Inférieure, 30 May 1791, ADSM, 1 QP 924; Bellamy, *Bénédictins et Annonçiades*, 24–25; Martin, *Histoire de Fécamp*, II, 119; Guéry, *Deux bénédictins normands*, 2; Montier, "Les Moines de Fécamp," 136–210; Bellamy, "La Vie religieuse," 49.

to champion monastic prerogatives. When the suggestion of suppressing the religious orders was introduced in the National Assembly, their adamant protestations in favor of their Congregation, which they addressed to the Ecclesiastical Committee, illustrated that their fraternization with secular society had not chilled their zeal for their monastic professions. Despite the monks' fervor for the preservation of their order, the deputies of the Assembly decreed the end of this illustrious group of French Benedictines, along with the rest of the regular clergy. In declaring to secularize or to continue the communal life in some form, the Maurists often reiterated their devotion to their vocations although the circumstances convinced most to leave their cloisters. Yet, whichever choice they made, many of these members of the Congregation of Saint-Maur preserved connections to their abbeys, their fellow Maurists, or their religious vocations throughout the Revolution and beyond.

CHAPTER 4

THE MAURISTS IN THE SECULAR REALM

ALTHOUGH DRIVEN FROM THEIR MONASTERIES by the decrees of the National Assembly, these monks found ways to maintain some connection with their former religious identities. Some continued their ecclesiastical careers as secular clergy (see Chapters 5 and 6). Others chose to remain steadfast in their monastic lifestyle by joining a house of union. Still others opted for complete laicization, but even these did not completely turn their backs on their religious experiences. In various ways, they maintained contact with their monastery or their fellow brothers.

Those who moved into a house of union found life in this monastic hodgepodge anything but typical of their monastic experience before the Revolution. As an appendage to Article Two of the suppression decree, letters patent of the king on 26 March 1790 required that each department designate one religious establishment as the collective residence for those who wished to continue living the communal life. This monastic retirement home of sorts was to receive monks from any rule or order and provide all the necessary amenities. The letters patent also granted the men of these institutions an annual pension even though the 13 February 1790 law had only agreed to pay such an indemnity to the religious who secularized. Since the decree provided no further descriptions or regulations for the houses of union, the lack of information contributed to many of the indecisive and vague declarations of monks during the initial municipal inspections of the monasteries in April-May 1790.[1]

Five months after the last declarations, on 14 October 1790, the National Assembly dispatched to the departmental governments more specific details regarding the houses of union. Departments would select which of its suppressed institutions would become a house of union based on the expanse of the complex, the condition of the structures, and the viability of the buildings to accommodate at least twenty monks and their personal effects. All religious who chose to live in such an establishment would gather—immediately upon their arrival and in the

---

1. "Lettres patentes du roi," p. 2, ADE, 56 Edt 5 P 1.

presence of a municipal official—to elect the house's superior and procurer (who would assume the paramount task of distributing the pensions) for a term of two years. The inhabitants of these houses, a heterogeneous blend of orders, would then vote on the regulations for meals, religious observance, "and generally all the other objects of their interior policy." The local municipal government would then ensure the implementation of the chosen regime. Stripped of their monastic rule, they were stripped of their religious habits as well according to the law. The National Assembly expected all departments to have fully functioning houses of union by April 1791.[2]

Perhaps as a testament to the Maurist building and reconstruction projects of the seventeenth and eighteenth centuries, the governments of both upper Norman departments selected establishments of the Congregation as their houses of union. The rather prosperous Maurist monasteries in Seine-Inférieure presented several options for that department's house of union, and monks from each institution lobbied vigorously for their abbey. In the declarations from Valmont, all but one of the residents tried to convince the local administration to petition in favor of their abbey for this distinction. An examination of the buildings, conducted by the municipal officials of Valmont, concluded that the monastery could house at least sixteen monks, but the wooden walls of the individual cells rendered it incommodious as a house of union.[3] The more spacious Saint-Wandrille also received some consideration, but the abbey's structures required too many critical and costly repairs.[4]

Jumièges on the other hand seemed the ideal location for Seine-Inférieure's house of union. Most of the twenty Maurists had expressed their intention of pursuing their cloistral life if that abbey remained in operation, and the townspeople appeared favorably disposed to welcoming other religious into the area. About two weeks after the National Assembly had delineated the guidelines for these monastic retirement homes, the laity and monks of Jumièges sent a letter to the departmental administration which described the abbey's suitability as a house of union. Its well-constructed buildings required no repairs, and it had ample room for all of the religious of the department who had already declared their desire to continue their monastic life. Furthermore, the establishment had little value as anything other than a residence for retired monks. The rocky terrain surrounding the abbey definitely provided little agricultural benefit, and unlike so many other abbeys across France, Jumièges' isolated location and distance from the Seine River made it impractical as a factory.[5] This petition must have convinced the directory of the department; on 3 March 1791, it announced to the

---

2. "Loi concernant les religieux," p. 5–8, ADE, 57 L 1; Lohier, *L'Inventaire,* 155; Cousin, *Précis d'histoire,* 475. In 1790, the National Assembly redesigned the administrative divisions of France by eliminating the old provinces and dividing the nation into smaller, more accessible units called departments. These were further subdivided into districts, cantons, and at the lowest level, communes.

3. AN, F[19] 611[3].

4. Ibid.; "Tableau général des traitements et pensions," ADSM, L 1709; Lohier, *Dom Louis-François Le Brun,* 14.

districts that any monks who wished to live in Seine-Inférieure's house of union should relocate to the abbey of Jumièges as soon as possible.[6]

Of the Maurists who had expressed their desire to live communally if an abbey of the Congregation became the house of union, most never moved to Jumièges. Only three Fécamp monks took up residence in the abbey although nearly all of their *confrères* from Sainte-Trinité had told their local administration that they could only give firm indications of their intentions when they had more information about Seine-Inférieure's house of union.[7] These three, combined with the eight men still living at Jumièges and five Maurists from other establishments, brought the total number of inhabitants at this house of union to sixteen in the spring of 1791.[8] A Maurist from outside Normandy, Dom Jean François Nicolas Lelaisant (dit Castel), had stated his wish to leave his priory of Saint Robert-de-Cormillon near Grenoble and retire to Jumièges. Although he had no apparent family ties to upper Normandy, the administration of the department of Isère granted his request.[9] No religious from other orders appeared on the resident roster at Jumièges.

These stalwart men who resolved to live out their monastic vows whatever the price made an effort to reestablish conventual life at Jumièges. On 17 June 1791, in the presence of the town administration, they elected Dom Jean-Baptiste Huard as their prior, Dom Jacques François Alexis Crespin as subprior and Dom Louis Bréant as cellarer. They even continued to receive the grain, cider, and fruit from the farms which had once belonged to the abbey even though such quasi-feudal donations should have ceased after the night of 4 August 1789.[10] On the exterior, monasticism appeared to revive at this house of union, but internally, contention—particularly from one individual—prevented the complete resurrec-

5. Mayor, municipal officers, prior, and religious of Jumièges to the department of Seine-Inférieure, 31 October 1790, ADSM, 1 QP 428; Directory of the district of Rouen to the administration of the department, 18 April 1791, ADSM, L 1195; "Tableau général des traitements et pensions," ADSM, L 1709.

6. Directory of the department of Seine-Inférieure to the directory of the district of Gournay, 23 April 1791, ADSM, L 1807; Administration of the department of Seine-Inférieure to Roland, Minister of the Interior, 2 May 1792, ADSM, L 1195; ADSM, 1 QP 428.

7. Mayor and municipal officers of Jumièges to [?], 26 June 1792, ADSM, L 6195; "État des religieux mendiants et non mendiants qu'ont préféré la vie privée qui sont residens dans le district de Montivilliers," ADSM, 1 QP 910; ADSM, L 1594; Bellamy, *Bénédictins et Annonçiades,* 82, f. 2; Montier, "Les Moines de Fécamp," 163–66.

8. "État des sommes à payer au quartier d'octobre aux cy devant religieux residents dans ce district," ADSM, L 1709; Dom de Quane to the administration of the department of Seine-Inférieure, 29 June 1791, ADSM, L 1327; "Premier registre des délibérations et arrêtes," p. 20r, ADSM, L 1562. Doms Louis François Lebrun and Nicolas Dubois may have also lived at the house of union for a while ["État des religieux," ADSM, 1 QP 910; Lohier, *Dom Louis-François Le Brun,* 15].

9. "Bureau des domaines nationaux certificats changement de domicile des prêtres, religieux et religieuses de 1791 à vendémiaire An IV ou Septembre 1795 vieux style," p. 15v, ADSM, L 1594; "Extrait du registre du directoire de district de Grenoble," ADSM, L 6195; "État des sommes," ADSM, L 1709; Bellamy, *Bénédictins et Annonçiades,* 25. Dom Nicolas Jean François Lelaisant (dit Castel) made his profession at Jumièges on 28 March 1753 ["Les Religieux de la Congrégation," 57, no. 232 (July-December 1967): 194].

10. de Quane to the administration of the department of Seine-Inférieure, 29 June 1791, ADSM, L 1327; "Premier registre des délibérations et arrêtes," p. 20r, ADSM, L 1562.

tion of ascetic life according to the Rule of Saint Benedict. Before 1789, Dom Outin had wearied the Maurist leadership with accusations of cloistral tyranny, and his reputation for criticizing his superiors may explain why most of the monks from Seine-Inférieure who had wanted to continue the communal life did not move to Jumièges.

Dom Outin persisted in exhausting Jumièges' paper supply by beleaguering the local, departmental, and national governments with demands for a pension increase and a stipend so that he and his *confrères* could buy new clothing. Monks who chose to leave their abbeys sometimes received a vestiary fund, a clothing allowance to purchase laymen's apparel. Dom Outin argued that the monks in the houses of union should receive similar remuneration since the law did not allow them to wear their habits.[11] When denied his requests, he enlisted the new arrivals in his letter-writing campaigns, but as they became aware of his disruptive character, they refused to sign their names to his petitions.[12] This abandonment fanned the fires of Dom Outin's paranoia, and in his letters to every level of government he railed against his unjust treatment at the hands of his "enemies," who included the abbey's new prior and officers, the rest of his Maurist brothers, and the local administration.[13]

Dom Outin's presence at the abbey became so disruptive for the other inhabitants that he drove away several of his brothers. Although the house of union had originally contained about sixteen men when it opened in April 1791, the abbey began losing residents. In July 1791, Dom de Saulty appeared before the district directory of Caudebec to inform them that his fellow ex-Maurist, Dom Guillaume Picheré, wished to move out of Jumièges and into the house of union in the department of Eure. Although not explicitly stated, Dom Outin's perpetual tirades undoubtedly influenced Dom Picheré's decision to leave—Dom Outin had denounced him as one of his enemies.[14] The *procureur syndic* for the district of Caudebec reported the situation more bluntly. He specifically blamed the rantings of this monk for the dissension and disorganization at Seine-Inférieure's house of union: "His *confrères* consider him a man of dangerous society because there is not one who has not known his malice and his blackness."[15] By September of 1791, the number had diminished by half, and some of those remaining isolated themselves in their cells.

The discontent which Dom Outin inflicted on his fellow inhabitants of Jumièges lasted eighteen months. In the world beyond the Norman cloister though, France faced threats from the outside and the inside as the Revolution turned more

---

11. Outin to the council of the district of Caudebec, 17 August 1792, Outin to the directory of the department of Seine-Inférieure, 8 September 1792, Outin to the directory of the department of Seine-Inférieure, 3 November 1792, ADSM, L 6195.

12. Dom Lepicard to the district of Caudebec, 10 December 1792, Lelaisant (dit Castel) to the district of Caudebec, 10 December 1792, ADSM, L 1327; ADSM, L 6195.

13. See ADSM, 1 QP 428 for more of Dom Outin's rants; Lohier, *Dom Louis-François Le Brun,* 15; Montier, "Les Moines de Fécamp," 163.

14. ADSM, L 1706, p. 347; ADE, 57 L 62; Montier, "Les Moines de Fécamp," 181.

radical. In September 1791, the king accepted the nation's first constitution which established a constitutional monarchy with a definite division of powers. With this monumental step, the National Assembly completed its primary goal, and its delegates went home, leaving the task of lawmaking to the representatives of the new Legislative Assembly. The inexperienced legislators of this body became more radical. Those known as the Girondins openly favored the dissolution of the monarchy and the establishment of a republic. Meanwhile, the émigrés, nobles who had fled France, issued threats and diatribes against the Legislative Assembly from the safety of France's other European neighbors. Insulted by these taunts, the Girondin-dominated legislature pressured Louis XVI to declare war on Austria in April of 1792. Other nations in Europe then joined the fray and France soon faced enemies on all sides.

With the nation at war and facing another season of poor harvests, the Parisian workers, the sans-culottes, became even more radical than the Girondins. On 10 August 1792, a Parisian mob stormed the Tuileries, city residence of the royal family, forced the Legislative Assembly to resign, and declared the establishment of a Republic. The Girondins set up a provisional government to prepare for a new legislature, the National Convention. During the elections for this body, the Girondins made their final attempts to curry favor with the sans-culottes—whose sympathies lay more with the left-wing Jacobins led by Maximilien Robespierre. The Girondin platform included a parting shot at the monastic establishments as they decreed "the absolute extinction of the monastic life," and the complete evacuation of all remaining religious establishments, including the houses of union, by 1 October.[16] They presumed that this measure would pacify the anticlerical mob, provide the government with further sources of revenue, and "dissipate the remnant of fanaticism for which the former monasteries have become too easy a retreat." A new round of inspections and inventories by the municipal governments commenced, followed by another set of declarations by the inhabitants of the houses of union. This time, the monks had to state their intended residences after their last bastion of the regular life shut its doors permanently.[17]

At the time of the promulgation of this legislation, only four monks still lived within the walls of the abbey of Jumièges.[18] Three of these, including of course Dom Outin, beseeched the department administration to allow them to live in the house of union until the following spring or, at least, either allow them to remain until January, when they would receive the first quarter of their pension for

---

15. Fenestre, *Procureur syndic* of the district of Caudebec to the *procureur général syndic* of the department, 27 November 1791, ADSM, L 1327; Montier, "Les Moines de Fécamp," 163–64. Each canton had a chief executive officer called the *procureur syndic*. His colleague at the department level was the *procureur général syndic*.

16. "Loi donnée à Paris le 17 août 1792, l'An IV de la liberté," ADE, 56 Edt 5 P 1; Kessler, "The Suppression of the Benedictine Order," 52–53; Rousseau, *Moines bénédictins martyrs*, 63.

17. "Loi donnée à Paris, le 16 août, l'An IV de la liberté," décret de l'Assemblée nationale du 7 août, l'an quatrième de la liberté," ADE, 56 Edt 5 P 1.

18. Montier, "Les Moines de Fécamp," 164.

1793, or pay them this money in advance.[19] The department administration executed the provisional government's orders with unrelenting exactness and refused to extend the deadline for departure or issue any pension advances. In protest, the four disregarded the order to vacate the monastery. By December the district of Caudebec had lost patience with these obtuse regulars. It dispatched a warning to the municipal administration of Jumièges that if these monks did not leave immediately, the district would hold the local officials responsible and declare them in rebellion against the central government. The four who had persisted in pursuing their communal life, even with a personality like Dom Outin in their midst, finally gave up their cause, and the once prestigious abbey of Saint-Pierre-de-Jumièges was abandoned forever.[20]

Although Seine-Inférieure's house of union at Jumièges did not enjoy much success in reestablishing communal life, the house of union in the department of Eure did attract a greater number of religious refugees. After the inventories of the abbeys in the spring of 1790, the department administration narrowed the choice for the house of union to Notre-Dame-de-Lyre, a rather unpopulated, rural establishment, or Notre-Dame-du-Bec, the famous abbey which had produced three archbishops of Canterbury including Saint Anselm. Upon hearing the news of their local monastery's consideration, the lay inhabitants of the town of Bec-Hellouin, who had already unsuccessfully petitioned to convert the buildings into a national college, vigorously supported the case of their abbey to the directories of the district and department. "The house of Bec is quite vast, solid, extensive; . . . it can easily and conveniently lodge fifty or even sixty religious; their stay at Bec will produce a steady and profitable income for the inhabitants of Bec and for those of the neighboring parishes."[21] The prior of Bec, Dom Pierre Marye, certified to the departmental head that his abbey stood ready to receive the religious, of any order, who desired to observe fully their monastic vows. Nevertheless, Eure's government failed to act and let the National Assembly's April deadline for the houses of union pass unexecuted. Finally, in November of 1791, the department administration made a decision. Since Lyre's small buildings would not suffice to lodge the number of monks who had declared to retire to Eure's house of union, Bec would receive these men into its cloister.[22]

Despite the smaller population of Maurist institutions in the area, the department of Eure's house of union seemed to enjoy greater success in maintaining

---

19. Lepicard to the president of the department, 26 September 1792, Lepicard to the directory of the district of Caudebec, 16 September 1792, ADSM, L 1327; Lelasaint (dit Castel) to the directory of the district of Caudebec, [n. d.], Outin, Lelaisant (dit Castel), and Lepicard to the directory of the district of Caudebec, 13 December 1792, ADSM, L 6195; Montier, "Les Moines de Fécamp, 166.

20. Directory of the district of Caudebec to the municipality of Jumièges, 7 December 1792, as cited in ASWF (1967), 90; Montier, "Les Moines de Fécamp," 166

21. Municipal administration of Bec-Hellouin to the directory of the district of Eure, 8 April 1791, as cited in Veuclin, *Fin de la célèbre abbaye,* 16–17; Porée, *Histoire de l'abbaye,* I, 538–39; Guéry, *Histoire de l'abbaye,* 307–8.

22. Guéry, *Histoire de l'abbaye,* 308–9; Veuclin, *Fin de la célèbre abbaye,* 15. Porée erroneously claimed that Lyre became Eure's house of union [Porée, *Histoire de l'abbaye,* 539–40].

the contemplative atmosphere necessary for the monastic lifestyle. Although only eight of the twenty-eight religious present at Bec in 1790 had declared their desire to continue living the monastic life, eighteen opted to stay after learning of the selection of their abbey over Lyre.[23] A number of former residents of other Maurist establishments also decided to relocate to Bec. Among these, four came from the same department, one from lower Normandy and six others from monasteries in Seine-Inférieure, including the septuagenarian Dom Louis Valincourt who left Jumièges to reside at Bec. Apparently, he and his fellow monks had surmised that Eure's house of union would better serve the Rule of Saint Benedict than their department's own assigned establishment.[24] Maurists from beyond Normandy such as Dom Jacques Depoix from Saint-Serge d'Angers must have also held this abbey in high regard as they opted to live there rather than in the houses of union of their own regions. The district of Bernay recorded Depoix as residing at Bec although he had no apparent ties to upper Normandy.[25] Members of other orders, a Carthusian from Eure and a Cluniac from the department of Oise for example, also chose Bec as their retreat, making it the true image of the religious amalgamation conjured by Article Two of the suppression decree. With thirty inhabitants in 1792, the abbey actually contained more monks after the 1790 suppression decree than it did before the Revolution.[26] Its ability to attract Maurists from outside its jurisdiction and even members of other orders bore testament to the reputation which Saint Anselm's monastery and the Congregation still enjoyed.[27]

Monastic life seemed to survive better within the walls of Bec than within those of Jumièges. The inhabitants of Eure's house of union also seemed to have better rapport with local laity and government officials. The monks at Bec fostered these good relations by conforming to the legislation coming from Paris. When the outgoing Legislative Assembly required all clerical pensioners to take the Liberty-Equality oath in August of 1792, the monks of Bec complied since the pope had not condemned it.[28] This display of obedience to the laws of the nation did not go unnoticed by the department administration. Five days after the Legislative Assembly required the closure of all religious establishments by 1 October 1792, the general council of the department of Eure issued an addendum to the

23. "État des maisons religieuses des deux sexes actuellement subsistants dans l'étendu du district de Bernay, des noms des individus qui les composent, et des pensions dont ils jouissent," ADE, 95 L 1, dos. 1790–An III. This number included Dom Charles Vigneron, the prior of Notre-Dame-de-Bernay, who resided at Bec in order to recuperate from an illness.

24. "État des maisons religieuses," ADE, 95 L 1, dos. 1790–An III; ADE, 57 L 62; ADSM, L 1706, p. 309.

25. *Procureur général syndic* of Eure to the directory of the district of Gournay, 25 July 1791, ADSM, L 1346; ADE, 57 L 62; "Registre des déclarations passés au directoire of the district of Bernay par les ex-religieux et ex-religieuses auxquels est échu des succession," ADE, 95 L 1, dos. 1790–An III.

26. "État des maisons religieuses," ADE, 95 L 1, dos. 1790–An III; ADE, 86 L 7 bis.

27. "État des maisons religieuses," ADE, 95 L 1, dos. 1790–An III; ADE, 57 L 62.

28. "État des maisons religieuses," ADE, 95 L 1, dos. 1790–An III; Porée, *Histoire de l'abbaye*, I, 543–45; Rousseau, *Moines bénédictins martyrs*, 68–69; Kessler, "The Suppression of the Benedictine Order," 54.

execution of this decree. The monks could reside at Bec indefinitely, "provided that their gathering does not trouble the public order and under the prohibition . . . of inviting citizens to their offices."[29] Even with this approbation, the monks made yet another declaration regarding their intended residence if the department ever shut the abbey permanently. Of the twenty-six still living at Bec, seventeen provided specific locations while nine remained undecided.[30]

The department kept its word to leave the inhabitants in peace beyond the 1 October deadline. Records from 1792 and 1793 indicate that seventeen religious, some of whom had stated their desire to move out of the immediate vicinity if forced to leave Bec, still occupied the monastic grounds. Perhaps the general council of Eure had permitted them to stay out of pity since some suffered from illnesses, or in one case blindness, which made a departure difficult, if not impossible.[31] At the same time, five of those still living at the abbey enjoyed excellent health and even journeyed from Bec every Sunday and feast day to say Mass in various parishes around the department.

Since 1790, the national government had required the clergy to swear an oath of loyalty to the Civil Constitution of the Clergy in order to serve in the pastoral ministry. By the fall of 1792, any parish priest who had refused this oath could face arrest and deportation. For the Bec residents who offered Mass outside the monastery, no confirmation was made of their status vis-à-vis this oath. The government's knowledge and apparent acquiescence of their activities, though, indicates that they must have sworn the oath to the Civil Constitution of Clergy. Furthermore, government documents described one of the infirm monks still residing at the abbey in 1792 and 1793 as non-juring, meaning he had not taken the constitutional oath. Had those providing pastoral care failed to demonstrate their allegiance to the constitutional church, the documents would surely have indicated this in a similar manner.[32] Just as they had done with the Liberty-Equality oath, these men showed their obedience to the government by accepting the Civil Constitution. This in turn must have convinced the departmental government to allow them to reside at their old abbey long after the Legislative Assembly had decreed its final closure.

The monks who chose to live in the houses of union wished to persevere in the communal life regardless of the conditions imposed upon them. Among all

---

29. "Extrait du registre des délibérations du conseil général du département de l'Eure," ADE, 57 L 2, dos. 1790–An VI.

30. ADE, 57 L 13.

31. "Registre des declarations," ADE, 95 L 1, dos. 1790–An III, 86 L 7 bis. Porée gives 1 October 1792 as the date of departure for the last monks of Bec while Ernes-Victor Veuclin says 8 October 1792, but the archival evidence seems to indicate otherwise [Porée, *Histoire de l'abbaye,* 545–46; Veuclin, *Fin de la célèbre abbaye,* 23]. Two of the monks who had lived at the Bec house of union, Doms Nicolas Bourdon and Jacques Depoix, were listed in 1793 as living in a house near the hamlet of Saint-Martin-du-Parc, two and one-half kilometers from the abbey. Dom Bourdon never ventured out of doors, and Dom Depoix only appeared in the village to buy provisions.

32. "Registre des declarations," ADE, 95 L 1, dos. 1790–An III. The departmental inquiry of the clergy in 1801 listed Doms Gilles Lechevallier and Louis Julien Benoit, two residents of Bec who

those affected by the suppression, they provided the most obvious display of attachment to their religious vocation. Those who did not choose this option, or who left the houses of union before their final closures, did not abandon completely all ties to their religious callings either. Some pursued careers in the secular clergy, as discussed in subsequent chapters. Those who laicized also remained connected to their former monastic lives by maintaining contacts with their fellow ex-Maurists, even living in the vicinity of their abbeys with their brother monks. Although Doms Louis Charles de Mésanges, de Saulty, Henri Hubert, Jean Jacques de Montigny, Louis Julien, Pierre Joseph Florentin Painblanc, and the former *frère commis* Jean-Baptiste Maillon had moved out of Seine-Inférieure's house of union before 1 October 1792—probably on account of Dom Outin—they still lived in the town of Jumièges. They may not have continued a communal lifestyle, but they certainly kept close ties with each other, and all swore the Liberty-Equality oath as a group in October 1792.[33] By 1793, Dom Norbert Joseph Gouillart, who had declared on 27 December 1790 that he intended to leave his lower Norman abbey of Sainte-Trinité-de-Lessay in order to live in the department of Seine-Inférieure, joined these monastic refugees.[34] These eight continued to inhabit the bourg throughout the Revolution, and by 1797 the names of all but two still appeared on the lists of state pensioners.[35] Like the Bec house of union residents, whose obedience to the state encouraged good relations with the local government, some of these former monks did likewise. While maintaining ties with his fellow ex-monks, Dom de Saulty occupied various seats in the local government, but his lingering religious sentiments must have superseded his devotion to the new regime. On suspicion of harboring refractory priests, he was suspended from his position as municipal agent in November 1797.[36] During the Consulate, he tried to buy the abbey buildings but lacked sufficient funds, and as mayor of the town from 1802 to 1808, he must have witnessed with horror the gradual decay of the once glorious edifices.[37] Although Dom de Saulty and his brother monks

---

served as desservants of parishes in Eure, as "attached to the government," and "enjoys confidence." This strongly suggests that they did take the constitutional oath [Sévestre, *L'Enquête gouvernementale,* I, 87–88].

33. "État des maisons religieuses des deux sexes actuellement subsistantes dans le district de Caudebec et les noms des individus qui les composent avec les pensions dont il a jouissent," ADSM, L 1709; "Délibérations de la municipalité de Jumièges," ADSM, L 6195; *Procureur général syndic* of Seine-Inférieure to the directory of the district of Caudebec, 1 June 1791, ADSM, L 1346; Savalle, *Les Derniers moines,* 26. *Frères commis* and *conversi* were laymen who lived at a monastery but did not take vows. According to the regulations, *frères commis* and *conversi* could live in the houses of unions, but only in a separate part of the monastery. They could not fraternize with the fully professed monks ["Loi concernant les religieux," ADE, 57 L 1].

34. "Bureau des domaines nationaux," p. 2v, ADSM, L 1594, L 1709.

35. For pension lists, see ADSM, L 1209, 1316, 1709, 3259, 1709. Dom Louis Charles de Mésanges died on 8 *frimaire* An V (8 November 1796), and Dom Julien disappeared from the pension lists after 1 *nivôse* An IV (22 December 1795) [ADSM, L 3259; Savalle, *Les Derniers moines,* 26–27; Montier, "Les Moines de Fécamp," 164].

36. De Saulty to unknown, 13 *frimaire* An III (3 December 1794), ADSM, L 6195; "Administration centrale, 1 vendémiaire An VI–29 ventôse An VI," ADSM, L 26.

did not reside in the Jumièges house of union until its end, their close connections with each other while living in the shadow of their abbey demonstrated a lingering attachment to their monastic identities.

A similar situation occurred at Saint-Wandrille. All but one of the monks there had followed the example of their prior and declared to leave the monastery. Yet, after its official closure, at least five still lived within the walls against the orders of the National Assembly. They and their *confrères* who had taken residences in the town of Saint-Wandrille still gathered in the abbey church on feast days to chant the divine office until a manufacturer purchased the buildings and dispersed the last of the monks in September 1792.[38] Nevertheless, the former residents of the abbey appeared reluctant to leave its environs. Doms Dechy and François Louis Joseph Lestievetz demonstrated their determination to reside near their former home by buying plots of the abbey's lands and establishing farms on them.[39] Doms Mathurin François Brixier, Dechy, and Emmanuel Catelain also inhabited the bourg of Saint-Wandrille throughout the Revolution. They must have also sustained and fostered their relationships with the former Maurist brothers who had served as parish priests as well. After resigning their posts as constitutional curés, Doms Louis Nicolas Grognet and Lestievetz moved back to Saint-Wandrille.[40]

At the same time, all of these ex-religious demonstrated their willingness to cooperate with the new regime by swearing the Liberty-Equality oath, receiving certificates of *civism* (proof of good conduct required of state pensioners and officials in 1793), and serving in the town's government.[41] Their positions in local politics even afforded them opportunities to protect other Maurists. As the president of the town's Committee of Surveillance, Dom Catelain agreed to allow Dom Étienne Joseph Mauger to fulfill the functions of the parish priest since the presiding pastor had abandoned his flock. Mauger had sworn the constitutional oath and had administered a parish in the department of Orne until the Jacobin-dominated national government proscribed him for his active federalist sympathies. He had fled to Saint-Wandrille where his Maurist colleagues, apparently unaware of his political leanings, welcomed him and allowed him to serve temporarily as Saint-Wandrille's curé.[42]

Like Dom de Saulty, Dom Catelain sat in various municipal seats until his election as mayor of his former abbey's town on 7 November 1804. He held

37. Savalle, *Les Derniers moines,* 29, 67.

38. "Registres des délibérations du district de Caudebec," ADSM, L 1562; Lohier, *Dom Louis-François Le Brun,* 13; Lohier, "L'Inventaire," 185–86; Frère H. L., "Dom Antoine Fidèle Dechy: Le Dernier cellérier de Saint-Wandrille avant la Révolution," ASWF (1980), 11.

39. "Extraits de premier registre des délibérations de conseil municipale de Saint-Wandrille," ASWF (1950), 51, 53; ASWF (1950), 80b.

40. "État des cy devant religieux de deux sexes et ecclèsiastiques domiciliés dans l'arrondissement de ce canton, jouissant d'un secours ou pension à la charge du trésor national, d'après la loi du second jour complémentaire An II," ADSM, L 3119.

41. "Extraits du premier registre des délibérations du conseil municipale de Saint-Wandrille," ASWF (1950), 61, 64; ASWF (1950), 80b.

42. ADSM, L 1579; "Extraits du premier registre des délibérations du conseil municipal de Saint-Wandrille," ASWF (1950), 65–66, 68. A few ex-Maurists did not always support their brothers. Dom

that office until 1823.[43] Dom Catelain eventually chose to completely laicize and marry, but he still kept contacts with his monastic brothers. Dom Brixier, who had become the secretary of Saint-Wandrille's sister town, Rançon, witnessed and received Dom Catelain's act of civil marriage to Marie Lhérondel on 30 August 1796.[44] After the 11 *prairial* An III decree, passed on 30 May 1795, allowed Catholic priests to resume their ministry, Dom Grognet fulfilled the functions of Saint-Wandrille's pastor and, as such, baptized Dom Catelain's firstborn in 1797.[45] As some from Jumièges had done, monks from Saint-Wandrille showed themselves obedient to the law and played prominent roles in local politics. At the same time, they continued to reside in the area or move back to it. They maintained their relationships with their former Maurist brothers and in this way, preserved their ties to their former monastic lives. With the presence of the two major Maurist establishments, Saint-Wandrille and Jumièges, it is not surprising that in the rural district of Caudebec during January 1793, thirty-seven religious, of the nearly fifty who had lived there in 1790, still lived in the area, and many of these names persisted on pension records through 1799.[46]

At Fécamp, the municipal administration had petitioned the National Assembly to allow the monks to carry on with their charitable work. As a result, at least some religious resided there until the abbey permanently shut down in July 1791. The directory of the department had also granted Sainte-Trinité's Maurists permission to open their church to lavish liturgies on special feast days.[47] The prior and his monks took advantage of this to further cultivate their amicable relations with the townspeople by offering Te Deums and Masses during municipal elections and presiding over the 1790 *fête de la fédération*, celebrating the first anniversary of the fall of the Bastille. They even welcomed the town government to meet in the abbey buildings.[48] Even after the abbey finally ceased its operations, the monks chose to stay in the town. By 1798, at least three still received their

---

Capperon who had served in the army at the front returned to Saint-Wandrille and denounced Dom Étienne Joseph Mauger for his anti-Jacobin sentiments to the government in Paris. Dom Mauger was arrested, conducted to Paris, tried and guillotined. Neither Dom Emmanuel Catelain nor any of the other ex-monks at Saint-Wandrille seemed to suffer any consequences for harboring the political dissident. For the details of Mauger's career and execution, see ADSM, L 1597; Abbé Louis Dumesnil, *Ma Prison ou mes avantures pendant le terreur,* BMR, Mss mm 31, I, 136, 144; Vaultier, *Souvenirs de l'insurrection,* 11, 93, 168, 206, 297; Lohier, "Dom Étienne Mauger," 339–80.

43. ADSM, 2 M 14; "Extraits du premier registre des délibérations du conseil municipal de Saint-Wandrille," ASWF (1950), 78–80a; Lohier, "L'Inventaire," 160, f. 24.

44. "Extraits du premier registre des délibérations du conseil municipal de Saint-Wandrille," ASWF (1950), 74; ASWF (1950), 80d, f. 1.

45. "Extraits de premier registre des délibérations du conseil municipal de Saint-Wandrille," ASWF (1950), 57, f. 1; ASWF (1950), 80d, f. 1. For the details of the 11 *prairial* decree, see Chapter 8. Doms Grognet and Catelain had probably grown up together; Dom Grognet's governess, Marie-Marguerite Rouland, was Catelain's stepmother ["Extraits de premier registre des délibérations du conseil municipal de Saint-Wandrille," ASWF (1950), 57, f. 1].

46. "État des sommes à payer pour le quartier de janvier 1793, aux cy devant religieux résident dans le district de Caudebec," ADSM, L 1709; ADSM, L 3119.

47. Directory of the department of Seine-Inférieure to the directory of the district of Montivilliers, 18 October 1790, as cited in Bellamy, *Bénédictins et Annonçiades,* 25; Bellamy, "La Vie religieuse," 49.

pensions there, and Dom Louis Ambroise Blandin, who had fled the area in 1792 for refusing the Liberty-Equality oath, returned to Fécamp after the Terror.[49]

Monks from less celebrated establishments also proved tenacious in their desire to remain close to their former homes. Until 1798, at least one monk from each of the abbeys of Aumale, Conches, Ivry, and Valmont lived in the local municipalities.[50] Ex-Maurists who chose residences near their old establishments usually gathered in groups with other confreres, as at Saint-Wandrille and Jumièges. Such a colony of monastic exiles developed around the obscure establishment of Saint-Pierre-de-Préaux in Eure. Three of its eight monks along with five from other Maurist institutions resided in the same district as the abbey through October 1794 although only one had familial or occupational ties to the region.[51] Though forced out of their conventual life, these men obviously found ways to preserve in some capacity their monastic fraternity.

Monks from urban establishments also continued to reside within their abbey or in the same city after the suppression. Évreux's Saint-Taurin, which had contained only a few monks in 1790, remained open and occupied for some time after the decreed suppression, and an eyewitness even claimed that the bishop of Eure, Thomas Lindet, no friend of the monastic orders, said Mass there with the Benedictines on 25 March 1791.[52] Pension records further indicate that the former prior, Dom Laurent François Dergny, and the octogenarian, Dom Bréant, lived in the city of Évreux until December 1794.[53] In Rouen, parts of the abbey of Saint-Ouen were rented out as apartments, but Dom Placide Deleyris managed to retain his cell indefinitely in the structure without paying rent.[54] Records reveal that he, six of his brothers from Saint-Ouen, and one religious from Bonne-Nouvelle maintained residences in the city through 1800.[55]

---

48. Bellamy, *Bénédictins et Annonçiades,* 22; Bourrienne-Savoye and Desjardins-Menegalli, *Marins, moines, citoyens,* 36; Fallue, *Histoire de la ville,* 441, 450; Bourrienne-Savoye, "Les Fecampois," 81; Montier, "Les Moines de Fécamp," 189.

49. "État des cy devant ecclésiastiques religieux et religieuses de la commune de Fécamp," ADSM, L 2095; ADSM, L 1316; Montier, "Les Moines de Fécamp," 198.

50. ADSM, L 1316, 1538; ADE, 107 L 14. These were Doms Pierre Bourlier, Pierre Martin Mullet, Louis Alexandre Théodore Beaussart, and Pierre Jean François Sta respectively. Dom Louis Joseph Cambier, Valmont's procurer at the time of the Revolution, listed the town of Valmont as his residence until An II.

51. "Registre servant à relever ses mandats délivrés aux pensionnaires et pensionnaires cy devant ecclésiastiques commencée du premier trimestre l'année trois," p. 37, 44, 48, 73, 127, ADE, 149 L 30; p. 2, 4, 6; ADE, 149 L 29.

52. Tribout de Morembert, *La Révolution dans l'Eure,* 24.

53. "État des cy devant religieux des deux sexes et ecclésiastiques domiciliés dans l'arrondissement de ce district, jouissant d'un sécours ou pension à la charge du trésor national, d'après la loi du second jour sans culotte An II," ADE, 107 L 13. Dom Adrien Lainé, who seemed to float between communities of monastic remnants in both departments, may have joined them in 1794.

54. de Chastenay, *Mémoires de Madame,* I, 186–88, 190; de la Bunodière, *Derniers jours de l'abbaye de Saint-Ouen,* 36; Deries, "La Vie d'un bibliothécaire," 218. Madame de Chastenay claimed that Dom Placide Deleyris was arrested but released two days later. He did not swear the

Fewer than ten from upper Normandy sought refuge in their hometowns or moved in with relatives immediately after the suppression. Instead, they seem to have preferred living in the proximity of their abbey and with other Maurists.[56] Yet, even those who moved away still exhibited signs that they had not completely abandoned a religious career. Dom Jacques François Huard and Dom de Maurey vacated their monastic cells, but rather than return to their parents, both chose to assist their siblings who became curés after the Civil Constitution of the Clergy decree.[57] Dom Letellier reappeared in his hometown of Goderville in Seine-Inférieure, but he moved there with Dom André Joseph Petit, his fellow monk from the abbey of Bonneval.[58] The two must have cultivated a rapport with other religious in the area since Letellier functioned as power of attorney for Fécamp's Dom Adrien Lainé in May 1791.[59] Ex-monks frequently served as each other's powers of attorney, illustrating another way by which they maintained contact with their monastic brothers after the suppression. Perhaps Doms Letellier and Petit assumed that they could live a quiet, semi-communal life in the obscure town whose nearness to Fécamp provided them with other comrades with whom to share their monastic exile. (This arrangement dissolved shortly after their arrival, though, as the monastic brothers found themselves in opposing camps after the promulgation of the Civil Constitution of the Clergy.)

Monks who completely laicized may not have overtly preserved some semblance of their monastic identities, but the careers which they chose often revealed the penchant for scholarship and education which the Congregation of Saint-Maur had inculcated in them. Examples of this tendency include Dom Bardel, who moved from Fécamp to Paris where he served on the National Assembly's Committee of Public Instruction, and Dom Alexandre Joseph du Bocquet from Lyre, who taught Latin in the primary school of Breteuil until the Directory prohibited any clergy from teaching in public schools.[60] Dom Armand Jean

---

Liberty-Equality oath, but no archival sources indicated that he was arrested.

55. "État des mandats delivrés aux pensionnaires ecclésiastiques pour le second semestre de l'An VII," ADSM, L 1316.

56. Only Dom Marie Antoine Lavieuville returned to the home of his parents in Eu where he became the manager of a hotel ["État des mandats," ADSM, L 1316; de la Bunodière, *Derniers jours de l'abbaye de Saint-Ouen*, 20; Deries, "La Vie d'un bibliothécaire," 218].

57. "Du registre des délibérations de la commune de Saint-Georges-sur-Fontaine," ADSM, L 1205; ADE, 57 L 62, 57 L 13, 129 L 9; Sévestre, *Le Personnel de l'église*, 119, 244; Montier, "Les Moines de Fécamp," 210.

58. Marnier, *procureur syndic* of the district of Montivilliers, to the *procureur général syndic* of the department, 30 April 1791, ADSM, L 1346; "État des sommes," "État des cy devant religieux des deux sexes et ecclésiastiques domiciliés dans l'arrondissement de ce district," ADSM, L 2097; ADSM, L 2095.

59. "Du registre des declarations passées par les religieux de quitter la vie commune," ADE, 57 L 62. For three other examples of this practice, see Doms Étienne Alexis Trémauville, de Saulty, and Lebrun acting as powers of attorney for colleagues ["Bureau des domaines nationaux," p. 5v, ADSM, L 1594; ADE, 57 L 62]. Although he did not choose to live with other ex-monks, Dom Desmares from Fécamp did appear to cling to his religious vocation by moving to Triel-sur-Seine, near Paris, where he lived with a community of priests [Dom Desmares to the *procureur syndic* of the district of Montivilliers, 28 April 1792, ADSM, L 2098; Bellamy, *Bénédictins et Annonçiades*, 79, f.

Froger also became a public school instructor at Yvetot at the behest of the local administration (which included the ex-Maurist constitutional curé Dom Legrand). In addition to teaching math, Latin, and French, Dom Froger also established a library for the district.[61]

Dom Gourdin's secular career allowed him to engage in an occupation well suited for a former member of the Congregation and to maintain close connections with his monastic past. The National Assembly declared all abbatial buildings and everything which they contained property of the nation and prohibited secularizing monks from taking anything but their personal belongings from their monasteries. The Assembly had included instructions to local officials on sealing doors and windows and stationing guards at the abbey doors to protect the contents of the vacated buildings. But, as the theft at the abbey of Lyre illustrated, such inadequate measures could not long deter looters. Therefore, the legislature ordered all departments to transport the libraries and works of art from these houses to a central depot for classification and storage. In August 1790, Dom Gourdin, the former librarian of Saint-Ouen, had written to the department directory requesting the preservation of the abbey's library which he had so meticulously maintained. Deciding that a well-educated Maurist with extensive experience in library work could best perform the collection and cataloging of the literary treasures of the suppressed institutions, the directory of Seine-Inférieure appointed Dom Gourdin as the department's first librarian. Since his expertise extended only over the realm of written materials, at his request the directory granted him an assistant, the Rouen painter Charles Louis François Le Carpentier, to assess and classify artwork.[62]

Dom Gourdin and Le Carpentier traveled throughout the department collecting books, manuscripts, sculptures, and paintings from religious houses of all orders. According to the instructions of the National Assembly, these two *commissionnaires des arts et belles lettres* were to enter an establishment with the municipal administration; count the books, manuscripts, and artwork present; select

---

20; Montier, "Les Moines de Fécamp," 168].

60. AN, F[19] 1217; Central administration of the department of Seine-Inférieure to the municipal administration of Bolbec, 28 *prairial* An VI (16 June 1798), ADSM, L 2798; ADE, 57 L 16; Chaussy, "Les Derniers moines," 266.

61. "Compte que rend l'administration du département de la Seine-Inférieure au comité de legislation de l'application des loix," AN, F[1cIII] Seine-Inférieure 7; Central administration of the department of Seine-Inférieure to the municipal administration of Bolbec, 28 *prairial* An VI (16 June 1798), ADSM, L 2798; "État des traitements et pensions des bénéfices ecclésiastiques des deux sexes," ADSM, L 1709, L 1212, 1181; Ledré, *Le Diocèse de Rouen*, 107; de la Bunodière, *Derniers jours de l'abbaye de Saint-Ouen*, 18; Tougard, *La Révolution à Yvetot*, vol. 2, 8, 141, 169; Deries, "La Vie d'un bibliothécaire," 218; Denis, "Les Bénédictins de la Congrégation," 312; Dubuc, "Bibliothèques et œuvres d'art," 145–49, 154.

62. AN, F1[cIII] Seine-Inférieure 7; ADSM, L 1181; de Chastenay, *Mémoires de Madame,* I, 186; Deries, "La Vie d'un bibliothécaire," 210, 219; Dubuc "Bibliothèques et œuvres d'art," 143–45, 149. Dom Aubin, who had assisted Dom Gourdin in the library of Saint-Ouen, returned to his hometown of Saint-Omer in the department of Pas de Calais after the suppression. The municipal administration appointed him the town librarian. His duties, similar to those of Dom Gourdin, included preserving

the items worthy of preservation; seal them in sacks and transport them back to Rouen. The directory had chosen the former convent of the Jacobins as the depot for these items, but the quantity of materials soon surpassed the space available, and the more spacious Saint-Ouen became the depot, no doubt to Dom Gourdin's delight. The department administration allowed him to live there and personally guard his collection. He even received permission to carry a loaded pistol in case of a break-in.[63]

Dom Gourdin's initial foray into the religious communities of the Rouen district produced 100,000 volumes and over one hundred works of art. The inspection of abbeys in the rest of the department proved even more fruitful as the vast libraries of Jumièges and Saint-Wandrille were loaded onto barges and sailed up the Seine River to Rouen.[64] These collection missions did not always proceed without obstruction or opposition. Upon his arrival at the Cistercian abbey of Valasse, he found some of the library already auctioned off, contrary to the decree of the National Assembly. In another incident, the mayor of Neufchâtel had visited the monasteries of Saint-Martin-d'Auchy-les-Aumales and Notre-Dame-de-Foucarmont ahead of Dom Gourdin and had shipped the contents to the public library of Neufchâtel.[65] At Fécamp, Dom Gourdin and Le Carpentier discovered a rich store of materials still in the town's religious institutions; however, when their carts of objects tried to leave, the local commandant of the National Guard blocked the road. Demanding that the objects of their abbeys stay in their community, the townspeople rioted and refused to let the carts pass. Nevertheless, with the authority of the directory of the department behind him, Dom Gourdin finally succeeded in transferring Fécamp's works to his Rouen library.[66]

Despite these difficulties, the constant threat of theft, the lack of supporting staff, irregular pension payments and even a brief imprisonment during the Terror, Dom Gourdin managed to assemble one of the most magnificent collections of the written word outside of Paris. His position as monastic librarian at Saint-Ouen had prepared him to assume this same role in the secular world. Although he did not persist in performing his religious faculties, his occupation after the suppression allowed him to preserve at least the scholastic element of his former Maurist identity. Furthermore, not only did this position allow him to maintain a connection with his former lifestyle and live in his old abbey, but by 1796, he had safeguarded and cataloged more than 300,000 volumes of precious books and manuscripts from the libraries of religious houses, émigrés, and

---

and classifying the volumes from local religious institutions. He retained this position throughout the Revolution and the reign of Napoleon. After producing a three-volume, handwritten catalog of the works which he had assembled, he resigned in 1827 at the age of 80 [Bled, "Les Origines," 208–17].

63. AN, F1ᶜᴵᴵᴵ Seine-Inférieure 7; ADSM, L 1181; Deries, "La Vie d'un bibliothécaire," 219–21; Dubuc, "Bibliothèques et œuvres d'art," 147–48; ASWF (1946), 59, 61.

64. ADSM, L 1181; Savalle, *Les Derniers moines,* 32.

65. ADSM, L 1181; Dubuc, "Bibliothèques et œuvres d'art," 150.

66. ADSM, L 1181; Deries, "La Vie d'un bibliothécaire," 223; Dubuc, "Bibliothèques et œuvres

deported priests. In many other departments such works were sold or, worse yet, destroyed.[67]

Although the National Assembly had ordered the closure of their abbeys, this did not prevent ex-Maurists from preserving ties with their former vocations. Those who refused to abandon the communal life joined the houses of union until these were abolished in 1792. Others, who laicized, maintained a connection with their monastic identities by living near (or, in some cases, even within) their abbeys, and by keeping in close contact with their old brothers. Members of both of these groups also sought to foster good relations with secular society as Maurists had done before the Revolution. As the inhabitants of Bec demonstrated, this rapport often benefited them in the preservation of their religious identities. A few monks chose secular careers in academia. But even in the performance of these occupations they drew upon their past Maurist training and scholarship. While serving in a temporal occupation, Dom Gourdin even continued to live at his abbey and executed a valuable service for the state and for religion. In various ways, Maurists demonstrated that the government could take the monks out of the monasteries but could not eradicate the monastic attachments from the monks.

---

d'art," 153

67. AN, F1ᶜⁱⁱⁱ Seine-Inférieure 8, dos. An II–III; ADSM, L 1180 and 1181; Deries, "La Vie d'un bibliothécaire," 224–25, 228–29, 232; Dubuc, "Bibliothèques et œuvres d'art," 146; Cooney, "'I Have Not Compromised Myself in Anything,'" 25–33.

CHAPTER 5

MAURISTS AND THE
CIVIL CONSTITUTION OF THE CLERGY

ONLY A FEW MONTHS AFTER JEAN-BAPTISTE TREILHARD had first presented his reforms for the regular clergy to the National Assembly, he again participated in the Ecclesiastical Committee's efforts to reform the secular clergy. While the Assembly's deputies formulated a political constitution which delineated the rights and duties of the government and its citizens, on 29 May 1790, Treilhard and his fellow committee members proposed a constitution for the French clergy. After six weeks of debates, the National Assembly, without a formal vote, implemented the Civil Constitution of the Clergy. The final draft of this document again proved more radical than the proposal offered by the Ecclesiastical Committee.[1]

Since Pope Leo X had granted Francis I the right to nominate the bishops of France in 1518, the kings of France had exercised extensive control over the Church in their domain. For two centuries, the Gallican clergy looked more to the French king than to the pope for its jurisdiction, financial security, and appointment of ministers. Yet, just as the National Assembly had usurped the monarch's lawmaking functions, so it also assumed control of the French Church with the Civil Constitution of the Clergy. With this legislation, the deputies attempted to completely subordinate the Church to the French state. In so doing, they hoped to inaugurate a more rational and egalitarian structure to the ecclesiastical body and eliminate clerical corruption. The Civil Constitution of the Clergy cut the last thread which bound the Gallican clergy to Rome by forbidding a newly selected bishop to seek papal approval for his appointment.[2] To complement the department divisions (the new administrative units of France established in 1790), the Civil Constitution of the Clergy abolished the old ecclesiastical boundaries and made the new dioceses correspond to the department borders. For example, the former diocese of Évreux and the archdiocese of Rouen became the dioceses of

---

1. *Moniteur,* 30 May 1790, 12 June 1790; Aston, *Religion and Revolution,* 140–41.
2. Tackett, *Religion, Revolution, and Regional Culture,* 16; Aston, *Religion and Revolution,* 143.

Eure and Seine-Inférieure.[3] The king no longer enjoyed the privilege of nominating bishops for these dioceses; the laity, regardless of their own religious denomination, elected the bishops and parish priests for their department. Cathedral chapters and canonical orders had to surrender their roles as the advisors of the bishop in favor of an elected episcopal council which approved all episcopal proceedings.[4]

The Civil Constitution of the Clergy leveled the church hierarchy by abolishing the archbishoprics, ending the nobility's monopoly on bishoprics and opening the episcopate to any clerics who had served as parish curés for at least fifteen years.[5] In response to the cahiers of the parish priests who had complained of the unequal distribution of the Church's wealth between the upper and lower clergy, all ministers of religion were included under the category *fonctionnaire public* and, as such, received quarterly salaries from the government in place of tithes, feudal dues, benefices, and revenues from Church property. The Civil Constitution of the Clergy reduced bishops' salaries, which during the ancien régime could exceed 500,000 livres per year, to an average of 40,000 to 50,000 annually. For curés and vicars, this legislation established a graduated salary scale based on parish population, but even the lowest-paid parish priest saw his yearly income raised from 700 livres before 1789 to 1,200 after the Civil Constitution.[6]

The National Assembly's initial promulgation of the Civil Constitution of the Clergy, which the king endorsed in August 1790, evoked little initial opposition. In many regions of France this legislation produced only a ripple in the sea of correspondence which flooded the offices of the novice departmental governments. The reorganization of the Gallican Church began to receive more attention in October 1790 when a number of clerics sitting in the Assembly expressed their disapprobation for the Civil Constitution claiming that it represented temporal encroachment on the spiritual realm.[7] On 27 November 1790, without the blessing of the Ecclesiastical Committee, the reporter of the Committee for Research and Reports, Jean-Georges-Charles Voidel, proposed legislation that would require all public functionaries to swear on oath of allegiance to the Civil Constitution or lose their positions. Taking such an oath would serve not only as a sign of acceptance of the Assembly's ecclesiastical meddling but also as implicit recognition that the National Assembly had replaced the king as the sovereign power in France.

---

3. The department of Seine-Inférieure changed its name to Seine-Maritime in the twentieth century. This book will refer to the department by its Revolutionary name, Seine-Inférieure, but the Archives départementales de Seine-Maritime refer to the archives of the same department.

4. Aston, *Religion and Revolution,* 141–42; Tackett, *Religion, Revolution, and Regional Culture,* 14–16.

5. The ten senior French bishops, which included the bishop of Rouen, received the honorific title of constitutional metropolitan [Aston, *Religion and Revolution,* 141].

6. ADSM, L 2097; ADE, 57 L 1; Tackett, *Religion, Revolution, and Regional Culture,* 13–14; Aston, *Religion and Revolution,* 142. See Appendices 5 and 6 for a list of salaries for curés and vicars.

7. Tackett, *Religion, Revolution, and Regional Culture,* 21.

The legislators passed the proposal the same day with the amendment that all clergy swear their oaths without restrictions or explanations. After the beginning of the new year, the deputies expected the forty-four bishops within their own midst to take the oath; however, only two—Talleyrand, the bishop of Autun and Jean-Baptiste Joseph Gobel, the bishop of Basle—complied, and only about one third of the lower clergy in the Assembly followed their example. The breech between those who swore (the juring, or constitutional, clergy) and those who refused (the non-juring, or refractory, clergy) became official on 4 May after Pope Pius VI issued his brief *Caritas quae* which declared the oath schismatic and excommunicated anyone who took it.[8]

The rest of the bishops of France proved as opposed to the oath as their episcopal brothers in the National Assembly; only seven out of 160 accepted the deputies' decree.[9] The prelates who refused to swear the oath lost their sees to lay-elected, juring clerics. The non-juring François de Narbonne-Lara, bishop of Évreux, condemned his replacement, a curé-deputy to the National Assembly named Robert Thomas Lindet, as an *intrus* and forbade any priest in the diocese to recognize the legitimacy of Lindet. Furthermore, he declared "suspended from all sacerdotal functions" any priest who ascribed to the Civil Constitution of the Clergy or who replaced a non-juring cleric. The former archbishop of Rouen, Cardinal de La Rochefoucauld, also refused to become a constitutional prelate and condemned his replacement, the Lyonnais priest Louis Charrier de la Roche.[10]

---

8. Ibid., 22, 25–26; Aston, *Religion and Revolution,* 157–58, 168. With the beginning of the Revolution and the collapse of royal authority, the pope may have had the opportunity to recapture the authority to nominate and invest French bishops. The National Assembly on the other hand had no intention of giving the pope greater influence in France; if anything, the delegates proved that they wanted to limit papal intervention when they abolished the annates with the rest of the feudal dues on the Night of 4 August. The progressively more radical legislation passed by the Assembly during the first year of the Revolution, especially the refusal to declare Catholicism the state religion, alarmed Pius VI, and he tried to put a stop to it. His actions came rather belatedly since he did not anathematize the oath to the Civil Constitution of the Clergy, and those who swore it, until almost one year after its promulgation. By that time, many priests had already made their decisions regarding the oath, and the battle lines over the constitutional church of France had already been drawn [Aston, *Religion and Revolution,* 143–51].

9. Tackett, Religion, Revolution, and Regional Culture, 44.

10. François de Narbonne, "Lettre pastorale et ordonnance de Mgr l'Évêque d'Évreux, au clergé séculier et régulier, et à tous les fidèles de son diocèse, 12 June 1790," ADE, 57 L 1; La Rochefoucauld, *Ordonnance de M. le Cardinal,* 1–11; Loth, *Histoire du Cardinal,* 231, 287–94; *Clérembray, La Terreur à Rouen,* 118; Dupuy, "Ordre et désordre," 462. Curé of the parish of Sainte-Croix in his native town of Bernay, Robert Thomas Lindet, was the brother of Jean-Baptiste Robert Lindet, one of the members of the Committee of Public Safety. Louis Charrier de la Roche, the first constitutional bishop of Seine-Inférieure, resigned shortly after his appointment. According to the refractory cathedral canon Abbé Guillaume-André-René Baston, Charrier de la Roche may have recanted his constitutional oath at the feet of Pope Pius VI. J.-B.-G. Gratien, a constitutional vicar general from the diocese of Eure-et-Loir, replaced him. After he refused to promulgate the Legislative Assembly's law allowing priests to marry, Gratien lost his office and was imprisoned. He resumed his episcopal seat after the Terror and died in office in 1799. Jean-Claude Leblanc-Beaulieu became the last constitutional bishop of the department of Seine-Inférieure. After the Concordat in 1801, he was replaced by the former non-juring archdeacon of Montpellier, Étienne-Hubert Cambacérès, the brother of the nineteenth-century statesman who authored the Napoleonic Code [Baston, Mémoire, 360–66; Loth, *Histoire du Cardinal,* 671, 684–86, 719].

The curés and vicars of France split into nearly equal parts between the constitutionals and the refractories, though regional acceptance or rejection varied widely throughout France.[11] The departments of upper Normandy illustrate the extremity of the dichotomy. In Eure, refractory priests outnumbered the constitutional ones in nearly every district, whereas the number of juring and non-juring clergy for the department of Seine-Inférieure as a whole followed the national average of fifty-fifty.[12] A study of Seine-Inférieure's statistics, district by district, reveals the variances which existed even between areas of similar economic conditions or population distributions. Only about one-third of the priests in the urban district of Rouen refused the oath, while the number of non-jurers in the district of Montivilliers, which included the busy port of Le Havre, reached about eighty percent.[13] Rural districts, such as Neufchatel and Gournay in the *pays de Bray*, counted a strong juring portion. The directory of the *pays de Caux* district of Caudebec, though, did not have enough priests to replace the seventy-four refractories (out of a total of 141) and had to allow eighteen non-jurers to remain at their posts.[14]

The local governments of upper Normandy, as elsewhere, recognized the danger of allowing non-juring priests to continue their pastoral duties, especially after the pope's condemnation of the Civil Constitution. This new religious legislation provided ammunition to opponents of the Revolution who used the Civil Constitution of the Clergy to attack the new regime as threatening the Church and even people's salvation. Already, civil strife threatened to erupt in areas where widespread rejection of the oath had forced local officials either to deprive parishes of their pastors or to allow refractories to continue administering to their flocks. Thus, the district directories scrambled to diffuse the tension by filling the posts of the non-jurers with constitutionals throughout the spring and summer of 1791.[15] With a refractory population of eighty-two priests, the *procureur syndic* of the Montivilliers district complained to the head of the department of Seine-Inférieure that he had only sixty constitutional candidates to replace the non-jurers

---

11. See Tackett for approximate figures for each department.

12. Bonnenfant and Huard, *Histoire générale*, II, 62; Sévestre, *Le Personnel de l'église*, 91–140. On 12 March 1791 the National Assembly required a list of juring and non-juring clergy from all departmental governments. Although for many regions of France, these lists were incomplete, erroneous, or have since disappeared, the tables for upper Normandy remained relatively intact and comprehensive. For problems using these lists as gauges of clerical or public opinion on the Civil Constitution of the Clergy or the Revolution in general for Normandy, see Sévestre, *Le Personnel de l'église*, 1–27 and for France, see Tackett, *Religion, Revolution, and Regional Culture*, 303–6.

13. *Procureur général syndic* to the procureur syndic of the district of Montivilliers, 21 May 1791, ADSM, L 2092; ADSM, L 2097; Ledré, *Le Diocèse de Rouen*, 7; Gisèle Tellier, "L'Émigration des curés Normands en 1792" in Lemaitre, *Journal de route*, 1; Sévestre, *Le Personnel de l'église*, 235–44, 253–61; Dupuy, "Ordre et désordre," 462.

14. Ledré, *Le Diocèse de Rouen*, 7–8; Tougard, *La Révolution à Yvetot*, vol.1, 171; *La Révolution à Yvetot et dans* (unpaginated); Dupuy, "Ordre et désordre," 462. The electoral assembly listed about eighty-five curates in need of constitutional clergy, but this number also included parishes where the priest, regardless of his juring status, was too old or infirm to continue his pastoral duties ["Etat des fonctionnaires publics du district de Caudebec," June 1791, ADSM, L 1709].

15. Tougard, *La Révolution à Yvetot*, vol.1, 170; Dupuy, "Ordre et désordre," 463.

and that some of these jurers "are not worthy to be placed at the head of a parish." The *procureur* begged for suggestions on where he could recruit more clerics.[16] The department's *procureur général syndic*'s response suggested that perhaps the directory of Montivilliers had not tapped a potentially rich vein of juring curés, "among your resources have you calculated the subjects which the houses of Valasse, Grasville [*sic*], and Fécamp and especially all the diverse religious communities of Havre, could furnish you? . . . By including these various resources it does not appear to us that there will be the scarcity of subjects which you seem to fear."[17]

In the debates over the suppression of the religious orders, Garat had indicated that the Church would benefit from the elimination of the regulars because it would gain secular priests. After passing the 13 February 1790 decree, the National Assembly suggested that secularizing male religious might become curés and vicars. The Maurist general superior echoed this recommendation in his letter to all the Congregation's members, urging them to "be zealous and fervent ministers of the Church" despite the abolition of their order.[18] In this way, monks who left their abbeys could at least continue their religious vocations, even if they could no longer pursue the conventual life. Nevertheless, the Civil Constitution of the Clergy posed a problem for regulars who wanted to become seculars: Did the 27 November 1790 decree ordering the constitutional oath apply to former monks? It seemed that those who did not want a curate or vicarate did not have to swear the oath; however, any man who wanted to live out his religious commitment as a state-recognized parish priest or vicar most definitely would have to raise his right hand and promise to uphold the Civil Constitution.[19]

Bishop Lindet of the Eure diocese offered to bestow the authority to hear confessions and oversee a parish to any former member of a religious order, and the bishop of Seine-Inférieure seemed equally accommodating, but many of the ex-religious in both upper Norman departments took no initial steps to continue their active service to the Church.[20] Yet, when faced with the paucity of suitable candidates to replace the refractories, these men of excellent reputation and education did not escape the attention of local officials for long.[21] The election of constitutional curés for the district of Caudebec in Seine-Inférieure officially

---

16. *Procureur syndic* of the district of Montivilliers to the *procureur général syndic*, 18 May 1791, ADSM, L 1191.

17. *Procureur général syndic* to the procureur syndic of the district of Montivilliers, 21 May 1791, ADSM, L 2092; *Le Révolution à Yvetot et dans* (unpaginated). Valasse was a Cistercian establishment, and Graville-Sainte-Honorine was a Benedictine priory belonging to Notre-Dame-du-Bec.

18. "Loi concernant les religieux," p. 10, ADE, 57 L 1.

19. Both Tackett and Rousseau state that the national government did not require ex-religious to swear the oath [Rousseau, *Moines bénédictins martyrs,* 64; Tackett, *Religion, Revolution, and Regional Culture,* 24]. Some did so—even those who did not take positions in the constitutional church.

20. "Lettre circulaire de M. Lindet à clergé de son diocèse," p. 12, ADE, 57 L 4.

21. ADSM, L 1579, dos. V; Tougard, *La Révolution à Yvetot,* vol.1, 181–82; Lohier, "L'Inventaire," 184.

commenced on Sunday 29 May 1791 as the local electors chanted the *Veni Creator* and assisted at a votive Mass of the Holy Spirit. Afterwards, the *procureur syndic* Fenestre impressed upon the active citizens seated in the church's choir the necessity of filling the eighty-five vacant parishes of the district with individuals "commendable for their morals and their wisdom, lovers of peace and sincerely attached to our felicitous constitution."[22] The electors must have judged the Maurists as projecting these qualities since they chose several former Benedictines for posts in the district's churches.

The first position to fill was the parish of Yvetot, the second largest municipality in the district and the *chef-lieu* of a canton. The previous curé, Nicolas-Louis-Edmond Coignasse-Desjardins, had never actually stated whether he refused the oath or not; each time the municipal officials questioned him, he found new excuses for delaying. His indecision put his church of Saint Pierre d'Yvetot on the list of vacant parishes.[23] By a vote of sixty-five to three the electors chose to offer Dom Ruault, the last prior of Saint-Wandrille, their district's first elected constitutional post. The following day, Desjardins submitted his formal resignation and denunciation of the Civil Constitution, and Dom Ruault sent his letter of acceptance.[24]

The electors then proceeded to select a curé for another canton *chef-lieu*, Bolbec. The curé, Jean-Nicolas Lambert, and his three vicars had refused to abide by the oath decree, but he had shown his opposition to the Revolution long before the oath controversy. In August 1790 when members of the National Guard asked him to bless its standards and celebrate a Mass for them on the feast of Saint-Louis, he refused, claiming that he would not give a Catholic blessing to a flag which might be carried by one of the Protestants in the regiment. His constitutional replacement, Dom Bride, the former prior of Jumièges, was elected by a vote of sixty-one to nine.[25]

In the election of constitutional curés and vicars over the next two weeks, the assembly at Caudebec seemed to prefer Maurists over any other former religious order since the electors offered them thirteen secular pastorships in the district.[26] Unlike Doms Ruault and Bride, these monks were not always the electors' first choice. Dom Jean François Dabout received his appointment to Lintot only

---

22. ADSM, L 11901, L 1709.

23. Tougard, *La Révolution à Yvetot,* vol. 1, 172, 178–79. The central commune of each department, district and canton was called the *chef-lieu.*

24. ADSM, L 11901; Marquis de Bailleul to Toustain, 11 February 1791, Hébert, ed., *La Révolution à Rouen,* 3; *La Révolution à Yvetot et dans* (unpaginated); Tougard, *La Révolution à Yvetot,* vol. 1, 180; Lohier, "L'Inventaire," 156, f. 3.

25 . "Proclamation de la Garde Nationale et des habitants de Bolbec contre le curé de la même ville, sur un refus de célébrer la Messe le jour Saint-Louis, le 25 août [1790]," BMR; ADSM, L 11901; Pigout, Bolbec, 3–4; Pigout, *La Révolution en Seine-Maritime,* 104. The abbeys of Jumièges and Saint-Wandrille had once possessed over one-half of Bolbec's lands.

26. "État des fonctionnaires publics du district de Caudebec," ADSM, L 1709. Two Penitents, one Cistercian and one Cordelier, were also elected as clerics. The Maurists included Dom Jean

after the Cistercian Dom Simon Bonnel had declined the position the day before in favor of the parish nearest his former abbey.[27] On the other hand, in a testament to the widespread renown of the Maurists, some monks received nominations in more than one district; Dom Xavier Fidèle Moniez from Notre-Dame-du-Bec turned down a position in the district of Montivilliers because he had already accepted the parish of Saint-Clair-sur-les-Montes given him by the electors assembled at Caudebec.[28] One Maurist, Dom Huard of Saint-Georges-de-Bocherville, turned down his offer, citing feeble health and old age; the electors replaced him the following day with a Maurist from the department of Eure.[29]

The relatively high number of Maurists elected in the district of Caudebec does not seem unusual since monks from that region's two prominent establishments, Jumièges and Saint-Wandrille, had fostered good relations with local laity through their charitable work, political activities and participation in secular sociability such as the freemason lodge *L'Union Cauchoise*. Likewise, in the district of Montivilliers which contained the vibrant house at Fécamp, the electors heeded the prompting of the department's *procureur général syndic* to use secularized regulars as constitutional clergy. After attending Mass and intoning the *Veni Creator* at their initial assembly, the electoral assembly chose ten ex-religious, including two Benedictines, as replacements for refractories.[30] Regions not permeated by such a strong Maurist rapport with secular society seemed less likely to prefer ex-monks of the Congregation for positions in the constitutional church. In a district of Dieppe whose modest Maurist house contained only seven occupants in 1790, the electors chose eight former Carmelite, but only one Maurist, to fill their vacancies.[31] The lack of a Maurist community in the Gournay district meant that the assembly, although it had the fewest posts to fill of any district in Seine-Inférieure, looked instead to the Norbertine priory of Bellozanne to provide five

---

Alexander Ruault for Yvetot, Dom Pierre-Armand Bride for Bolbec, Dom Guillaume-François Dabout for Lintot, Dom Jacques François Huard for Allouville (refused), Dom Xavier Fidèle Moniez for Saint-Clair-sur-les-Monts, Dom François Joseph Levacque for Allouville, Dom Louis Charles François Bricque for Saint-Sylvestre, Dom de Quane for Bielleville, Dom Pierre-Michel Duvrac for Beuzevillette, Dom Jean-Baptiste Ferey for Lanquetot, Dom Louis Nicolas Grognet for Auzebosc, Dom François Louis Joseph Lestievetz for Bois-Himont, and Dom Louis François Joseph Lengaigne for Autretot [ADSM, L 11901, 1327, 1707]. See Appendix H for a list of all ex-Maurists who became constitutional clerics in upper Normandy.

27. ADSM, L 11901.

28. Dom Moniez to the president of the electoral assembly of the district of Montivilliers, 16 June 1791, ADSM, L 2092; *procureur syndic* of the district of Caudebec to *procureur général syndic* of the department of Seine-Inférieure, 14 August 1791, ADSM, L 1346; ADSM, L 11901.

29. ADSM, L 11901.

30. "Procès-verbal des séances de MM les électeurs du district de Montivilliers," 9 June 1791, ADSM, L 2091. The other electees included two Augustinians, two Capuchins, one Carmelite, one Cordelier, and one Cistercian. Among the Maurists elected to parishes were Dom Moniez to Villemenil (refused), and Dom Letellier to Fécamp.

31. "Liste de MM les curés élus par l'assemblée électorale du district de Dieppe, pour remplacer ceux qui n'ont pas prêté le serment, ou dont les curés sont vacantes par décès," ADSM, L 11901. One of these, Dom Philippe André-Joseph Surmont, came from the district's only Maurist establishment, Saint-Michel-de-Tréport.

of its constitutional priests.[32] In the department of Eure where the juring clergy equaled sixty-two percent, only three ex-Maurists became shepherds for the revolutionary Church.[33] Since Notre-Dame-du-Bec stood as the only monastery of its order to maintain an appearance of vitality, discipline, and cooperation with the townspeople, the lack of a Maurist contingent active beyond its walls probably contributed to the minuscule number of its former members among Eure constitutional clergy. Thus, Maurists who became constitutional clergy appear to have benefited from their connection with secular society in obtaining their positions.

While it appears that citizens in areas where the Congregation's monks made an effort to interact with the temporal world tended to employ more of these men in the service of the constitutional Church, the electors in these regions did not always choose monks from the monasteries within their districts—or even departments. Passing over monks from the famous abbey of Sainte-Trinité in Fécamp, Montivilliers' assembly appointed the Maurist Dom Étienne Tissier, a native of the department of Seine-et-Marne and living at the Chartres monastery Josaphat in 1790, as curé of Saint-Antoine-la-Forêt.[34] These same electors did not select a former resident of Sainte-Trinité to serve in the abbatial church, converted into one of the town's two parish churches. After electing a secular priest who refused the nomination, the district chose Dom Letellier, the Maurist from the monastery at Bonneval who had moved to upper Normandy with Dom Petit, despite the continued presence of a number of Sainte-Trinité's former inhabitants in Fécamp.[35] Concerned that his life in the cloister had ill prepared him for the responsibilities of parish work, Dom Letellier initially declined the nomination, "Never have I had the vocation nor the aptitude for the public functions of the ecclesiastical ministry. I have only lived until recently in the private life of the religious state and . . . I believe therefore that it would be detrimental and more than imprudent if I took on duties of this importance." Yet, he must have acquiesced. About two months after his election, he received his canonical institution from Bishop Charrier de la Roche and was installed as the constitutional curé on 28 August 1791.[36]

---

32 . "Procès-verbal de l'assemblée de MM les électeurs pour la nomination des curés à remplacer dans le district de Gournay," 4 October 1791, ADSM, L 1191; Tackett, *Religion, Revolution, and Regional Culture,* 355.

33 . ADE, 57 L 23; ASWF (1980), 98; Tackett, *Religion, Revolution, and Regional Culture,* 324, 355.

34. "Procès-verbal des séances," 10 October 1791, ADSM, L 2091.

35. "Procès-verbal des séances," 8 June 1791, ADSM, L 2091; ADSM, L 1205; Bourienne-Savoye and Desjardins-Menegalli, *Marins, moines, citoyens,* 39; Montier, "L'Abbaye de la Sainte-Trinité," 335 f. 79.

36. "Procès-verbal des séances," 8 June 1791, "Extrait des minutes de greffe de l'hôtel de ville de Fécamp," 28 August 1791, ADSM, L 2091; Dom Guillaume Dominique Letellier to the administration of the district of Montivilliers, 5 September 1791, ADSM, L 2095; Dom Letellier to Monsieur President [of the electoral assembly of the district of Montivilliers], 8 June 1791, as cited in Montier, "L'Abbaye de la Sainte-Trinité," 335, f. 79; Montier, "Les Moines des Fécamp," 135; Bourienne-Savoye and Desjardins-Menegalli, Marins, moines, citoyens, 39. The canonical institution granted a priest permission to hear confessions and serve as a parish priest in a bishop's diocese.

Few monks served parishes in the near vicinities of their abbeys in the early years of the Revolution. Only Dom Pierre Jean François Sta of Notre-Dame-de-Valmont became the secular curé for the parish of his monastery's location.[37] As mentioned previously, monks often took residences near their old abbeys, but the district electors appeared reluctant to let one of these monastic exiles become a constitutional priest in the local parish. Following the example of Dom Brixier who became the parish priest of Rançon (the sister municipality of the village of Saint-Wandrille), Dom Grognet wrote to the constitutional bishop of Seine-Inférieure, Charrier de la Roche, asking for permission to assist the juring curé of the parish of Saint-Wandrille. He even demonstrated his commitment to this desire by taking the constitutional oath in May 1791. The bishop, an amiable man, may have been willing to fulfill this request, but not the electoral assembly of Caudebec. By a vote of fifty-five to one, it removed Dom Grognet from his beloved abbey and sent him to Auzebosc. (He later returned to Saint-Wandrille during the Terror.)[38]

The district officials also seemed uneasy about the appearance of lingering signs of attachments to feudalism and the ancien régime in the appointment of constitutional clergy. Only one monk, Dom de Montigny, served as the constitutional priest of a chapel which had once paid feudal dues to his monastery. The villagers of Heuteauville, across the Seine from Jumièges, petitioned the district of Caudebec to keep open their chapel, the only one on the south bank of the river. Dom de Montigny, part of the group of Jumièges exiles still in the area, had acted as Heurteauville's *desservant* at the time of the Revolution, and since he swore the oath with the curé of Jumièges in February 1791, the district decided to allow him to continue his secular religious functions. In this way, the electors could provide the tiny church with a constitutional cleric without having to pay him a curé's salary or provide lodging since he lived with his fellow ex-monks while performing services for Heurteauville.[39] Nevertheless, most electoral assemblies

---

37. ADSM, L 2693; *Martin, Notes pour servir à l'histoire,* 66. While no former monk was ever elected as curé of the parish of his former abbey, some ex-cenobites did provide religious services in the area. Dom Mauger became the curé of Saint-Wandrille briefly in 1793 as he tried to escape the Jacobin's persecution for his active support of the Girondins (see Chapter 4). Dom Bourlier of Saint-Martin-d'Auchy-les-Aumales functioned as *desservant* of the parish of Villers-sur-Aumale "at the request of the inhabitants" [Bourlier to the administration of the revolutionary district of Neufchâtel, 26 *brumaire* An II (16 November 1793), ADSM, L 2267].

38. "Du Procès-verbal de l'assemblée du corps électoral du district de Caudebec département de la Seine-Inférieure en date du 29 mai consernant [sic] la nomination aux curés vacantes par le réfus des titulaires d'avoir satisfait de serment ou par le décès des derniers titulaires," 31 May 1791, ADSM, L 6196; "Extraits de premier registre des délibérations du conseil municipal de Saint-Wandrille," 19 May 1791, ASWF (1950), 56; Ledré, *Le Diocèse de Rouen,* 8; Lohier, "L'Inventaire," 158, f. 12.

39. "Directoire du département de Seine-Inférieure," 27 October 1791, ADSM, L 11902; "Délibérations du municipalité de Jumièges," 6 February 1791, ADSM, L 6195; "Registre des actes capitulaires de l'abbaye de Jumièges," p. 133r, ADSM, 9 H 37; "État des sommes," ADSM, L 1790; "Directoire de Caudebec," 14 September 1791, ADSM, L 1710; "État des sommes," ADSM, L 1709. A *desservant* served as a parish priest for a municipality without having received an official appointment or full salary.

followed the general pattern of the Caudebec district in using juring ex-religious to fill vacancies but not in the immediate vicinity of their former abbeys or former dependents.[40]

The district assemblies also did not appear eager to allow monks to become pastors in their hometowns. By becoming one of the educated elite in the Congregation of Saint-Maur, Dom Trémauville, the son of an illiterate farming family, must have been somewhat of a local success story in his native Froberville. Nevertheless, the electors of Caudebec chose him as the curé first of Ecretteville-sur-les-Baons and then of Cléville, rather than his birthplace.[41] Perhaps the reluctance on the part of the electors to allow ex-monks to become secular clergy near their former abbeys or birthplaces suggests that they still harbored some suspicions about the loyalty of these decloistered regulars. After all, many of them had protested the secularization or expressed their desire "to return to the religious order if I deem it suitable." The electors may have judged removing such ecclesiastics from the environs of their old monasteries or hometowns, where they undoubtedly enjoyed the esteem of family and neighbors, the path of greatest prudence.

The urban representatives appeared just as skeptical of the loyalty of these former monks. No Maurist became the constitutional curé of a district *chef-lieu*, nor did any shepherd parishes in the department's largest cities. While the electors from the Rouen district needed to fill about one third of their parishes with juring priests, they did not choose any Benedictines from either of the city's Maurist abbeys. The two monks from Saint-Ouen who did become constitutional curés administered rural parishes.[42] Furthermore, despite the conspicuous Maurist contingent in Seine-Inférieure, none served on the episcopal council. Only after the Terror did Dom Bride, the elected curé of Bolbec, and Dom Letellier, serving the parish of Sainte-Trinité at Fécamp, become candidates for the position of the

---

40. ADSM, L 11901.

41 . "Du procès-verbal de l'assemblée du corps electoral du district de Caudebec," 9 October 1791, ADSM, L 6196; Trémauville to the president of the electoral assembly of Caudebec, 12 October 1791, ADSM, L 1710; "Procès-verbal des séances de l'assemblée électorale de Caudebec," 1 December 1792, ADSM, L 6194; ADSM, L 1206; ADE, 57 L 62.

42. "État des sommes," ADSM, L 1709. Dom Nicolas Joseph Louis Mesnard shepherded Saint-Marie-des-Champs, and Dom Antoine-Joseph Fortier became the constitutional curé of Beuzevillette, both in the district of Caudebec.

43. "Extrait du registre tenu à l'agent municipal de la commune de Bolbec canton du même nom," 11 brumaire An VIII (2 November 1799), ADSM, L 2890; Montier, "L'Abbaye de la Sainte-Trinité," 336 f. 79. An undated document in ADSM, L 11901 lists Doms Bride and Letellier under the heading "Pour le conseil de l'évêque," but this could refer to their nomination for the bishopric of Rouen in 1799. Coming in third and fourth place with 410 and 372 votes respectively, Doms Letellier and Bride were not really even in the running since the winning candidate, Jean-Claude Leblanc de Beaulieu, received 4,154. Dom Alexis Davoust, who had represented the First Estate of Rouen at the Estates-General, secured a prominent position in the constitutional church outside the department of Seine-Inférieure as episcopal vicar of the bishop of Orne in lower Normandy. Kessler erroneously listed him as the constitutional bishop of Orne [Deries, "La Vie d'un bibliothécaire," 209–10; de la Bunodière, *Derniers jours de l'abbaye de Saint-Ouen,* 11–12; Kessler, "The Suppression of the Benedictine Order," 104].

last constitutional bishop of that department.[43] This evidence may suggest that although the Maurists had cultivated a bond with lay society before the Revolution, the lay officials simply did not fully trust the former monks when they swore to uphold the Civil Constitution.

If the members of the assemblies still surveyed the ex-regulars with skeptical eyes, officials from the rural municipalities appeared all too willing to receive their new constitutional clerics with open arms. Upon hearing the news that Dom Lestievetz had agreed to serve as their curé, the administration of Boishimont publicly expressed its enthusiasm for the ex-monk and allowed him to move into the rectory ten days before his formal installation.[44] The town of Yvetot actually demanded the appointment of another Maurist as its curé after Dom Ruault was elected as a deputy to the National Convention, the legislative body that replaced the Legislative Assembly after the declaration of the First Republic in August 1792. "There is certainly no citizen of this city who does not know how worthy Dom Legrand is. . . . His morals, his knowledge, his assiduousness have earned him the veneration of all true partisans of religion."[45] Legrand first served as *desservant* of the town, while Dom Ruault sat in the Convention. But, as foreign armies surrounded France and civil war threatened from the royalists in the Vendée and even from the exiled Girondins in Normandy, the National Convention decided to hold sessions every day and eventually around the clock. At that time, Dom Ruault decided that he could not serve two masters, religion and the nation, and so he wrote to the local officials at Yvetot to resign his post since "the dangers to the fatherland seem to require the National Convention to meet continually."[46] The municipality's general council then drew up a proposal to officially install Legrand as its curé to replace Dom Ruault. When the administrators put this motion before the rest of the town assembled in the parish church, they responded affirmatively "in the most determined manner." Escorted by Yvetot's detachment of the National Guard, Dom Legrand took his place as the town's second constitutional curé on 27 October 1792.[47]

A year or more of service by Maurists in the constitutional church (combined with the lack of other, more suitable candidates) seemed to provide enough evidence of their loyalty to the Civil Constitution to dispel any doubts. Electors seemed to trust these men to such a degree that they began assigning ex-monks to municipalities where the counterrevolutionary activities of the refractory priests had led to unrest and sedition among the local inhabitants. At Ecretteville-sur-les Baons, the first constitutional priest had resigned shortly after his installation,

44. "Registre pour servir à l'inscription à donné par l'article 29 du titre 2 de la proclamation du roi sur un décret de l'Assemblée nationale pour le constitution civile de clergé et la fixation de son traitement du 24 août 1790," 9 June 1791, ADSM, L 6196.

45. "Registre des délibérations 1792–An II," AMY, 1 D 15.

46. "Registre des délibérations 12 juin 1792 au 20 décembre 1792," p. 38r, AMY, 1 D 14.

47. "Bureau des domaines nationaux," p. 50r, ADSM, L 1594; p. 480, ADSM, L 1706; "Registre des délibérations 12 juin 1792 au 20 décembre 1792," p. 38r, AMY, 1 D 14; Tougard, La Révolution à Yvetot, vol. 2, 8–10.

possibly due to opposition from partisans of the old curé. Dom Trémauville, for his part, proved his ability to shepherd this contentious and divided flock faithfully and delicately. After he had served this parish for about one year, the electoral assembly chose him as the new constitutional curé for Cléville on 1 December 1792 after a letter from the juring priest of Ricarville had requested the immediate assignment of a constitutional cleric for the town. The old curé, Pierre-François Miette, had taken the oath with restrictions, and although a former Cordelier from Rouen was chosen as his juring replacement, the people of the village had continued to attend Miette's Masses. Just as at Ecretteville-sur-les Baons, the first constitutional priest found his situation too daunting, but the Maurist Dom Trémauville persisted and had more success in winning support for the constitutional church despite Miette's continued presence in the area.[48]

The refractory situation at Saint-Jean-de-Folleville appeared even more critical for that town's revolutionary government. Louis-Henry Lemercier had served the parish for over thirty years, and by 1791 he had become so frail that he had to rely on his vicar, Nicolas-Victor Le Normand, to discharge the duties of the curé. Le Normand had refused the oath, but since the district of Montivilliers had not provided the town with a constitutional substitute, he persevered in his position. The old curé died on 26 March 1792, and the assembly wanted to seize this opportunity to replace the non-juring vicar. The bishop of Rouen, however, lamented that he had no candidates capable of dealing with the hostility which any juring priest would inevitably encounter as the unwelcome replacement of a beloved and well-respected refractory. The town officials of Saint-Jean-de-Folleville did have someone in mind; they wrote to the electoral assembly of the district "ardently desir[ing]" to have as its curé Louis Charles François Brique [*sic*] priest at Saint-Sylvestre."[49] Apparently, this former Maurist's devotion to the new regime, and his tactful handling of the refractory who had refused to vacate the rectory at Saint-Sylvestre, had earned him a reputation for bringing stability and tranquility to an otherwise perilous situation. Nevertheless, he still needed to rely on the local regiment of the National Guard for protection and vigilance against clandestine services by the refractory priest.[50]

The Civil Constitution of the Clergy and its oath had divided the French clergy between those who accepted this clerical legislation and those who rejected it. For some ex-Maurists, it provided the opportunity to continue their religious

---

48. Lion, curé of Ricarville to unknown, [n. d.], ADSM, L 1710; Directory of the district of Caudebec to the directory of the district of Seine-Inférieure, 26 March 1792, ADSM, L 1710; Procureur général syndic, 3 September 1791, ADSM, L 1710; "Registre d'arrêtes pris sur requêtes et autres pour l'exécution de celui du conseil général du 18 août 1792, l'an quatre de la liberté rélatif aux prêtres et religieux insermentés," ADSM, L 1250; "Procès-verbal des séances de l'assemblée électorale," 1 December 1792, ADSM, 6194; ADSM, L 11901, L 1223

49. Five people from Saint-Jean-de-Folleville to the citizens called to Montivilliers for the nomination of curés, [n. d.], ADSM, L 2094.

50 . "Mémoire de M. Le Normand desservant la dérnière paroisse," 27 June 1792, ADSM, L 2099; directory of the district of Montivilliers to the administration of the directory of the department of Seine-Inférieure, 3 April 1792, J.-B.-G. Gratien, Metropolitan Bishop of Rouen to the directory of

vocation as secular, juring curés and vicars.[51] The Maurists may have found the constitutional church particularly attractive because, as members of a strictly Gallican order under the patronage of the king of France, they may have seen themselves as merely joining their Gallican counterparts in the secular clergy.[52] The lay electoral assemblies of the districts in upper Normandy had enough confidence in these men to put them at the head of nearly thirty parishes, with the majority of these located in areas where Maurists enjoyed a long-standing reputation for cooperation with secular society. Electors may have shown their reluctance to assign these former monks to the municipalities of their abbeys or their birthplaces, but any residual distrust was eliminated by the Maurists' tactful handling of difficult situations, and their continued devotion to the service of religion and the laity seemed to dissipate any residual distrust.

the department of Seine-Inférieure, 8 April 1792, ADSM, L 1198; "Du registre de la municipalité de la paroisse de Saint-Sylvestre canton de Lillebonne, district de Caudebec, département de la Seine-Inférieure," 19 June 1791, ADSM, L 1707; directory of the district of Montvilliers to the directory of Seine-Inférieure, 3 April 1792, municipal officials of Saint-Jean-de-Folleville to the administrators of the directory of the district of Montvilliers, 28 March 1792, ADSM, L 2088; "Directory du district de Caudebec," 20 February 1793, ADSM, L 1709; Sévestre, *Le Personnel de l'église,* 256.

51. If constitutional curés were in short supply, the lower pay and longer hours of vicars made them even scarcer, as the bishop of Seine-Inférieure noted in 1791 and 1792. Yet again, the administrative and ecclesiastical officials of the department turned to the former monks to assist parishes with large populations. The few Maurists who did become constitutional vicars tended to accept positions in towns whose curé had been a member of the Congregation. Until his nomination as desservant of the vacant parish of Beuzevillette, Dom Fortier, as a vicar, assisted Dom Bride at Bolbec and Dom Mesnard did the same for the two Maurists who would successively serve as curés of Yvetot [Directory of the Department of Seine-Inférieure to the president of the Ecclesiastical Committee, 4 September 1791, AN, D XIX 45, 704 bis; Directory of the district of Montivilliers to the directory of the department, 2 July 1791, ADSM, L 11901; Bishop Gratien to the directory of the department, 1 March 1792, ADSM, L 1195; "État des sommes à payer aux fonctionnaires publics ecclésiastiques pour le quartier d'avril 1792," ADSM, L 1709; "État des sommes," ADSM, L 1709; État des sommes à payer aux fonctionnaires publics ecclésiastiques pour le quartier de janvier 1793," ADSM, L 1709; "Bureau des domaines nationaux," p. 30r, ADSM, L 1594; de la Bunodière, *Derniers jours de l'abbaye de Saint-Ouen,* 17].

52. Plongeron argued that ex-monks became constitutional clergy due to their exposure to eighteenth-century philosophic ideologies and mysticism while still in their abbeys, [Plongeron, *Les Réguliers de Paris,* 423–25]. As described in previous chapters, the evidence collected on the Maurists of upper Normandy does not support Plongeron's explanation.

CHAPTER 6

MAURISTS IN THE CONSTITUTIONAL CHURCH

IN THE PERFORMANCE OF SECULAR CHURCH FUNCTIONS, these former regulars turned constitutional priests demonstrated their commitment to their religious vocation while also showing their willingness to cooperate with the new regime. This included participating in celebrations which reinforced the priest's duties to the laity to whom he owed his position. Exposure to these ceremonies began upon the curé's arrival at his new post with a ritual to mark the installation of the new pastor in his parish church and rectory. The municipal body and the National Guard regiment of Ecretteville-sur-les-Baons knocked on the door of the rectory at 9:00 AM on the morning of 23 October 1791 to conduct the newly elected Dom Trémauville to his new parish church. The refractory curé, Antoine-François-Radulphe Robinay, had resided there as the parish priest for twenty years, and the shortage of constitutional replacements allowed him to continue to serve the municipality despite his refusal of the oath at the beginning of 1791. Finally, the electoral assembly found a suitable juring candidate in the ex-Maurist Dom Trémauville. The local officials were eager to install him as their new priest. Yet they also wanted to impress upon him that he, like all public functionaries, was at the service of the people first and foremost, and not to any ecclesiastical authority. As if to reinforce this point, Charles Quesnel, the town secretary, read aloud first the proclamation of Dom Trémauville's election by the electoral assembly of the district and then the canonical institution which the bishop of Seine-Inférieure had issued him after he had accepted his nomination. The former monk turned parish priest then swore the oath before the congregation and intoned the *Veni Creator* to begin the Mass. Afterwards, he processed back to the rectory with the National Guard and the municipal officials who gave him the keys to the residence. This procedure highlighted Dom Trémauville's role as servant of the people.[1]

---

1. "Copie du procès-verbal de la prise de possession de Monsieur Trémauville à la curé d'Ecretteville-sur-les-Baons," 23 October 1791, ADSM, L 6196; Aston, *Religion and Revolution,* 209.

Patriotic, rather than religious, aspects marked similar installation ceremonies involving former monks as constitutional curés. At the installation of Dom Lestievetz on Trinity Sunday, 19 June 1791, "many citizens of this place armed with rifles to show their patriotism" accompanied the priest and administrators to the church. Dressed in his chasuble and maniple the new curé knelt before the high altar during the proclamation of his nearly unanimous election and his letter of approval from the bishop. Dom Lestievetz then raised his hand and, before the congregation, pronounced his oath as if to acknowledge that he accepted the power vested in the people to name him as their curé.[2] This sequence of events—the reading of the secular election before the episcopal institution followed by the public swearing of the oath—became the standard formula for the installation of constitutional clergy.[3] The willingness of ex-Maurists to participate in such rituals exemplify their cooperation with the secular society of the Revolutionary regime. At his installation, Dom Grognet even tried to narrow the gap between the religious and the secular by emphasizing a virtue common to both realms. After performing his part before the congregation, he distributed 300 livres of bread to the poor of his parish at Auzebosc. This act of generosity showed his civic-mindedness but also perhaps betrayed his lingering connections with his monastic past. It must have reminded him of his previous alimentary service in the *pay de Caux*, during his days at Jumièges when the monastery dispensed similar poor relief.[4]

During his tenure as constitutional curé of Auzebosc, Dom Grognet continued to reconcile the spiritual with temporal society by adding religious rituals to the revolutionary commemorations. To honor the victims who had died in the first two years of the Revolution, the former monk offered a requiem attended by the municipal officials and the National Guard. As the Revolution turned more radical, Dom Grognet persisted in adding traditional sacred elements to patriotic displays. After evening vespers in March 1793, Auzebosc planted trees of liberty and fraternity and decorated them with tricolored ribbons. The curé gave a brief sermon and then recited his Liberty-Equality oath to the wild applause of the local citizens. After a rousing rendition of "La Marseillais," Dom Grognet ended the ceremony by chanting the Te Deum "in order to ask the Eternal One to confirm and strengthen their steps."[5]

The pastor of Auzebosc's ceremony seemed a meager affair compared to the expressive display of religious and patriotic fervor which accompanied the

---

2. "Registre pour servir à l'inscription," 19 June 1791, ADSM, L 6196; "Du procès-verbal de l'assemblée du corps électoral du district de Caudebec," 2 June 1791, ADSM, L 6196.

3. See also the installation of Dom de Quane at Bielleville on 19 June 1791 [ADSM, L 1205]; the installation of Dom Lengaigne at Autretot on 19 June 1791 ["Registre pour servir à l'inscription," ADSM, L 6196]; and the installation of Dom Bride at Bolbec [Pigout, *La Révolution en Seine-Maritime*, 118].

4. "Auzebosc: Délibérations 21 février 1790 au 18 juillet 1791," 12 June 1791, p. 131, ADSM, L 6219. Dom Grognet professed his monastic vows at Jumièges in 1764.

5. Ibid., 28 October 1791, p. 141, ADSM, L 6219; "Municipalité d'Auzebosc: Registre de délibérations commune le 5 février 1792 en fine le 3 octobre 1793," p. 131, ADSM L 6216

planting of Bolbec's tree of liberty. That celebration included a Mass in thanksgiving for ridding the nation of the traitor Dumouriez, an army general with Girondin sympathies who deserted to the Austrian army in March 1793. After the Mass, the constitutional curé of Bolbec, Dom Bride, intoned the Te Deum during the distribution of bread to the poor. The former prior of Jumièges described the event as symbolizing that "the citizens . . . enslaved to the false prejudices which had given birth to fanaticism, have broken the chain which held them captive and hastened to gather at the foot of the altars to offer to God the homage which is due to him." To the municipal officials and to Dom Bride, traditional sacred ritual and worship could play a part in revolutionary ceremonies without giving such occasions the appearance of "false prejudices" or "fanaticism."[6]

Indeed, Dom Bride played an active role in other national festivals as well; at the *fête de la federation* in 1791, before taking the Liberty-Equality oath, he exhorted his congregation to combine their patriotism with "those [sentiments] which your religion should inspire in you" and to ask God for protection against tyranny and injustice.[7] Dom Bride even indicated that spiritual worship went hand in hand with civic duties. While blessing the National Guard's flags which were to hang in the parish church, he affirmed for his congregation that "depositing them under the vaults of this temple attests to the patriotism which dedicates them." To further emphasize the role that the divine played in civic society, he concluded his discourse by calling upon his flock to ask God for peace so that "all united in the same sentiments, we will thank the same civil and religious law." Dom Bride obviously believed that religion had an integral role to play in the Revolution's new social order, and the officials of Bolbec must have agreed since time and again they reprinted Dom Bride's speeches in their municipal proceedings.[8] As Doms Trémauville, Grognet, and Bride exemplified, former monks who had become constitutional clergy used Revolutionary celebrations to perpetuate their rapprochement with the laity while still fostering their own religious vocations and nurturing the spirituality of their flock.[9]

While these monks turned constitutional clergy continued to enforce the important role which Christianity played in the new regime, they needed the items necessary to perform the rituals. Rural parishes often lacked sacred vessels, vestments, and artwork; therefore, the department of Seine-Inférieure distributed such articles to needy municipalities, including ones staffed by former Benedictines. In this way, rather than ending up in the molten vats of the Hôtel de Monnaie, sacred articles from closed religious houses still served their original purpose, sometimes

---

6. As quoted in Pigout, *Bolbec,* 70.
7. As cited in Ibid., 119.
8. As quoted in Ibid., 141–43.
9. "Municipalité d'Auzebosc: Registre de délibérations communé le 5 février 1792 en fin le 3 octobre 1793," 7 April 1793, p. 131, ADSM, L 6216. Dom Grognet left his post at Auzebosc at the end of An II and returned to Saint-Wandrille ["Extraits de prémier registre des délibérations du conseil municipal de Saint-Wandrille," ASWF (1950), 56, f. 1].

in the same consecrated hands that had used them before the Revolution. As constitutional curé of Bolbec, Dom Bride must have taken great pleasure in hearing the bell of Jumièges summoning his parishioners to Mass as it had once called his monks to prayer. He also said Mass on the very altar which he had used on so many feast days at the abbey. He saw to it that the grills from Saint-Wandrille and the funeral vestments, chandeliers, and the iron doors from the Cistercian abbey of Valasse received a safe home in his parish church, far from the pickaxe or the foundry.[10] Dom Ruault likewise acquired goods from suppressed houses by ordering the transfer of the magnificent marble altar from the Carthusian monastery in Rouen to his parish at Yvetot.[11] In the case of Fécamp, Dom Letellier obtained the entire abbey church, but acquiring such a structure did have its drawbacks. After the closure of the abbey, Sainte-Trinité had been so stripped of all its sacred articles that the pastor had to petition the municipality of Fécamp to supply him with even the most basic necessities for the Mass, including furniture, candles, and Communion wine.[12] Nevertheless, obtaining the articles or buildings, which they had once used at their abbeys, served as yet another way former monks, even though they had secularized, retained ties to their monastic past.

These regulars who became seculars experienced the same challenges as the rest of the constitutional clergy throughout France, but poor housing, inadequate supplies, and opposition from both sympathizers of the refractory clergy and the virulently anticlerical Jacobins did not deter these ex-monks from preserving their religious vocations in the Revolutionary church. Many presbyteries had fallen into disrepair in the latter half of the eighteenth century when the economic crisis in Normandy forced the Church to neglect critical renovations. After the establishment of the constitutional church, municipal officials seemed to take their magistracy over religious affairs seriously, and the municipalities of Auzebosc, Boishimont, and Saint-Sylvestre planned to rectify the state of their decrepit rectories after ex-Maurists had served as their constitutional curés for about one year. In some cases, the dilapidation resulted less from the ravages

10. "État des linges et ornements d'église, provenues des maisons religieuses et paroisses supprimées qui ont été delivrés aux paroisses conservées qui en avoient besoin," ADSM, L 11901; Pigout, *Bolbec*, 43; Pigout, *La Révolution en Seine-Maritime*, 118, 334. Occasionally, churches lacked sacred vessels and artwork because the non-juring curé had taken such articles with him when he left.

11. Tougard, *La Révolution à Yvetot*, vol. 1, 185, 288–89. For other examples of ex-monks whose parishes received goods from abandoned abbeys, see "État des linges et ornements d'église," ADSM, L 11901.

12. Dom Letellier to the mayor and municipal officials of the city of Fécamp, 29 February 1793; municipal bureau [of Fécamp] to the directory of the district of Montivilliers, 27 February 1793; Municipality of Fécamp [n. d.], ADSM, L 2099; Fallue, *Histoire de la ville*, 126–27. Robert Eude and Alphonse Martin credit Dom Letellier with saving Sainte-Trinité's church by converting it into a parish church, but when Dom Letellier took over his post in August 1791, the town had already reduced the number of parishes from nine to two and designated the former abbey church as the center of worship for the parish of Sainte-Trinité [Directory of the district of Montivilliers to the directory of the department, 2 July 1791, ADSM, L 11901; Mayor and municipal officers of the city of Fécamp to the department of Seine-Inférieure, 27 July 1791, ADSM, L 1194; Eude, "L'Église de la Sainte-Trinité," II, 268; Martin, *Histoire de Fécamp*, II, 127].

of time and neglect than from the attempts at passive opposition from outgoing refractories.[13] The broken doors, leaky bedroom ceiling and holes in the floor which Jean-Nicolas Lambert bequeathed to his constitutional successor rendered the presbytery "at least on par with the worst lodging" when Dom Bride arrived in 1791.[14] The non-juring priest of Allouville likewise appeared to resent handing over the keys of his home to Dom François Joseph Levacque; the latter found the door to the bedroom locked and still full of the refractory's belongings when he moved in on 12 June 1791. By October, the parish's vicar had still not claimed his personal effects, and the municipal officials ordered their confiscation.[15] Dom Grognet seemed to have no problems moving into his new residence in the *pay de Caux* village of Auzebosc, but he would have trouble saying Mass. On the pretext that he had purchased the church's sacramentals himself, Dom Grognet's predecessor had stripped the sacristy of all but one cope and one chasuble.[16]

Like many of the constitutional priests, the ex-religious who took the oath endured passive resistance as well as active opposition from the non-juring clergy. Lambert, the former curé of Bolbec, and his three vicars may have vacated the rectory of Bolbec, albeit not without first damaging it, but they stayed in the area. The initial laws regarding enforcement of the Civil Constitution decrees permitted non-jurers the freedom to celebrate private Masses wherever they chose. This allowed Lambert to continue his residence at Bolbec where his persistent presence attracted other refractories to the town. Emboldened by the number of their clerical and lay supporters, the former curé and vicars began issuing threatening statements against Dom Bride which escalated into demands for his blood.[17]

In some areas, refractories did not actively seek vengeance against their replacements, but their continued existence and immunity from punishment allowed them to say Mass in private homes. Such clandestine worship depleted the numbers at the ex-monks' Masses. Despite nightly patrols by the National Guard, the municipal administrators of Allouville discovered an altar, vestments, sacred vessels, and consecrated hosts in the cellar of a local residence. They assumed that their former vicar, Samuel-Isidore Turbel, and his fellow refractories used the makeshift chapel to say Mass. Dom Levacque transferred the hosts to

---

13. Procurer général syndic of the district of Montivilliers to the directory of the department of Seine-Inférieure, 2 June 1791, directory of the district of Montivilliers to the directory of the department of Seine-Inférieure, 22 June 1791, ADSM, L 11901.

14. Pigout, *La Révolution en Seine-Maritime,* 118; Pigout, *Bolbec,* 43.

15. "Registre pour servir à l'inscription," 12 June 1791, ADSM, L 6196; "Registre pour servir aux officiers municipales de la paroisse de Saint-Quentin d'Allouville," [n. d.], 30 October 1791, ADSM, L 6198.

16. ADSM, L 1710, 6196.

17. Municipal officers of Bolbec to the directory of the department of Seine-Inférieure, 5 August 1792, ADSM, L 1596; Toustain to Marquis de Bailleul, 11 May 1791, Hébert, ed., La Révolution à Rouen, 5; Pigout, Bolbec, 35, 43; Pigout, *La Révolution en Seine-Maritime,* 120. Lambert's inflammatory rhetoric against Dom Bride eventually subsided; when faced with the possibility of deportation to Guyana, Lambert voluntarily went into exile in England.

the tabernacle of the parish church, and the National Guard dismantled the cellar chapel. Yet, this did not stop Turbel from persisting in his covert rituals until the general council of the department prohibited refractory clergy from residing in their former parishes in August 1792.[18] The district of Caudebec even forced Dom Pierre-Michel Duvrac to grant his refractory predecessor access to the parish church of Beuzevillette before the August 1792 regulations went into effect. Perhaps this explained why he resigned his curate to the directory of the district of Caudebec—rather than to the municipal administration—in October 1791.[19] The municipality of Lintot realized the aggravations which the refractory priest caused for their juring curé, Dom Dabout, and they petitioned the district of Caudebec to change the laws regulating non-jurers' residences in their former parishes and to impose harsh penalties for noncompliance. Yet, refractory activity lingered in the town.[20]

Juring monks also encountered passive resistance from some laity. While not publicly condemning the constitutional priests, partisans of the refractory clergy most frequently refused to attend the juring curé's Masses. Dom Thomas Antoine Jean Despinose complained to the directory of Caudebec that in addition to having to supply his own lodging at the parish of Saint-Aubin-de-Cretot, he could no longer perform funerals or even say Mass since none of the townsfolk appeared to assist him at his services.[21] If Dom Levaque's Allouville parishioners refused to attend his Mass, then he went to them. On the afternoon of 10 April 1792, he knocked on the door of Catherine Le Grande, a homebound widow. He explained to her daughter that he had come to offer the woman the opportunity to perform her Easter duty (the yearly confession and reception of the Eucharist). The daughter's resistance went from passive to active as she proceeded to denounce Dom Levacque as an imposter. The abuse became so vehement that the National Guard threatened to arrest her. The constitutional priest ordered the soldiers to stand down and succeeded in convincing the mother to receive the consolation of the sacraments the following week.[22]

Abstention from the sacraments represented the most common form of nonviolent defiance which these ex-Maurists confronted. Yet, while spurning the

---

18. "Registre pour servir aux officiers," 24 July 1791, 4 September 1791, 30 October 1791, 10 March 1792, ADSM, L 6198.

19. "Arrête du conseil général du département de la Seine-Inférieure rélatif aux prêtres et aux ci-devant religieux insermentés," 18 August 1792, p. 2, BMR, U4 1281; Directory of the district of Caudebec to Dom Duvrac, curé of Beuzevillette, 24 September 1791, ADSM, L 1710; p. 339, ADSM, L 1706; ADSM, L 1710.

20. Guerit to unknown [directory of the district of Caudebec], [n. d.], ADSM, L 1710. In some cases, refractory priests did not obstruct the functions of their constitutional successors. When Dom Lengaigne became the parish priest of Autretot, he and the municipal assembly did not detect any degradations to the edifices or thefts from the rectory or the church ["Autretot: Délibérations, 11 novembre 1788 au 9 pluviôse An II," p. 16r, ADSM, L 6212; Gisèle Tellier, "L'Émigration des curés Normands en 1792" in Lemaitre, *Journal de route,* 1].

21. Dom Despinose, curé of Saint-Aubin-de-Cretot to the directory of the district of Caudebec, 3 October 1792, ADSM, L 1707.

22. "Registre pour servir aux officiers," 10 April 1792, ADSM, L 6198.

Eucharist and confession remained a matter of personal piety, Pierre Lebourg, a clothier from Yvetot, found out that refusing to have his children baptized by the constitutional vicar and former monk Dom Nicolas Joseph Louis Mesnard could incur civil punishment in the form of a fine or jail time. Lebourg never stated whether he opposed Dom Mesnard in particular or religious practice in general, but he tried to argue that baptism was a private matter. The National Guard, a representative of the town government, two midwives and a locksmith (in case they had to force the door open) marched to the clothier's home and finally convinced him to proceed to the church of Saint-Pierre. Dom Mesnard, with water and oil in hand, administered the sacrament to Lebourg's two children and appointed two of the guardsmen as godfathers.[23]

Some Norman supporters of the non-juring clergy even rejected the liturgies of ex-Maurist constitutional priests for the services of self-proclaimed clerics with spurious credentials. Dom Dabout accused the Lintot mayor and some of the municipal officials of granting asylum to a priest named Campion and attending his clandestine Masses in local farmhouses instead of supporting the constitutional curé. The Lintot administration even seemed to extend its protection to a certain illiterate thatcher named Louis Louvel who posed as a Catholic priest and performed religious rituals.[24] A similar individual—named *Abbé Desjardins* by the local residents, because he chose to live in a garden—appeared at Bolbec and began offering an alternative worship service which attracted a number of followers from among those who judged Dom Bride a schismatic. Having acquired some literacy skills along with knowledge of the Divine Office, Abbé Desjardins recited prayers, read the Gospel and even preached sermons, but his Latin deficiency seemed to prevent him from actually saying Mass. While not overtly displaying hostility toward the constitutional priests, opponents of the Civil Constitution of the Clergy seemed to prefer any option to attending the services of the juring monks.[25]

In addition to non-attendance at services and other forms of passive resistance, former religious who replaced seculars as constitutional clergy endured bold displays of overt antagonism from both supporters of the refractories and anticlerical factions. Madame Leclerc of Yvetot directed her verbal venom against juring ex-monk curés, like "that rogue Ruault" whom she accused of consorting with atheists and of encouraging children to attack the homes and persons of those who refused to participate at his Masses.[26] The situation at Yvetot became so critical that the directory of the district wrote to the departmental government

---

23. Tougard, *La Révolution à Yvetot,* vol. 1, 240
24. Dabout to general council of the commune of Lintot, 21 *thermidor* An III (9 August 1795), ADSM, L 1597; Tougard, *La Révolution à Yvetot,* vol. 1, 291.
25. Abbé Louis Dumesnil, *Ma Prison ou mes avantures pendant le terreur,* BMR, Mss mm 31.
26. Tougard, *La Révolution à Yvetot,* vol. 1, 263–64.
27. Directory of the district of Yvetot to the directory of the department of Seine-Inférieure, 12 *messidor* An III (30 June 1795), ADSM, L 334.

warning that if such incidents continued, "fanaticism is going to grow and we fear the torches of a new Vendée will occur in our area."[27]

Elsewhere in upper Normandy, constitutional ex-Maurists bore verbal invectives and disruptions during the performance of their liturgies. According to Dom Bride, the Bolbec inhabitants who remained loyal to the local refractory "showered [him] with bitterness and humiliation upon his arrival."[28] A domestic servant in Allouville verbally assaulted Don Levacque on 2 February 1792. The town government sentenced the offender to a public apology.[29] Less than one week later, a servant interrupted the singing at Allouville's Sunday Mass. On the same day, Dom Levacque appeared before the municipal assembly to ask them to disregard a petition which certain townsfolk had circulated against him. The local government, deciding on this occasion to support its constitutional curé, fined the servant thirty *sols* (payable to the town, not Dom Levacque or the parish church), shelved the complaints against the ex-monk and ordered the National Guard to patrol the streets at night and during Mass.[30]

If the adversaries of the constitutional clergy displayed outward hostility to these ex-monks, those in the camp of the juring curés could prove equally vehement and violent in their support. While some priests may have taken it upon themselves to exhort their wayward parishioners to return to the good graces of the constitutional church, as Dom Levacque had done with Madame Le Grand, lay Yvetot supporters of their juring curé Dom Ruault attempted to bring such strays back to the fold by force. Bands of young men coerced women into attending Dom Ruault's Masses since his arrival. On 6 April 1792 though, these displays of popular support for the constitutional clergy turned more violent.[31] A mob stormed into the courtyard of Robert Roullard's residence and demanded that his wife follow them to the Good Friday liturgy of the constitutional priest. As Roullard's wife fled out the back door, the rioters broke into the residence, smashed furniture, broke windows and doors and looted the house. The municipal officers and a detachment of the National Guard appeared on the scene to shut the gates to the courtyard and arrest the perpetrators. In all, the Guard took about one hundred people into custody including twenty-two women and about thirty-five people from neighboring villages.[32] One month after the Good Friday incident, another mob invaded the home of the Yvetot lawyer Closet under the pretext of forcing him to attend Mass. When the National Guard and local officials arrived, they found overturned furniture in the house and some of Closet's belongings tossed into the pond in his yard. The municipal government condemned these acts of religious vigilantism although Dom Ruault neither denounced nor applauded

---

28. As quoted in Pigout, *La Révolution en Seine-Maritime,* 330.
29. "Registre pour servir aux officiers," ADSM, L 6198.
30. Ibid.
31. Tougard, *La Révolution à Yvetot,* vol. 1, 266–67.
32. ADSM, L 334; "Registre des délibérations 20 janvier 1792 au 12 juin 1792," AMY, I D I3; Tougard, *La Révolution à Yvetot,* vol. 1, 264–66; *La Révolution à Yvetot et dans* (unpaginated).
33. Closet to the procureur syndic of the district of Caudebec, 14 May 1792, ADSM, L 334; Tougard, *La Révolution à Yvetot,* vol. 1, 240, 263, 267; *La Révolution à Yvetot et dans* (unpaginated).

the efforts of his self-proclaimed supporters. This silence led some of his detractors to claim that he had incited these disturbances.[33]

Assaults against these juring Maurists also came from the anticlerical deists. They apparently harbored a particular resentment toward ex-religious for having belonged to a body of men which they perceived as an especial example of archaic superstition and fanaticism. Dom Mesnard, who did not seem to enjoy a particularly edifying record when it came to baptisms, encountered such hostility at the baptism of Pierre Lefebvre's baby on 17 December 1791. Three times the constitutional vicar asked the godfather, Thieulent, if he "believed in the Roman, Catholic, and apostolic religion." Each time, Thieulent replied, perhaps even with a spit, that the National Assembly had exterminated Catholicism. When Dom Mesnard inquired a fourth time, Thieulent responded in the affirmative, no doubt just to get on with the ceremony. The disturbed vicar reported the incident to the local administration which ordered Thieulent to pay a 100-livres fine, post one hundred copies of his apology to the vicar throughout the town, and pay Dom Mesnard a fee for any inconvenience which the layman's behavior may have caused.[34]

Yvetot's town government was exemplary in patronizing its constitutional clergy, but other municipal officials often did not show such support, even turning against the constitutional clergy.[35] Allouville's administrators may have supported Dom Levacque during the incident with the servant in February 1792, but at the first available chance, the local administration betrayed him. Agitation against Dom Levacque had steadily escalated when in the spring of 1793, two members of the municipal council and a notable—all secret supporters of the nonjuring curé—abducted Dom Levacque and threatened to shoot him in the stomach.[36] Later that year, Dom Levacque took a leave of absence from his position at Allouville in order to seek medical care. The municipal authorities, more radicalized than the year before, alleged that their curé had used his illness as an excuse to flee the country as an émigré. They apparently overlooked the inconsistency between their assumption and Dom Levacque's previous service to the town, both as a parish priest and as Allouville's mayor. Rather, they saw Dom Levacque's absence as an opportunity to make revenue. When he returned on 7 *ventôse* An II (25 February 1794), he found his belongings placed under seals, and some even added to the auction list of the furnishings from the Château d'Allouville. The national agent of the commune had even put his name on the list of suspects deserving imprisonment. Before reciting the *Judica me, Deus* to begin the Mass on the Sunday following his return, Dom Levacque demanded justice for himself

34. "Registre pour servir aux délibérations et audience de police de la municipalité d'Ivetot [sic]," AMY, 1 D 12; Tougard, *La Révolution à Yvetot*, vol. 1, 239–40.

35. Tougard, *La Révolution à Yvetot*, vol. 1, 291.

36. Dom Levacque to Citizen Fenestre, *procureur syndic* of the district of Caudebec, 25 April 1793, ADSM, L 1596.

from his parishioners, whom he rebuked for their precipitous assumptions: "My sickness was not imaginary, it was all too real to me. Was it really necessary to be so inhumane, dare I say barbarous, to treat me as a stranger, a suspect, and enemy, like a Turk, a Moor, I who sacrificed everything daily for the aid of the unfortunate? For that the bold and the malicious refuse me the honored title of a true republican."[37] Even though a monk had sworn the oath and joined the ranks of the juring clergy, this did not guarantee him respect or support from those officials of the government he had sworn to uphold. Yet, the assaults of refractories, their supporters and the anticlerical faction did not daunt these former Maurists from pursuing their religious vocations in the constitutional church.

During the ancien régime, Maurists like Dom Ruault from Saint-Wandrille and Dom Lemaire from Fécamp had held positions in local politics, but in spite of these examples, Barnave had declared the monastic vow unjust because it required the monks to renounce their participation in civil life. Yet, it turned out to be the pension given the former religious, and not the elimination of their orders, that guaranteed these men the right to participate in the new regime. The deputies of the National Assembly set the requirements for active citizenship—the right to vote and serve in government—at twenty-five years of age and the payment of a tax equal to the salary for three days of work. Any ex-religious whose pension exceeded 400 livres had to pay a patriotic tax (contribution patriotique), equivalent to one month's pension. This tax in effect rendered all former regulars active citizens.[38] In particular, former monks who joined the constitutional clergy appeared on the lists of active citizens for the departments of upper Normandy. Dom Bride's name figured on the list of 160 active citizens of Bolbec while Dom Lestievetz's name is conspicuously placed at the head of Boishimont's table of eligibility.[39]

As some of them had done before the Revolution, ex-monks who became constitutional curés often held prominent positions in local government. Parish priests had played influential roles in local politics during the eighteenth century, and, when the National Assembly restructured municipal administration

---

37. "Registre des délibérations de la municipalité d'Allouville 4 août 1793 au 17 brumaire An IV," p. 31v, 36r, 43r, ADSM, L 6199.

38. "Mémoire au district de Montivilliers," [n. d.], ADSM, L 2098; "Arrête du directoire du département de la Seine-Inférieure concernant la contribution patriotique du clergé régulier et séculier," 8 April 1791, ADSM, L 1808; ADSM, L 1579; "Arrête du conseil général," 18 August 1792, p. 2, BMR, U4 1281; ADE, 107 L 13; Lohier, Dom Louis-François Le Brun, 15–16; Lohier, "L'Inventaire," 185, f. 133. A decree passed on 18 February 1791 also required all recipients of state funds to pay a capital tax (contribution mobilière) before receiving any portion of their pensions for 1792 [Jean-Bernard Tarbé de Vauxclairs, minister of public taxes to the procureur général syndic of the department of Eure, December 1791, ADE, 95 L 1: Correspondance 1791–92]. According to the law of 18 September 1793, a former monk who became a constitutional priest could not receive a pension as an ex-religious and a salary as a public functionary [Assemblée nationale constituante, Journal des débats, (September 1793), 251].

39. ADSM, L 1579. Jean Pigout counts 602 active citizens at Bolbec in 1792 [Pigout, Bolbec, 50]. Although most ex-monk curés, such as Dom Lengaigne, received certificates of civism after they resigned their ecclesiastical posts or abdicated the priesthood, Dom Legrand received his while still serving the parish of Yvetot ["Registre des délibérations 1792–An II," AMY, 1 D 15].

in 1790, curés often occupied seats on the town councils or even served as mayors. It seemed perfectly reasonable, therefore, when constitutional former Maurists participated in secular politics by assuming civic functions.[40] Dom Dabout participated in the 1791 electoral assembly of Lintot, just as his non-juring predecessor had done the previous year.[41] Both Doms Lestievetz and Hubert took over the civic duties of the refractory curés of Boishimont and Bouville by serving as presidents of their parishes' electoral assemblies. Unlike their predecessors, they had the new responsibility of swearing an oath of fidelity to the nation and then administering the same to the other active citizens.[42] Dom Bride indeed took advantage of his selection as president of the Bolbec electoral assembly on 20 June 1791 to "pronounce a speech which proved his zeal, his patriotism, his religiosity, and his devotion to the state."[43] Upon his reelection to the same position five months later, he could not resist the urge to harangue his fellow citizens again on the "august function" of participating in a democratic government. The former prior of Jumièges must have convinced his fellow Bolbec residents of "his devotion to the state" since they chose him as one of the municipality's twelve notables. He was reelected to this position twice more, and in 1792 he even became a member of the commune's council.[44]

Dom Bride's fellow monks who had followed him through the doors of the constitutional church also served as either notables or members of local administrations in addition to their positions on electoral assemblies. Dom Gaspard Léon Gobard, one of the few ex-monks to become a constitutional curé in the department of Eure, enjoyed enough respect from his parishioners to sit on the municipal government in 1792.[45] A few ex-Maurists were even reelected more than once. Dom Grognet, who had become a notable of Auzebosc in December 1792, retained a position in town government until 1793.[46] In another example, the Yvetot inhabitants regarded Dom Legrand's commitment to their parish and to the national government so highly that they made him a member of the municipal council only two months after his installation as Dom Ruault's replacement.[47]

These constitutional ex-regulars rarely achieved the highest local office. Although Bielleville's local administrators may have welcomed Dom Charles de Quane as their constitutional curé, they wanted to avoid the turmoil which had

40. Aston, *Religion and Revolution*, 131, 208; Tackett, *Religion, Revolution, and Regional Culture*, 18, 96.

41. ADSM, L 1579.

42. Ibid.

43. Ibid.

44. Ibid.; Pigout, *Bolbec*, 60.

45. ASWF (1980), 98.

46. "Municipalité d'Auzebosc," p. 82, ADSM, L 6216; "Auzebosc: Subsistance: 16 thermidor An II (3 August 1794) au 5 brumaire An IV," ADSM, L 6222; "Délibérations 7 fructidor An II au 28 brumaire An IV," p. 10, 28, ADSM, L 6220.

47. "Registre des délibérations 12 juin 1792 au 20 décembre 1792," AMY, 1 D 14; Tougard, *La Révolution à Yvetot*, vol. 2, 9. Dom Ruault also served as a notable and municipal officer ["Registre pour servir aux délibérations," p. 25r, AMY, 1 D 12; Tougard, *La Révolution à Yvetot*, vol. 1, 185; Tougard, *La Révolution à Yvetot*, vol. 2, 37; *La Révolution à Yvetot et dans* (unpaginated)].

recently rocked the town. The mayor had to renounce his civil post because, as the parish priest, he had refused the oath. The municipality therefore allowed Dom de Quane to serve as president of the electoral assembly and a town notable, but nothing more. Article Six of the Civil Constitution of Clergy actually forbade curés from achieving the mayoral office, although parish priests and Maurists had done so before the Revolution.[48] Whatever the scruples of the National Assembly for inserting this provision, the example of Dom Levacque proved the measure's wisdom. In violation of the Civil Constitution of the Clergy, Allouville elected the ex-Maurist as its mayor in 1792. As the constitutional curé, he had endured the insults of the old priest, but after his election as mayor, he suffered from a barrage of criticism directed at his ecclesiastical and civic offices. At the end of his term, he took his sick leave, perhaps hoping to diffuse the tempest which had arisen during his period in office. Unfortunately, he learned that time and distance did not extinguish the volatile mixture of political and religious unpopularity.[49]

As members of local administrations, constitutional curés often received special commissions from the other members of the municipal council. For ex-Maurists, these assignments further illustrated their enduring association with their religious vocations. The tasks nearly always involved functions traditionally fulfilled by parish clergy or enterprises which employed the aptitude for charity and education which they had acquired as Maurists. On 20 September 1792, in one of its last acts before its dissolution and the establishment of the National Convention, the Legislative Assembly ordered the parish clergy to relinquish their duties as record-keepers of baptisms, burials, and marriages. The municipal governments assumed the responsibility of keeping these registries, known as the *état civil*.[50] In the case of Yvetot, however, the collection of data remained in ecclesiastical hands—the municipal council voted unanimously on 18 December 1792 to award its curé Dom Legrand the task of inscribing births, deaths, and marriages in the *état civil*. (The council tactfully assigned a layman to register divorces.) Thus, Dom Legrand, as a member of the local administration, continued in a capacity which parish clergy had performed for centuries.[51]

At Yvetot, the *ci-devant* Maurist clerics carried out formal roles in secular education. During Dom Ruault's tenancy in the rectory, he and four other local officials served on the committee which designated a schoolmaster for the town's public school system. When Dom Legrand became curé, the local administration asked him to develop a primary school. Once the first school bell rang, he even taught some of the classes alongside his fellow ex-Maurist Dom Froger.[52]

---

48. ADSM, L 1327, 1579; Lohier, "Dom Étienne Mauger," 351
49. "Registre pour servir aux officiers," ADSM, L 6198; "Registre des délibérations de la municipalité d'Allouville," ADSM, L 6199.
50. "Municipalité d'Auzebosc," p. 131, ADSM, L 6216; Pigout, *Bolbec,* 50.
51. "Registre des délibérations 12 juin 1792 au 20 décembre 1792," AMY, 1 D 14; Tougard, *La Révolution à Yvetot,* vol. 2, 9.
52. "Registre des délibérations 12 juin 1792 au 20 décembre 1792," p. 7r, AMY, 1 D 14; "Registre des délibérations 1792 au An II," AMY, 1 D 15; Tougard, *La Révolution à Yvetot,* vol. 2, 11, 37, 168.

In 1790, the National Assembly deputy Garat had argued that if the state assumed the responsibility of charity from the religious orders, "the fate of the poor will be less precarious."[53] Yet, when faced with a potential famine in the spring of 1793, the officials of Yvetot called on the alimentary expertise of their former Maurist curé, Dom Legrand, to direct their newly formed alimentary agency, *bureau de bienfaisance*. Indubitably, when he journeyed to Paris in order to petition the National Convention for a grain dole, he put to good use the experience he had gained in Maurist poor relief. Upon his return to Yvetot, the national government sent the town an emergency shipment of wheat. Dom Legrand then had the task of distributing the sustenance in an orderly fashion, according to greatest need. Once all the grain had been doled out, the town asked its curé to compose a plan for preventing this hazardous situation in the future.[54] In addition, Dom Legrand and his constitutional predecessor Dom Ruault contributed a portion of their incomes to provide weapons and equipment for some of Yvetot's cavalry volunteers who did not have enough money to supply their own equipment. Dom Legrand also set the example of civic duty for his parishioners by donating part of his meager pension to the national funds for the parents of army volunteers who died in combat.[55] Undoubtedly, these generous donations intensified the already warm relations between these former regulars and the lay town government.

When the department announced the convocation of two electoral assemblies, at Caudebec and Rouen, to select deputies to the National Convention, the individual cantons and districts convened to elect their delegates for these assemblies. As in the past, the curés of Bolbec and Yvetot played important roles. At the assembly for the canton of Bolbec, the delegates chose Dom Bride as the president of the election, and once again moved by "the sentiments with which you have just honored the president," Dom Bride burst into an eloquent discourse. The old cleric exhorted his audience to select deputies of uncontested and unassailable devotion to the *patrie*. At the same time, he reiterated his belief in the kinship of patriotism and religion, a theme which he had evoked in his previous orations and which spanned the gap between his religious vocation and his duties as a citizen. "Religion and the fatherland aid each other," he declared, "let us therefore sustain the one with true Christians and the other with the sentiments of sincere patriotism." The deputies must have shared his beliefs as they greeted his entreaty with wild applause and voted to append it to the assembly's

---

Dom Grognet may have also briefly taught at the local public school of Auzebosc after abdicating the priesthood on 24 ventôse An II (14 March 1794) ["Copie du procès-verbal de la commune d'Auzebosc relativement à la nomination d'un instituteur par le conseil général de la commune," ADSM, L 6192].

53. *Moniteur,* 14 February 1790.

54. "Registre des délibérations 1792–An II," AMY, 1 D 15; Tougard, *La Révolution à Yvetot,* vol. 2, 9, 71. Dom Ruault signed the municipal proceedings authorizing Dom Legrand to chair the *bureau de bienfaisance*.

55. Tougard, *La Révolution à Yvetot,* vol. 2, 9, 304.

56. ADSM, L 1579.

proceedings.[56] Meanwhile, the canton of Yvetot gathered at the end of August 1792 to elect its sixteen delegates to the district assembly. With the new regulations which allowed all males over the age of twenty-one to vote; Dom Ruault's election as a delegate bears testament to the esteem with which the majority of the townspeople regarded him and to their confidence in his patriotism. Dom Ruault reinforced their trust in him by drafting a letter of approbation and respect to the Convention on behalf of the citizens of Yvetot.[57]

At the district assembly of Caudebec, the delegates further certified that Dom Ruault's reputation as a good citizen had traveled beyond Yvetot. They selected him as one of the sixteen to represent Seine-Inférieure at the National Convention. Although ex-monk curés often played roles in local and regional politics, few clerics achieved Dom Ruault's position, with the opportunity to directly influence national policy. Yet, given the large population of former Maurists in the constitutional church of upper Normandy and given the rapport which many of them had enjoyed with secular society even before the closure of their abbeys, it does not seem surprising that one of their number joined the Norman lawyers, shopkeepers, and craftsmen who took seats in the National Convention at Paris.[58]

In the Convention's meeting hall, the Salle des Machines, Dom Ruault sat in the middle with fellow clerics Abbé Emmanuel Joseph Sieyès and Bishop Grégoire. Among the issues facing Dom Ruault and his fellow deputies were the king and what to do with him. The Jacobin radicals in the Convention, who sat on the left in the Salle des Machines, wanted to try Louis XVI for treason and conspiracy against the nation. The moderates, including some Girondins, suggested that a national referendum should decide the king's fate. The Jacobins won out and declared that the National Convention itself would try the monarch. The trial lasted about one month, until 15 January 1793, when the deputies declared a guilty verdict by a vote of 693 to 0. The Girondins again proposed putting the verdict to a national referendum, but the measure went down in defeat. Then came the fatal decision of the king's sentence—execution or exile. By a margin of 70, the Convention voted to execute Louis XVI. Dom Ruault, for his part, voted against putting the king's fate to a national referendum. At the same time, he also resented the hypocrisy of those who demanded the death sentence according to penal law when they had violated judicial law by holding the trial in the National Convention instead of a court of law. He eventually cast his ballot in favor of imprisonment, and future banishment, rather than execution.[59]

---

57. "Registre des délibérations 12 juin 1792 au 20 décembre 1792," p. 24v–26r, AMY, 11 D 14; Tougard, La Révolution à Yvetot, vol.1, 307–80; Loth, Les Conventionnels, 358; La Révolution à Yvetot et dans (unpaginated).

58. "Tableau alphabétique des députés à la convention, 1792," BMR, Mss m 225, dos. Horcholle; ADSM, L 1709; Rousseau, Moines bénédictins martyrs, 70; Tougard, La Révolution à Yvetot, vol.1, 308; Tougard, La Révolution à Yvetot, vol. 2, 7, 8, 131, 307.

59. Loth, Les Conventionnels, 54; Tougard, La Révolution à Yvetot, vol. 2, 40–42; La Révolution à Yvetot et dans (unpaginated); Lohier, "L'Inventaire," 156, f. 3.

As a National Convention deputy, Dom Ruault served on various committees, but he held firm to his seat in the Center. With the beginning of the Reign of Terror in 1793, Dom Ruault's centrist position garnered him the animosity of radicals like Marat who denounced him as a supporter of the condemned Girondin minister of the Interior, Jean-Marie Roland. Before the end of 1793, he was imprisoned at La Force for his political leanings. Upon his release, after the overthrow of Robespierre known as the coup of 9 *thermidor* (27 July 1795), he rejoined the Convention and became a member of the Council of Five Hundred in the Directory government.[60]

As a Norman representative, he looked after the religious and economic interests of his constituency. Before he left for Paris, he suggested that his fellow ex-monk, Dom Legrand, take over as *desservant* of the parish in his absence. The respect which Dom Legrand enjoyed from juring and non-juring partisans alike, as well as his speech on toleration in April 1793, earned him the admiration of his parishioners. Thus, by providing a worthy replacement before his departure, Dom Ruault spared his parish the trouble of searching for another constitutional cleric when the National Convention's round-the-clock sessions forced the old prior to resign his curé position.[61] Furthermore, during the unrelenting threat of famine in 1793, Dom Ruault, at the request of Dom Legrand and the members of Yvetot's municipal council, intervened with the *Comité des subsistances* to secure grain doles for the town. For his efforts to maintain religion and sustenance in Yvetot, the local officials voted a letter of thanks to the deputy on 22 September 1793.[62]

Maurists who chose to serve as constitutional clergy carried on with their ecclesiastical callings while also interacting with secular society. They displayed their willingness to cooperate with the new regime by the celebration of Revolutionary festivals and rituals. At the same time, they took advantage of such occasions to remind their flocks that "religion and the fatherland aid each other." Holding political offices, as secular and regular clergy had done before the Revolution, afforded them the opportunity to nourish their lay relations while also influencing local policies which affected the Church, education, and poor relief. However, like most constitutional priests, these former monks had to endure the jibes and ridicule of opponents. But neither this nor even persecution by the government to which they had sworn fidelity could shake their devotion to pursuing their vocations and serving the spiritual needs of the laity.

---

60. Tougard, *La Révolution à Yvetot,* vol. 2, 38–39, 81, 125, 131.
61. "Bureau des domaines nationaux," p. 50r, ADSM, L 1594; "Registre des délibérations 1792– An II," AMY, 1 D 15; Tougard, *La Révolution à Yvetot,* vol. 2, 9, 37, 126.
62. "Registre des délibérations 1792–An II," AMY, 1 D 15; Tougard, *La Révolution à Yvetot,* vol. 2, 46, 71, 126. The municipal assembly delayed sending him this letter since one of the councilmen argued that a person in prison for crimes against the Republic did not deserve their gratitude. Dom Ruault received the commune's thanks after his release.

CHAPTER 7

MAURISTS DURING THE TERROR

Both the ex-Maurists who did not join the constitutional church and those who did became the targets of active persecution as the policies from Paris took a more radical and anticlerical turn in 1792 and 1793. For failing to take the Liberty-Equality oath, some monks faced imprisonment, deportation, and even death. Those who had demonstrated their willingness to cooperate with the new regime by swearing fidelity to the Civil Constitution did not see their goodwill reciprocated. They witnessed the stripping and closure of their churches, and then they found themselves under assault for continuing their religious vocations. In some cases, they endured the same persecution as the refractory clergy whom they had replaced. Nevertheless, this persecution afforded ex-Maurists, both juring and non-juring, the opportunity to again manifest their commitment to their religious identities.

The monks who chose not to serve as parish clergy did not have to swear the oath to the Civil Constitution of the Clergy. However, as pensioners of the state, they did have to swear the Liberty-Equality oath.[1] In one of its final sessions before handing over the reins of power to the National Convention, the Legislative Assembly decreed on 14 August 1792 that anyone enjoying a pension from the government who did not swear the Liberty-Equality oath within fifteen days would lose their payments and perhaps suffer more serious consequences. As already mentioned, several ex-religious living separately or in groups felt that they could pledge "to be faithful to the Nation and to maintain liberty and equality, or to die while defending them" without bruising their consciences.[2] Some monks, though, still viewed even this apparently innocuous vow as hazardous to their eternal salvation and refused to take it.

In April 1793, Seine-Inférieure's Committee of Surveillance, established to ferret out anti-revolutionary activity in the area, began rounding up former ecclesiastics for refusing the Liberty-Equality or Civil Constitution oath and detaining them in the old seminary of Saint-Vivien.[3] The internment of Maurists began on 5

---

1. Lohier, "L'Inventaire," 187.

101

April 1793 with the arrest of the former prior of Saint-Lucien-de-Beauvais, Dom Charles Gabriel Cardon, who had moved to upper Normandy after the suppression of his abbey. Then, Dom Lebrun of Saint-Wandrille, hiding at his brother-in-law's home in Rouen, voluntarily turned himself over to the department administration on 19 *brumaire* An II (19 November 1793). He did not want to risk the lives of his family members since any lay person caught harboring a clerical renegade would share his fate.[4] By 25 and 26 *brumaire* An II (15 and 16 November 1793), the dates of Doms Outin and Lelaisant (dit Castel)'s arrests, the Committee of Surveillance of Seine-Inférieure had incarcerated five former Maurists.[5]

On 21 October 1793, the National Convention ordered the deportation to France's overseas colonies of ex-clergy and ex-religious who had failed to fulfill their Liberty-Equality or constitutional oath obligations by 23 March. After forcing the Rouen prisoners to spend the winter in the drafty old seminary with insufficient food, the Committee of Surveillance began loading the eighty-one clerics subject to deportation into carts as early as 16 *ventôse* An II (6 March 1794), for transport to the port of Rochefort. For the next two weeks, convoys of the condemned left Rouen at three-day intervals.[6] The group which departed on 22 *ventôse* An II (12 March 1794) included Dom Nicolas Dubois.[7] By the Convention's decree, which exempted from deportation the infirm or prisoners over the

2. Rousseau, *Moines bénédictins martyrs,* 68–69; Loth, *Liste des prêtres,* 6; Lohier, *Dom Louis-François Le Brun,* 16; Kessler, "The Suppression of the Benedictine Order," 37, 54. Originally, the National Assembly had required all pensioners of the state to swear a civic oath "to maintain the constitution of the kingdom" which implied acceptance of the Civil Constitution of the Clergy. Since individuals who did not accept positions in the constitutional church were not bound by the Civil Constitution, the civic oath was changed to the less offensive Liberty-Equality oath [Lohier, *Dom Louis-François Le Brun,* 16].

3. Assemblée nationale constituante, *Journal des débats,* (1 October 1793–21 October 1793), 277–80; Clérembray, *La Terreur à Rouen,* 83; Lohier, *Dom Louis-François Le Brun,* 16–17, 19; Rousseau, *Moines bénédictins martyrs,* 70. The initial decree of deportation required that at least six citizens denounced the accused; this number was eventually reduced to one. None of the monks from upper Normandy appeared to emigrate voluntarily during the Reign of Terror. The district of Montivilliers did cancel the pensions of seven former Maurists because "they are believed to be in England." None of those listed, however, emigrated ["État des fonctionnaires publics ecclésiastiques et des pensionnaires que l'on propose de retirer des états du trimestre de juillet 1793," ADSM, L 2097]. Dom Michel Barthélemy Gobard turned up in Guadalupe in 1792 and served there as the curé of Port-Louis. Whether he swore the constitutional oath or fled France to avoid it is unknown although his monastic and blood brother Dom Gaspard Léon Gobard became the juring curé of Saint-Quentein-des-Isles in the department of Eure [ASWF (1980), 13]. Only one Maurist, Dom Louis Dominique Lecomte, appeared to emigrate first to England and then to Germany [Guéry, *Deux bénédictins normands,* 37].

4. Dom Lebrun to the administration of the department of Seine-Inférieure, 19 brumaire An II (19 November 1793), ADSM, L 1222; Lohier, *Dom Louis-François Le Brun,* 17–18. The records from the prison listed Dom Lebrun's date of internment as 18 *vendémiaire* An II (9 October 1793) ["Maison de réclusion des prêtres," BMR, Ms p 110]. The date of his letter to the department though disputes this.

5. "Maison de réclusion des prêtres," BMR, Ms p 110. The ex-Maurists arrested at this time were Doms Charles Gabriel Cardon, Lebrun, Dubois, Nicolas Jean François Lelaisant (dit Castel) and Outin.

6. Horcholle, "Anecdotes de ce qui s'est passé dans la ville de Rouen depuis l'établissement des états généraux dont l'ouverture s'est faite à Versailles le 4 mai 1789," in Chaline and Hurpin, ed., *Vivre en Normandie,* II, 536; Hérissay, *Les Pontons de Rochefort,* 151; Lohier, *Dom Louis-François Le Brun,* 21–22; Loth, *Liste des prêtres,* 1–3, 35; Rousseau, *Moines bénédictins martyrs,* 229; Montier, "Les Moines de Fécamp," 146.

age of sixty, three of the six imprisoned Maurists escaped the merciless fate which awaited their less fortunate clerical brothers in Rochefort. They remained in the prison of Saint-Vivien until after the fall of Robespierre—with the last, Dom Lelaisant (dit Castel), finally set free on 17 *ventôse* An V (7 March 1797).[8] Their suffering did not end with their release though; they found themselves destitute of everything except their prison clothes since the government had confiscated what few goods they had possessed at the time of their arrests.[9]

Along the 503 kilometer trek to Rochefort, Doms Lebrun, Dubois and the other bound and gagged prisoners endured poor food rations, exposure to the elements—sometimes sleeping on the steps of deconsecrated churches—and the ridicule of passersby.[10] Upon arriving at the port city on 22 *germinal* An II (11 April 1794), the three Maurists from upper Normandy boarded the slave ship *Deux-Associés*. They assumed that the vessel would soon set sail for Madagascar or the Americas.[11] In the meantime, the Committee of Public Safety had dispatched new instructions,

> We see with regret that their transport to Madagascar will be very expensive . . . and that these criminals do not merit all the care which the National Convention has taken to assure their arrival in a fertile place and so near the European possessions; therefore we believe that it will be more convenient . . . to drop them on the shores of Barbary (North Africa) . . . in order to do penitence, among the Moors, for the crimes which they have committed toward humankind.[12]

In the end, the priests and the religious never set foot on the coast of Africa or any other continent. Blocked by the English ships prowling the water just beyond the Bay of La Rochelle, the ship sailed back and forth between Rochefort and La Rochelle for three months. Meanwhile, the prisoners below deck suffered days

---

7. "Maison de réclusion des prêtres," BMR, Ms p 110; Rousseau, *Moines bénédictins martyrs,* 245; Montier, "Les Moines de Fécamp," 145–46.

8. "Tableau des ecclésiastiques dans la maison de réclusion," ADSM, L 1257; "Registre d'arrêtes pris sur requêtes," ADSM, L 1250; ADMS L 1244; "Maison de réclusion des prêtres," BMR, Ms p 110; Assemblée nationale constituante, *Journal des débats,* (1 October 1793–21 October 1793), 279; Lohier, *Dom Louis-François Le Brun,* 19; Rousseau, *Moines bénédictins martyrs,* 71; Bellamy, *Bénédictins et Annonçiades,* 78, f. 8; Kessler, "The Suppression of the Benedictine Order," 85; Montier, "Les Moines de Fécamp," 183–84, 281 f. 155. Only two former Maurists were incarcerated in the department of Eure, and both escaped deportation because of their age. They regained their freedom after the fall of Robespierre on 9 *thermidor* An II (27 July 1794) ["Compte que rend l'administration du département de l'Eure au comité de législation," AN, F[1cIII] Eure 7].

9. Of course, only Dom Outin dared to complain to the government about this [Outin to the administration of the department, 4 March 1797, Outin to the administration of the department, 18 August 1797, Central administration of the department to the central administration of the canton of Rouen, [n. d.], ADSM, L 1244].

10. Horcholle, "Anecdotes de ce qui s'est passé dans la ville de Rouen depuis l'établissement des états généraux dont l'ouverture s'est faite à Versailles le 4 mai 1789," in Chaline and Hurpin, ed., *Vivre en Normandie,* II, 536; Lohier, *Dom Louis-François Le Brun,* 24–25; Montier, "Les Moines de Fécamp," 146.

11. The *Washington and Bonhomme Richard* also transported deportees, but the three Maurists from upper Normandy embarked on Deux-Associés [Rousseau, *Moines bénédictins martyrs,* 235].

12. AN, AF II 172 D p. 60.

13. For a detailed account of the excruciating conditions on the ship, see Hérissay, *Les Pontons de Rochefort.*

with little sunlight, meager food rations, and threats from the ship's captain and crew. Poor sanitary conditions and pervasive vermin made the ship a breeding ground for parasites and infection which spread rampantly and claimed a number of the clerics.[13] As conditions on the ship deteriorated and the crew threw more and more bodies of dead prisoners overboard, the administration of the Rochefort port began to fear that the epidemic would spread to the mainland population. After inspecting the vessel on 6 *thermidor* An II (24 July 1794), an appalled health official reported, "This is not how men should be treated! If, in the evening, four hundred dogs were put in this place, they would all be dead or have gone mad by the next day!"[14] The administration decided to dump the lingering captives on one of the harbor's islands, the Ile Madame (renamed the Ile Citoyenne), where it had set up a makeshift hospital. For Doms Dubois, Lebrun, and most of their fellow prisoners, their illnesses had advanced too far to hope for a recovery; they died on the island.[15] One of the other remaining prisoners from *Deux-Associés*, Labiche de Reignefort, in his memoirs of the ordeal, mentioned the heroism and saintliness exhibited by Dom Lebrun in his final days, and for this reason, the Catholic Church opened his cause for beatification.[16] Thus, by enduring imprisonment, deportation, and even death, these ex-Maurists provided the ultimate testimony of their adherence to their religious convictions.

Although none of the ex-monks who swore the constitutional oath were deported at this time, they did suffer from the oppressive measures implemented by the National Convention and the Committee of Public Safety—the oligarchic executive branch of the French government during the Terror. The policies of the national government aimed to de-Christianize France and replace Catholicism with the cult of the goddess of Reason and the deistic religion of the Supreme Being. Throughout the nation, the exteriors of Catholic churches were denuded of their Christian accouterments, while the interiors were converted to temples for the Revolutionary deities. Streets and even towns which bore names with religious connotations received secular appellations. For example, the town Saint-Antoine-la-Forêt, where Dom Tissier had served as the constitutional curé, assumed the desacralized name Pomone.[17]

As for the monks who had sworn the constitutional oath "to uphold with care the constitution," the revolutionary governments did not reward them

---

14. Béraud to the *conseil de santé*, 6 thermidor An II (24 July 1794), Archives du port de Rochefort, D p. 116, as cited in Hérissay, *Les Pontons de Rochefort,* 290–91.

15. Lohier, *Dom Louis-François Le Brun,* 29; Hérissay, *Les Pontons de Rochefort,* 292, 312–13; Loth, *Liste des prêtres,* 2, 17; Rousseau, *Moines bénédictins martyrs,* 243; Bellamy, *Bénédictins et Annonçiades,* 25; Montier, "Les Moines de Fécamp," 146, 149.

16. Lohier, *Dom Louis-François Le Brun,* 29. Since Labiche de Reignefort did not provide any information about Dom Dubois, his cause for beatification has not been considered [Montier, "Les Moines de Fécamp," 151].

17. Aston, *Religion and Revolution,* 259–76. The National Convention also ordered the abolition of the Gregorian calendar and replaced it with the Revolutionary one which symbolized the triumph of the Republic over the tyranny of the old regime. The names of the days and the months were renamed to reflect their "natural" attributes, such as *frimaire*–the cold month, and year calculations

for their devotion to the state. As the de-Christianization policies spread from Paris to the departments, the increasingly radical, anticlerical legislation of the National Convention began to affect the constitutionals as well as the non-jurers. The monks who faithfully served the constitutional church endured the same harassment and persecution as their monastic brothers who had rejected all of the oaths. Despite the local support and admiration for Dom Legrand and despite his presence on the town council, the municipal administration stripped him of the outward signs of his ordination by forbidding him to wear his vestments, conduct processions, or administer the sacraments beyond the church doors. While he complied with these orders, he diplomatically intervened on 12 *frimaire* An II (2 December 1793) when, in compliance with the de-Christianization measures, the municipal administration wanted to remove two corpora from crucifixes on the exterior of Saint Pierre church and replace them with representations of the Republican allegories of Liberty and Reason. The curé did succeed in convincing the council to allow him to transfer these images to the interior of the church as long as he operated alone and without ceremony.[18] In this way, he used his good lay relations to save sacred images.

Some constitutional ex-monks witnessed the insides of their parish churches converted into Temples of Reason. The devastation of the church at Bolbec began on 18 *ventôse* An II (8 March 1794) when the commune government ordered the destruction of all "signs of the former Catholic cult."[19] Dom Bride—who at every opportunity had so eloquently orated on the compatibility between religion and the new regime—must have looked on with impotent horror as soldiers threw statues into the streets and tore out the grills which he had brought from Saint-Wandrille. A few items from Dom Bride's church survived the iconoclastic fury and were rebaptized as Revolutionary symbols, such as an image of the Virgin Mary which escaped vandalism after someone painted the inscription "De la Déesse de la Raison" above it.[20] Dom Grognet, on the other hand, did not stand by impassively in September 1793 as his parish church was made a shrine to the Revolutionary deity. He adamantly protested this sacrilege, even though the local administration did permit him to continue to offer Mass in the choir. For resisting the conversion of the church into a temple of Reason, the town council declared that Dom Grognet's intolerance for the new religion "wounds the principle of equality which he seems to misunderstand." Evidently, despite taking the oath, saying a requiem for the fallen heroes of the Revolution, and serving as a town notable, Dom Grognet could still be accused of intolerance—the capital

---

began with 1792, the date of the proclamation of the First French Republic. Each month had three ten-day weeks, beginning with the day of rest, *décadi*. For a detailed account of the de-Christianization, see Vovelle, *The Revolution against the Church*.

18. "Registre des délibérations 1792–An II," AMY, 1 D 1₅; Tougard, *La Révolution à Yvetot*, vol. 2, 11–12. Saint-Pierre d'Yvetot was closed and used for grain storage by decree of the municipal assembly on 19 nivôse An II (8 January 1794) [Tougard, *La Révolution à Yvetot*, vol. 2, 12].

19. As quoted in Pigout, *La Révolution en Seine-Maritime*, 333.

20. Ibid., 333–34, 337.

sin of revolutionaries—for daring to defend the prerogatives of the constitutional church and his religious vocation.[21]

At Fécamp, the Popular Society, an army of the Jacobin Club in Paris, had begun holding its meetings in Dom Letellier's parish church in November 1793, but the de-Christianization measures did not commence with fury until December.[22] On 5 December, Dom Letellier tried to imitate Legrand by petitioning the municipal council of Fécamp to allow him to place a statue of Saint Suzanne inside the church. The administrators refused to even debate the issue, and two days later they decreed that the first fête to the goddess of Reason would take place on the following *décadi* in the old abbey's church.[23] Initially, the curé could prolong his use of Sainte-Trinité for Catholic Mass, but the Popular Society soon eliminated this concession—even though Dom Letellier enjoyed their respect, as they later illustrated during his imprisonment. In an effort to stamp out the remaining vestiges of Catholic worship in the seaside parish, the Society ordered the closure of all churches and chapels on 21 March 1794.[24] Dom Letellier had said his last Mass in the abbey church, at least for awhile.

As commune governments closed churches throughout upper Normandy, Maurist curés tried to save the sacred objects from their churches. But as the de-Christianization progressed, their very religious vocations came under fire. They faced the dilemma of persisting in their active, ecclesiastical functions and attracting the suspicion of the municipal government, or resigning their constitutional positions and retiring into private life. The first resignation of ex-monk curés began shortly after the initial elections of constitutional clergy in 1791. But at the end of 1793, the growing Jacobin suspicion of even the constitutional clergy, and the consequent de-Christianization policies, caused a stream of resignations by ex-Maurists. Amid cries of "Long live The Mountain!" (a reference to the National Convention's radical delegates, known as The Mountain), the citizenry of Bolbec celebrated their first *décadi* fête with a procession from the Temple—the former parish church—to the meeting place of the Popular Society. Arriving at their destination, the crowd paused as Dom Bride stepped up to the podium to

---

21. "Municipalité d'Auzebosc," p. 179, ADSM, L 6216. Dom Grognet's name disappears from the municipal records of Auzebosc c. 22 *ventôse* An III (12 March 1795). He did not sign the council's decree of 1 *floréal* An III (20 April 1795) transforming the parish church into a temple for the Supreme Being ["Auzebosc: Délibérations 7 *fructidor* An II au 28 *brumaire* An IV," p. 32, 40, ADSM, L 6220].

22. Found in many municipalities during the Revolution, Popular Societies were political clubs which usually sided with one of the major Parisian political clubs such as the Jacobins or the Cordeliers. Under the Terror the most radical policies of the National Convention and the Committee of Public Safety were often implemented by municipal administrations in the provinces at the instigation of the local Popular Societies. [Aston, *Religion and Revolution*, 186].

23. de Beaurepaire, *Fécamp pendant la Révolution*, 46, 48; Bourienne-Savoye and Desjardins-Menegalli, *Marins, moines, citoyens*, 41; Bellamy, *Bénédictins et Annonçiades*, 27; Martin, *Histoire de Fécamp*, II, 144. The Maurist monastery church of Saint-Ouen in Rouen was also converted into a temple for Republican cults [Ledré, *Le Diocèse de Rouen*, 100–1].

24. Martin, *Histoire de Fécamp*, II, 150–51; Bellamy, *Bénédictins et Annonçiades*, 28; Loth, *Histoire du Cardinal*, 523; Bourienne-Savoye and Desjardins-Menegalli, *Marins, moines, citoyens*, 52; Montier, "L'Abbaye de la Sainte-Trinité," 336, f. 79.

declare his renunciation of the parish. Employing his oratory skills one last time, he described how his desire to serve his fellow citizens had led him to accept the curé position at Bolbec. But, since he had pledged his obedience to the general will, and since the general will seemed to have turned against Catholicism, he chose this first celebration of the revolutionary holiday to step down as curé.[25]

Not all resignations went as smoothly as that of Dom Bride. Dom Levacque's renunciation "in order to conform to the wishes of the people" probably came as no surprise to the local administration of Allouville, given the harassment which they had inflicted on him as the town curé and mayor.[26] Similarly, Dom Moniez handed over the keys to the church of Saint-Clair-sur-les-Monts on 27 *vendémiaire* An II (18 October 1793) and moved to Dom Louis Charles François Bricque's former parish Saint-Sylvestre after enduring two harsh winters in a dilapidated rectory with no apparent aid from the municipal administration of Saint-Clair.[27]

The Terror and the de-Christianization measures induced some ex-monks to relinquish their positions in the constitutional church, but the National Convention's decrees went further—requiring them to abandon all signs of their religious vocations by abdicating their positions and handing over their letters of priesthood (*lettres de prêtrise*) to the local administration. On 19 *brumaire* An II (9 November 1793), Bishop Lindet set the example by renouncing his bishopric and his priesthood.[28] Claude Siblot, the representative on mission to upper Normandy, viewed the bishop's behavior as worthy of imitation and issued an ultimatum on 18 *germinal* An II (7 April 1794) to the Norman priests who had not already followed Lindet's example.[29] Regardless of "very pronounced *civism*, their advanced age, their infirmities, the cessation of their functions, their marriage even," all clerics who had not resigned all ecclesiastical functions and handed over their *lettres de prêtrise* to their municipal or district governments within four days would face imprisonment. In pursuing and detaining those who had not already abandoned their religious vocations, Siblot knew that he would indiscriminately criminalize the constitutional priests (who had proven their loyalty to the new regime) along with the refractories, but this did not trouble him:

25. Pigout, *La Révolution en Seine-Maritime,* 330–31; Pigout, Bolbec, 82. Doms Étienne Tissier and de Quane were among the other priests of Seine-Inférieure who resigned their ecclesiastical functions at the end of 1793 [Tissier to the administration of the district of Montivilliers, 3 *floréal* An III (22 April 1795), ADSM, L 2097; "Tableau des pensionnaires dits ecclésiastiques des deux sexes domiciliés dans le canton de Goderville et du montant de la pension et du secours au qu'il chacun a droit," ADSM, L 1205].

26. "Registre de délibérations de la municipalité d'Allouville," p. 44r, ADSM, L 6199.

27. "Bureau des domaines nationaux," p. 31r, ADSM, L 1594; "Du registre de la municipalité de Saint-Sylvestre," ADSM, L 6196.

28. "Extrait du procès-verbal de la séance de la société des sans-culottes de la commune d'Évreux," ADE, 57 L 2, dos. 1790–An III.

29. The representatives on mission were sent out from the National Convention to parts of France embroiled in political and social unrest. These representatives had complete authority to take whatever measures they deemed necessary to end the civil strife. They gained a reputation for their ruthlessness as well as their lack of understanding of the areas in which they operated.

"If, on the one hand, some patriots will lose momentarily the precious benefit of their liberty, on the other hand, many enemies of the Republic will be sequestered from society."[30] Desperate times required desperate measures, and he needed to do whatever necessary "to terminate the threatening gatherings [of the Catholic worship] for the liberty and security of the department."[31]

Despite the constitutional clergy's previous loyalty to the Revolution, Siblot's decree refused to recognize any priest as a true friend of the new order, "For all time, the priests have been the scourge of society . . . they are the natural enemies of the Republic . . . they are at the head of all the intrigues and plots which are hatched against liberty."[32] Therefore, even those who had sworn the constitutional oath had to provide ultimate proof of their devotion to the state by renouncing their ecclesiastical calling in favor of the Republic. Dom Trémauville had proven his patriotism by swearing the oath, and he even reconciled the feuding religious factions in the parishes of Ecretteville-sur-les-Baons and Cléville. Yet, he had to prove his loyalty again by handing over his letters of priesthood. Along with these documents, he also relinquished the same canonical institution and proclamation of election which had been read aloud at his first installation. He accepted this decision without protest, only desiring to retire to his farm and "no longer exercise the functions of Catholic worship."[33] Doms Bricque and Bride— two of Seine-Inférieure's most prominent ex-Maurists turned constitutional clerics—also submitted their *lettres de prêtrise* to their local governments, but they did not make public statements abnegating their religious beliefs.[34]

Most juring ex-monks had handed over their letters of priesthood before the representative on mission's demand. Dom Gobard imitated his superior, the Bishop of Eure, and gave up his priesthood on 22 *germinal* An II (11 April 1794).[35] "In order to respond to the will of the nation and to not leave any doubt of my civism," Dom Lestievetz deposited his *lettres de prêtrise* along with the keys to the parish church at the town hall of Boishimont on 23 *ventôse* An II (13 March 1794).[36] Yet, in perhaps a clever ruse, the former Saint-Wandrille monk Dom Louis François Joseph Lengaigne and Dom Moniez from Notre-Dame-du-Bec acted "as good Republican(s) protesting [their] submission to the laws" while not abandoning their holy orders. They presented the officials of their municipalities with their

30. Administration of the revolutionary district of Dieppe to the communes of its arrondissement, 4 *floréal* An II (23 April 1794), ADSM, L 6365; Representative in Seine-Inférieure and Eure to the Committee of Public Safety, 18 *germinal* An II (7 April 1794), Comité de salut public, *Recueil des actes,* XII, 442; Aston, *Religion and Revolution,* 268; Pigout, *La Révolution en Seine-Maritime,* 334–35. Pigout erroneously gave the date of Siblot's decree as 12 *germinal* An II (7 April 1794). Siblot did exempt from his decree priests who promised to abandon the priesthood and who 1) had married or 2) were over sixty years old as long as they eventually handed over their *lettres de prêtrise.*

31. National agent of the revolutionary district of Dieppe to the citizens, mayor, municipal officers and agent of the commune of Eu, 22 *prairial* An II (10 June 1794), ADSM, L 6365.

32. As cited in Pigout, *La Révolution en Seine-Maritime,* 334–35.

33. Mayor and municipal officers of the commune of Ecretteville to unknown [directory of the district of Caudebec], [n. d.], ADSM, L 6196; Trémauville to the Montagnard district of Yvetot, 16 *ventôse* An II (6 March 1794), ADSM, L 6196.

34. ADSM, L 2088; Pigout, *La Révolution en Seine-Maritime,* 332; Pigout, Bolbec, 83.

canonical institutions as curés, but they could not do the same with their *lettres de prêtrise* which they claimed still remained in the hands of their former Maurist priors. Considering that Dom Lestievetz, who had also resided at Saint-Wandrille at the time of the suppression, handed over his letters of ordination, Doms Lengaigne and Moniez may have tried to present themselves as good Republicans while finding an excuse to avoid relinquishing the last bond to their religious vocations.[37]

Dom Pierre Bourlier appeared prepared to abandon his spiritual duties, which he had earlier claimed to have performed only at the behest of the good citizens of Villers-sur-Aumale. But, this former prior of Saint-Martin-d'Auchy-les-Aumales did not break faith completely with his religion. He presented himself on 20 *ventôse* An II (10 March 1794) to the local administration of Villers-sur-Aumale, where he had fulfilled the duties of *desservant*, to renounce his ecclesiastical position. Claiming obedience to the principles of the Republic as his motivation, he sought to affirm his devotion to the radical government in Paris by declaring to have "always regarded the dogmatic part of the Christian religion as beneath his intelligence and his reason." Still, he did not completely turn his back on the faith in which he had professed his vows. Rather, he tried to reconcile his religious beliefs with the current situation by asserting that "the moral part [of Christianity] which ought to regulate the conduct of the Christian conforms to the sacred principles of the Constitution which have been given to us by the National Convention." [38]

While monks who did not wish to become parish clergy did not have to swear the constitutional oath, they still had to surrender their letters of priesthood. Although never functioning as a curé or vicar, Dom de Saulty promised the municipal government of Jumièges on 9 *ventôse* An II (27 February 1794), to no longer say Mass "so as to not trouble the public order" and deposited his letters of priesthood.[39] One week later, his fellow ex-Maurists Doms de Mésanges, Julien, and Painblanc, part of the group of monastic exiles at Jumièges, had only "said Mass when they had been required or obliged to do so." Since they did not want to upset the local community, they followed Dom de Saulty's example.[40]

As the representative on mission, Siblot carried out his mandate with rigorous exactness. His 18 *germinal* An II abdication decree required constitutional

35. "État nominatif des ex-religieux, ex-bénéficiers et congregationnaires et vicaires épiscopaux qui ne sont attachés à aucun service," ADE, 95 L 1, dos.1790–An III. Forty-one ex-Maurists abdicated their priesthood. Since he was over sixty years old, Dom Alexandre Joseph du Bocquet was allowed by Siblot's decree to hand over his *lettres de prêtrise* after 18 *germinal* An II. He later claimed that he did so "by weakness and by fear of persecution . . . but without motive of act of irreligion" [ADE, 57 L 16]. Dom Ruault probably abdicated his priesthood while in prison for his Girondin sympathies during the Terror [Tougard, *La Révolution à Yvetot,* vol. 2, 129].

36. ADSM, L 6196.

37. "Extrait du registre des délibérations et arrêtés de la commune d'Ecretteville-les-Baons, district Montagnard d'Yvetot," ADSM, L 6196; "Du registre de la municipalité de Saint-Sylvestre," ADSM, L 6196. Apparently, Dom Lengaigne had moved to Ecretteville-les-Baons after he had resigned as curé of Autretot.

38. "Extrait du registre des délibérations des officiers municipales de la commune de Villers-sur-Aumale," ADSM, L 227; Dom Pierre Bourlier to the administration of the revolutionary district of Neufchâtel, 26 *brumaire* An II (16 November 1793), ADSM, L 2267.

ex-monks and those who had not engaged in any ecclesiastical occupation to abandon the priesthood or face incarceration.[41] Some of these men appeared willing to suffer imprisonment rather than divest themselves of the last vestige of their religious calling. Dom Gourdin's employ as the department's librarian did not exempt him from Siblot's intractable demands, and when the bibliophile failed to relinquish his letters of priesthood, he was ordered to Rouen's Saint-Vivien prison.[42] Dom Tissier resigned as curé of Saint-Antoine-la-Forêt and gave up all of his papers except for his *lettres de prêtrise*. Although he had sat in the electoral assembly of his district of Montivilliers, this did not suffice to exempt him from the representative's severity. Nine days after the publication of Siblot's 18 *germinal* An II abdication decree, Dom Tissier was arrested and imprisoned in Montivilliers' house of detention. Even though the Popular Society of Pomone (formerly Saint-Antoine-la-Forêt) attested to his *civism*, he remained in prison for two months until his release at 5:00 AM on 19 *floréal* An III (8 May 1795) by the authority "of Siblot of happy memory" (as Dom Tissier later sarcastically commented).[43]

Some constitutional ex-monks not only resisted the order to relinquish their *lettres de prêtrise* but even persisted in their guardianship of the Church's sacred objects despite the threat of jail or worse. On 12 *frimaire* An II (2 December 1793), one week before Fécamp's first festival of Reason, the town council issued a certificate of *civism* to Dom Letellier, and affirmed that "the ex-Benedictine has always manifested and manifests still both by his conduct and his morals the most pure *civism* and true patriotism."[44] Yet, his arrest only four months later showed that, apparently, his certificate of *civism* as well as his presidency of Fécamp's Jacobin Club did not excuse him from the crime of trying to protect his church's most sacred possession, a relic of the Precious Blood.[45]

---

39. "Registre des délibérations du conseil général de la municipalité de Jumièges," ADSM, L 6195. De Saulty was listed in January 1793 as the desservant of the parish of Launay in the department of Eure, but he does not appear to have been officially elected by the department ["État des sommes," ADSM, L 1709].

40. "Registre des délibérations du conseil général," ADSM, L 6195; Amand, mayor of Jumièges to unknown [directory of the district of Caudebec], 30 *germinal* An II (19 April 1794), ADSM, L 6195. According to Savalle, the names of Dom de Mésanges and Dom Jean Jacques de Montigny appeared on a list of denunciations for the town of Jumièges. Dom de Montigny's *lettres de prêtrise* did not appear in the department's archives, but since Dom de Mésanges did relinquish his, it seems most probable that this story was the product of Savalle's embellishment [Savalle, *Les Derniers moines,* 58–59]. Citing AN, F19 883, Dom Y. Chaussy placed Dom Julien in the department of Pyrénées-Atlantiques where he abdicated his priesthood on 18 *germinal* An II [Chaussy, "Les Derniers moines," 256–57]. The documents at the Archives départementales de Seine-Maritime, however, clearly affirm his presence in the commune of Jumièges during the Terror.

41. Hérissay, *Les Pontons de Rochefort,* 83.

42. Deries, "La Vie d'un bibliothécaire, 228–29; Dubuc, "Bibliothèques et œuvres d'art," 146.

43. "État des ecclésiastiques du district de Brutusvilliers (ci-devant Montivilliers) qui ont abdiquée leur profession de prêtre et renoncé à l'exercice de leur fonctions depuis le 27 brumaire jusques et compris le 15 *germinal* An II," ADSM, L 2095; "État des prêtres mis en état d'arrestation tant en conséquence des ordres du citoyen Briquel commissaire du comité de sûreté général qu'en exécution de l'arreste du représentatif du peuple Siblot du 18 germinal," "État des prêtres élargis par l'agent national du district de Brutusvilliers (Montivilliers) en exécution de l'arrêt du représentatif de peuple Siblot sous la datte du 15 prairial," ADSM, L 2098; Tissier to the administration of the district of Montivilliers, 3 *floréal* An III (22 April 1795), ADSM, L 2097; ADSM, L 2095.

As constitutional curé at the former abbey church of Sainte-Trinité, Dom Letellier—more than many other ex-regulars—must have been surrounded by constant reminders of his cloister days. No souvenir, however, could have compared to the priceless vial of Christ's blood. At the beginning of his curate, Dom Letellier had handed over the relic's gilded reliquary to the national foundry, as required by law, but he had kept the silver vial containing the actual Blood. He continued to safeguard it even after the Popular Society of Fécamp took over his church. He still had it in his possession on 8 *germinal* An II (28 March 1794) when he was arrested for failing to turn over all precious metal objects from the church. Even the downfall of Robespierre and his Committee of Public Safety on 9 *thermidor* An II (27 July 1794) did not bring about Dom Letellier's liberation until the Popular Society testified on his behalf. "He, who has always demonstrated to be a partisan of the Revolution, ought not to be regarded as a fanatic." The new representative on mission reviewed the case and judged the silver container not subject to confiscation. He decreed Dom Letellier's internment unlawful and ordered the ex-monk's release on 13 *ventôse* An III (3 March 1795). [46]

Siblot treated all priests, juring and non-juring, with contempt and suspicion; all could equally deserve incarceration. By the same token, all could receive emancipation after a few months, as in Dom Monthois' case. Barely had he escaped deportation in 1793 when he found himself imprisoned under Siblot's orders on 28 *germinal* An II (17 April 1794). After the suppression of his abbey of Valmont, this former prior had lived in the town of the same name where he said low Mass with Dom Sta. On 2 May 1793 he became the vicar of Auberville-la-Renault.

Dom Monthois insisted that as an ex-monk he did not have to swear the constitutional oath, and his retraction of the Liberty-Equality oath, which he had sworn both at Valmont and at Auberville-la-Renault, raised questions about his loyalty to the Revolution. The day after his arrival in Auberville-la-Renault, the *procureur syndic* of the Cany district dispatched to Valmont an order for his arrest.[47] Dom Monthois wrote letters to the department trying to explain the motivation of his retraction. After taking his Liberty-Equality oath, religious unrest broke out, and so he renounced the oath "because he preferred the public well-being to his particular interest." Although Dom Monthois did not protest his attachment to the Republic in his letters nor claim to have sworn the constitutional oath,

44. ADSM, L 2095; de Beaurepaire, *Fécamp pendant la Révolution,* 44; Martin, *Histoire de Fécamp,* II, 150, 152.

45. Clérembray lists Dom Letellier as the president of *Les Amis de la Constitution* from October to December 1791 [Clérembray, *La Terreur à Rouen,* 117, f. 1].

46. "État des secours accordés aux pensionnes de deux sexes détenus à raison des fonctions ou bénéfices ecclésiastiques supprimés qu'ils exerçaient sur reprise de quarante sols par jour, formé en exécution de l'article six de la loi du 2 sans cullotide dernier," ADSM, L 2098; Dom Dupont to the directory of the district of Montivilliers, 16 *frimaire* An III (6 December 1794), as cited in Fallue, *Histoire de la ville,* 475; de Beaurepaire, *Fécamp pendant la Révolution,* 54, f. 1, 54–55; Bellamy, *Bénédictins et Annonçiades,* 28; Bourienne-Savoye and Desjardins-Menegalli, *Marins, moines, citoyens,* 41; Martin, *Histoire de Fécamp,* II, 152, 159; Montier, "L'Abbaye de la Sainte-Trinité," 28, 336, f. 79. Arriving at Sainte-Trinité in the tenth century, the relic of the Precious Blood rendered

he did admit his mistake in retracting his Liberty-Equality oath and affirmed his desire to submit himself "to the law with the greatest sincerity."[48]

Dom Monthois' letters assured the local administration that he had never threatened the status or person of the constitutional priest.[49] This must have sufficed to ensure the former monk's freedom since no record exists of his deportation in 1793. However, after returning to Auberville-la-Renault and proceeding with his vicarial duties, the municipal council of the town heard rumors about the incident at Valmont and decided to verify his background.[50] Satisfied with the results of their inquiry, the officials of Auberville-la-Renault attested that "he has always shown himself to be the friend of order, obeying and submitting to the laws and to the constituted authorities."[51] This testament to his *civism* did not matter after the promulgation of Siblot's decree requiring priests to hand over their *lettres de prêtrise*. The former Maurist refused to comply with Siblot's orders and joined Dom Tissier in the house of detention for the district of Montivilliers. Less fortunate than his fellow inmate, Dom Monthois remained in prison until 28 *thermidor* An II (15 August 1794).[52] Perhaps the previous renunciation and his own admission of the retraction made him susceptible to a lengthier prison sentence. It does seem ironic that, under Siblot's decree which had allowed no distinction between constitutional and refractory priests, an ex-monk with a record of suspicious behavior eventually regained his freedom right along with former Maurists of known loyalty to the new regime.

In delivering his invective against the religious orders to the National Assembly on 13 February 1790, Barnave had accused the clerical vow of celibacy of violating natural law, and the Legislative Assembly had sought to correct so obvious a transgression of nature by encouraging all priests to wed. The National Convention even exempted married priests from deportation. Bishop Lindet of Eure, the very model of episcopal obedience to the national legislatures, set the

Fécamp a place of pilgrimage until the French Revolution. The Friday after Passion Sunday was designated as the solemn feast day of the Precious Blood, and the Maurist brothers of Fécamp–whose musical talent and expertise were well-known throughout France–performed the *Missa Sanguinis Christi* [Montier, "Les Moines de Fécamp," 28].

47. Monthois to the directory of the department of Seine-Inférieure, 10 November 1792, ADSM, L 1538; "Du registre de la municipalité de Vallemont [sic]," ADSM, L 2092; "Extrait du registre de la municipalité d'Auberville-la-Renault," ADSM, L 2092; Municipal officers of the commune of Valmont to unknown [*Procureur syndic* of the district of Cany], 28 November 1792, ADSM, L 2593; ADSM, L 1538.

48. "Extrait des registres des délibérations de la commune de Valmont," ADSM, L 1538; Monthois to the directory of the department of Seine-Inférieure, 4 April 1793 and [n. d.], ADSM, L 1538. The warrant from Valmont ordered the arrest of Dom Monthois as well as Dom Dubois who was apparently living, or hiding, with the vicar at that time. For his known rejection of the Liberty-Equality oath, Dom Dubois was later jailed and deported; he died on the pontoons of Rochefort [ADSM, L 1538]. Perhaps Dom Dubois' presence at Valmont further compromised Dom Monthois.

49. ADSM, L 1538.

50. "Extrait du registre de municipalité d'Auberville la Renault," ADSM, L 1538; Members composing the general council of the commune of Auberville-la-Renault to the administrators of the department of Seine-Inférieure, 1 September 1793, ADSM, L 1538.

51. ADSM, L 2097 and 2095.

example for his diocese by marrying in 1792. In the other department of upper Normandy however, this issue caused a rift in the constitutional church as the juring Bishop Gratien of Seine-Inférieure refused to promote such a practice and even condemned the Legislative Assembly for interfering in matters of ecclesiastical discipline. For publishing and promulgating his views on the issue, Gratien received the revolutionary's most detested label, *fanatic*, and his prohibition against the nuptials of one of his diocesan priests resulted in his removal from his episcopal office and his imprisonment.[53]

As Siblot had stipulated in his decree regarding letters of priesthood, priests who had married had a slight grace period in which to hand over their *lettres de prêtrise* before their arrest and imprisonment. Only one ex-Maurist curé took advantage of the representative's extension. Dom Gobard, who abdicated his priesthood on 22 *germinal* An II (11 April 1794), had followed Bishop Lindet's example a year earlier; he had married the daughter of a ploughman from his parish of Saint-Quentin-les-Iles.[54] However, Dom Gobard was the exception—fewer than twenty former Maurists from upper Normandy married at any time during the Revolution, and of this number only seven had taken positions in the constitutional church. Most of the ex-regulars who married had completely laicized after the suppression of their abbeys, and even then, they did not hasten to the altar with brides. Dom Evrard, the monk sentenced to live at Bec before the Revolution by *lettres de cachet*, had pronounced his nuptial vows in 1792, shortly after leaving the cloister of Bec. Both Dom de Maurey and Dom Catelain did not marry until An IV, and Napoleon had already created the First Empire by the time Dom Jean Michel Raoullet contracted a civil union in 1807.[55] Their low pension may explain some of their reluctance to marry. A monk who received 600–800 livres annually—and could not earn any other income without jeopardizing his pension according to the decrees of the National Convention—could hardly support himself, not to mention a wife and children. Furthermore, it seemed that most ex-religious waited to marry until after the Terror, when any possibility of reestablishing monastic life had been eliminated.

Those constitutional ex-monks who were not imprisoned tended to wait out the Terror in their former parishes. About thirteen chose to maintain their

---

52. "État des prêtres mis en état d'arrestation," ADSM, L 2098; "État des ci-devant religieux des deux sexes et ecclésiastiques domiciliés dans l'arrondissement de ce district jouissant d'un secours ou pension à la charge du trésor national, d'après la loi du 2 sans culottide An II (18 Septembre 1794)," ADSM, L 6380.

53. Baston, *Mémoires*, 360–66; Loth, *Histoire du Cardinal*, 514–15, 671; Pigout, *La Révolution en Seine-Maritime*, 335; Rousseau, *Moines bénédictins martyrs*, 49; Aston, *Religion and Revolution*, 213; Kessler, "The Suppression of the Benedictine Order," 95–96.

54. ASWF (1980), 98; ASWF (1967), 100. Doms Jean Jacques Henry Besserve, Mullet, and Duvrac married in 1794, but the exact dates are unknown. They would not have benefited from Siblot's extension since they had already abdicated their priesthood before their marriages ["État nominatif des ex-religieux, ex-bénéficières, ex-congrégationnaires et vicaires épiscopaux qui ne sont attachée aucun service," ADE, 57 L 14; "Les Religieux de la Congrégation," 56, no. 226 (October-December 1966): 120].

residences, and whether they resumed their ministry during the Directory or not, most of these continued to live among their flocks long after the coup of 9 *thermidor*.[56] Some of these monks even accepted positions in the local government; Doms Bride and Trémauville gained seats on the general councils of Bolbec and Cléville respectively, and Dom Mesnard became the head of the correctional police for his former parish of Auzebosc.[57] After abdicating his curate at Lanquetot, Dom Jean-Baptiste Ferey became the municipal agent. As such, he drew upon his expertise in education, acquired in the Congregation of Saint-Maur, to provide the municipality with information on improving the local public school.[58] Upon vacating the presbytery of his parish, Dom Grognet decided to join his fellow ex-Maurists in their monastic hometown of Saint-Wandrille where he also perpetuated his Congregation's tradition of scholarship by serving as the instructor for the town's public school.[59]

Serving in various political offices afforded former monks the opportunity to aid their fellow clerics. Yvetot's constitutional curé, Dom Legrand, remained in his town after abdicating his priesthood and, under the Terror, began his promising political career as the assistant to the national agent for the town of Yvetot.[60] This position, which included interrogating prisoners, allowed him to assist detained priests. Abbé Louis Dumesnil described Dom Legrand's kindness to incarcerated, non-juring clerics while they waited for audiences with the national agent. The former monk assured these refractories of their eventual freedom, and he may have even had a hand in their release. It was later claimed that Dom Legrand had placed the files of clerics at the bottom of the stack of those condemned to death. In this way, the cases of priests never rose to the top of the pile, and the sentences were not executed. Thus, ex-Maurists who chose to accept occupations in the Terror regime could still maintain ties with the ecclesiastical population even though such connections could put them at risk of suffering the same punishments as their imprisoned or deported former Maurist brothers.[61]

Regardless of their stance on the Civil Constitution, monks continued to provide evidence of their devotion to their religious vocations and principles during the de-Christianization period of the Revolution. Former Maurists who had not entered the secular clergy and had refused the Liberty-Equality oath could suffer

55. AN, AF^{IV} 1910, 1909; "Extrait du seconde registre des délibérations du conseil municipal de Saint-Wandrille," as cited in ASWF (1950), 74; Bellamy, *Bénédictins et Annonçiades*, 25; Montier, "Les Moines de Fécamp," 211.

56. ADSM, L 1202, 1205, 1209, 1211, 1316, 1539, 3119. Martin tells the story of Dom Sta being forced to flee Valmont during the Terror and hiding at the home of the curé of Thiergeville, but the department's record always indicated his residence as Valmont [Martin, *Notes pour servir à l'histoire*, 67].

57. ADSM, L 1202; de la Bunodière, *Derniers jours de l'abbaye de Saint-Ouen*, 18.

58. ADSM, L 2789.

59. ADSM, L 3119; Lohier, "L'Inventaire," 159, f. 15, 185.

60. Municipal officers of Cléville to the administration of the district, 17 *germinal* [An III] (6 April 1795), ADSM, L 1597; Pigout, Bolbec, 80; Tougard, *La Révolution à Yvetot*, vol. 2, 12. Dom Bride became the archivist of Bolbec after his abdication [Pigout, *Bolbec*, 83]. The position of national agent was roughly equivalent to that of town mayor [ASWF (1950), 80c].

imprisonment, deportation, and death. Some of the ex-Maurists turned constitutional clerics demonstrated their commitment to their ecclesiastical profession by protecting the art and relics of their parish churches and even incurring internment for refusing to turn over their *lettres de prêtrise*. Even those who did relinquish their letters of priesthood, however, did not necessarily reject their vocations, as exemplified by Dom Legrand. Besides, after the Terror, when ministers of religion could again fulfill their ecclesiastical duties, some of those who had handed over their letters of priesthood in order to avoid punishment vindicated themselves by reestablishing their ministries.

---

61. Abbé Louis Dumesnil, *Ma Prison ou mes avantures pendant le terreur,* BMR, Mss mm 31, I, 176; Dumesnil, *Souvenirs de la Terreur,* 68; Fromentin, *Essai historique,* 88, f. 1; Savalle, *Les Derniers moines,* 60, f. 1; Tougard, *La Révolution à Yvetot,* vol. 2, 15–17. Fromentin claimed that by putting their files on the bottom of the stack, Dom Legrand also saved the Marquise de Nagu and her daughter from the guillotine [Fromentin, *Essai historique,* 88; Tougard, *La Révolution à Yvetot,* vol. 2, 17, 19, 189, f. 13].

CHAPTER 8

MAURISTS DURING THE DIRECTORY

THE FALL OF ROBESPIERRE and his supporters on 9 *thermidor* brought a breath of fresh air to France which had labored under the oppressive Reign of Terror for over a year. During the following months of 1794, the National Convention, no longer under the thumb of the Committee of Public Safety, reconstituted itself as the lawmaking body of France. The moderates, like Dom Ruault, dominated the Convention and set about dismantling Robespierre's oligarchic Committee. They also annulled all extralegal pronouncements by the representatives on mission, thus ending Siblot's ruthless pursuit of priests in upper Normandy. The Convention then began working on yet another constitution, the Constitution of An III, which would establish the Directory government in the fall of 1795. With the new constitution, a bicameral legislature—the Council of Five Hundred and the Council of Elders—replaced the National Convention. A crippled executive branch—the Directory, consisting of five men chosen by the legislature—was established.

While working on the constitution, the National Convention needed to address some of France's more immediate concerns, including the religious tension that the previous legislation and the de-Christianization efforts had spawned. To alleviate the situation, the Convention issued the freedom of worship decree on 11 *prairial* An III (30 May 1795). Once again, priests all over France freely intoned the introit at their altars. Any priest living in France at the time could practice his ecclesiastical vocation if he simply pledged to obey the laws of the Republic. Deported or émigré priests could not reestablish their ministry on French soil, but clerics in prison or awaiting deportation were released and given the same freedom of worship.[1]

---

1. Assemblée nationale constituante, *Journal des débats,* (20 May 1795–18 June 1795), 584–85; Committee of legislation of the National Convention to the *procureur-général syndic* of the department of Seine-Inférieure, 22 *thermidor* An III (9 August 1795), ADSM, L 11901; Ledré, *Le Diocèse de Rouen,* 7–9, 17. The National Convention after the Terror was termed reconstituted because the members, including the former Maurist Dom Ruault, who had been imprisoned during the Jacobin purges, could reclaim their seats.

This freedom came with a price: the government ended the payment of clerical salaries. Priests could not wear their cassocks or vestments in public, and places of worship could not display any exterior symbols betraying the activities conducted behind their doors. The new decrees on religion also forbade using churches confiscated as national property for Catholic worship, but this last stipulation proved difficult to enforce, as the directory of Seine-Inférieure described to the reconstituted National Convention: "We believe that we should inform you that in our department rural commune churches are seized daily to reestablish worship."[2]

According to the freedom of worship law of 11 *prairial* An III, the National Convention no longer recognized the existence of the *lettres de prêtrise* so those who had relinquished them during Siblot's persecution did not need to retrieve them in order to resume their sacerdotal duties. Some districts of the department of Seine-Inférieure returned letters of priesthood to clerics who requested them, but some ex-monks began to exercise their priestly duties without their *lettres de prêtrise*. For example, Dom Dabout, who had abdicated his priesthood at his parish of Lintot on 17 *ventôse* An II (7 March 1794), signed his name as "minister of Catholic worship" in a letter to the town council just a year and a half later.[3]

Other former monks who had sworn to accept the National Assembly's Civil Constitution of the Clergy agreed once again to submit themselves to the laws of the nation—becoming known as *soumissionnaires*—in exchange for resumption of their parochial responsibilities. Dom Bride reconstituted his ministry in his old parish of Bolbec so quickly after the 9 *thermidor* coup that the future prefect of Seine-Inférieure, Jacques-Claude Beugnot, commented that in the area around Bolbec "the exercise of religion never ceased in the midst of the fire of persecution."[4] Dom Bride even became a candidate for the bishopric of Seine-Inférieure in 1799. One of his opponents in the episcopal race, Dom Letellier, the constitutional pastor of Sainte-Trinité at Fécamp, swore to "recognize that the universality of French citizens is sovereign and . . . promise submission and obedience to the laws of the Republic" as he began again to provide his former parishioners of Fécamp with the consolation of religion. In fact, the people of this

---

2. National agent of the revolutionary district of Dieppe to citizens mayor, municipal officers and agent of the commune of Eu, 22 *prairial* An III (10 June 1795), ADSM, L 6365; "Des registres des délibérations du district de Rouen," ADSM, L 1199; Directory of the department to the directory of the district of Cany, 8 *messidor* An III (26 June 1795), ADSM, L 1198; Assemblée nationale constituante, *Journal des débats,* (1 October 1793–21 October 1793), 277; Loth, Histoire du Cardinal, 671–74; Ledré, *Le Diocèse de Rouen,* 9, 14; Martin, *Notes pour servir à l'histoire,* 163.

3. Dabout to the general council of the commune of Lintot, 21 *thermidor* An III (8 August 1795), ADSM, L 1597; "État des sommes à payer aux ex-prêtres abdicataires par forme de secours annuel dans l'arrondissement de ce district pour le prorata du semestre de *nivôse,* seconde année Républicaine," ADSM, L 1709. He may have picked up his letters of priesthood at some point, but the Seine-Maritime archives contain his letter of deaconate [ADSM, L 1212].

4. "Extrait du registre tenu à l'agent municipal de la commune de Bolbec canton du même nom," ADSM, L 2790.

port city had demanded that the local government allow them to congregate with Dom Letellier at Sainte-Trinité, and despite the protests of the district directory, the townspeople got their wish.[5]

Some ex-Maurist constitutional clergy served at parishes other than those assigned to them by the electoral assemblies before the Terror. Dom Lengaigne moved a few kilometers away from his former parish of Autretot to the village of Ectot-les-Baons where the local government listed him as the Catholic minister in An VI (1797–98).[6] In spite of the problems that accompanied Dom Monthois' vicarship at Auberville-la-Renault, Dom de Quane began administering to the community's spiritual needs sometime around An V (1796–97).[7] Dom Grognet who had moved back to the town of Saint-Wandrille—his last monastic residence—swore his obedience to the laws of the Republic as the local priest on 6 *messidor* An III (24 June 1795).[8]

The law of 11 *prairial* An III only required an ecclesiastical minister to swear his loyalty to the Republic's laws and, therefore, any delving into his past oath-taking practices would constitute government oppression.[9] As a result, monks who had not pursued careers in the constitutional church before the Terror could engage in the secular ministry. Dom Jean-Baptiste Billard from Rouen's abbey Bonne-Nouvelle on the left bank of the Seine crossed the river to the *centre ville* and became the parish priest for the city's famous Gothic masterpiece Saint-Maclou.[10] Having disappeared during the Revolution after leaving Notre-Dame-de-Coulombs in the department of Eure-et-Loir, Dom Claude Justin Martel resurfaced in Fécamp around 22 *prairial* An III (10 June 1795) when he declared his obedience to the Republic and obtained permission to say Mass in the Fécamp church of Saint-Étienne although he had never sworn the constitutional oath.[11]

Refractories imprisoned but never deported could also freely exercise their functions as long as they swore the oath of submission.[12] A former resident of Fécamp's Sainte-Trinité, Dom Blandin, had lived with his blood brother at

---

5. AN, F[lclll] II Seine-Inférieure, dos. An II–III; "État des déclarations passées par les ministres de tout culte, lesquelles ont dû être inscrités sur un registre ouvert à cet effet conformément à l'article cinq du titre III de la loi du 7 vendémiaire An IV (29 Septembre1795)," ADSM, L 1253; Bellamy, *Bénédictins et Annonçiades,* 28; de Beaurepaire, *Fécamp pendant la Révolution,* 57; Martin, *Histoire de Fécamp,* II, 164; Fallue, *Histoire de la ville,* 478; Bourienne-Savoye and Desjardins-Menegalli, *Marins, moines, citoyens,* 14, 43; Loth, Histoire du Cardinal, 524; Montier, "L'Abbaye de la Sainte-Trinité," 336, f. 79. For the election of the last constitutional bishop of Seine-Inférieure, see Loth, *Histoire du Cardinal,* 684–86.

6. "Extrait des registres des délibérations de ladite municipalité du canton de Motteville," ADSM, L 1708.

7. ADSM, L 1205.

8. "Extraits de premier registre des délibérations du conseil municipal de Saint-Wandrille," ASWF (1950), 57, f. 1, 74.

9. Committee of legislation of the National Convention to the presidents, administrations of departments and *procureurs générals syndics,* 29 prairial An III (17 June 1795), ADSM, L 11901

10. "Extrait du registre des délibérations de l'administration municipale du canton de Rouen," ADSM, L 1211.

11. Martin, Histoire de Fécamp, II, 164; de Beaurepaire, *Fécamp pendant la Révolution,* 57.

12. Ledré, *Le Diocèse de Rouen,* 14.

Mortain in lower Normandy and had apparently continued his vocation as a refractory priest.[13] Proscribed in 1793, he fled from his brother's house and roamed
the countryside until his capture and detention in the prison of Les Nouvelles
Catholiques at Caen. After composing songs and poems to lift the spirits of his
fellow inmates and then barely escaping deportation due to an illness, he was
transferred to the Carmes in Paris to await his fate.[14] The coup of 9 *thermidor* led
to his liberation and when the National Convention proclaimed the freedom of
worship decree, even for once-incarcerated priests, he returned to the town of his
abbey. In exchange for his promise to comply with the decrees of the Republic on
20 *prairial* An III (8 June 1795), the municipal officials of Fécamp allowed him
to celebrate Mass at Saint-Étienne.[15] Thus, at Fécamp, both juring and non-juring
ex-Maurists, Doms Letellier and Blandin, helped to reestablish Catholic worship
after the Terror.

Although the law of 11 *prairial* An III seemed to draw no distinction
between constitutional and refractory clergy, the resentment that the Civil Constitution had bred between these two groups and their partisans lingered. Almost
as soon as Dom Dabout had restored Catholic worship at Lintot, he wrote to the
commune assembly complaining that the mayor and certain local officials pro-
tected a fugitive who refused to swear submission to the Republic's laws. Those
officials even attended the fugitive's Masses rather than those of Dom Dabout.[16]
After the Directory took office in 1795, the situation of unrest in the department
had so escalated that the newly elected commission of the executive directory for
Seine-Inférieure informed the minister of general police that "hatred of the government and contempt for the laws of the Republic are openly flaunted."[17]

The national government had foreseen the agitation which the freedom
of worship acts might create and had warned the departments against "the renewal
of old religious quarrels."[18] However, the susceptibility of the Directory government to fluctuate wildly from left wing to right wing policies complicated any
attempts to heal the nation's wounded, religious sensibilities. The measures that it
undertook to prevent future turmoil proved that neither the five Directors nor the

---

13. Guéry, *Deux bénédictins normands,* 1–5. 72; Rousseau, *Moines bénédictins martyrs,* 89–91;
Montier, "Les Moines de Fécamp," 198. Rousseau asserts that Dom Blandin's brother was arrested
and imprisoned for harboring him [Rousseau, *Moines bénédictins martyrs,* 91, f. 3].

14. Guéry, *Deux bénédictins normands,* 5–6, 7, f. 2, 20, 22; Bourienne-Savoye and Desjardins-
Menegalli, Marins, *moines, citoyens,* 47; Montier, "Les Moines de Fécamp," 198.

15. Guéry, *Deux bénédictins normands,* 23, f. 2; Lecroq, *L'Hôpital de Fécamp,* 213; Guéry, *Deux
bénédictins normands,* 22–23; de Beaurepaire, *Fécamp pendant la Révolution,* 57; Martin, *Histoire
de Fécamp,* II, 164; Fallue, *Histoire de la ville,* 478; Ledré, *Le Diocèse de Rouen,* 19; Bellamy, *Bénédictins et Annonçiades,* 79, f. 15; Montier, "Les Moines de Fécamp," 198. Dom Blandin and two
other priests shared the church of Saint-Étienne after the laws of 3 *ventôse* An III and 11 prairial An
III [de Beaurepaire, *Fécamp pendant la Révolution,* 57].

16. Dabout to general council of the commune of Lintot; 21 *thermidor* An III (8 August 1795),
ADSM, L 1597; Ledré, *Le Diocèse de Rouen,* 11.

17. As cited in Ledré, *Le Diocèse de Rouen,* 25–26. Under the Directory, the executive directory
replaced the department directory and the position of *procureur général syndic* became the commissioner of the executive directory.

legislature in Paris had learned the lesson of the failure of the repressive decrees against the clergy.

After a surge in threats from royalists in the summer and fall of 1795 (including the infamous Whiff of Grapeshot incident in central Paris), the outgoing National Convention passed the law of 3 *brumaire* An IV (25 October 1795). It reversed the freedom of worship measure and reimposed the persecution decrees of 1792 and 1793 against the non-juring priests. Refractory clergy no longer enjoyed equal status with constitutionals, and deported priests who had returned to France had fifteen days to leave or face execution.[19] During this period of renewed hostility towards the Church, Dom Despinose abandoned his feud with the non-juring partisans of Saint-Aubin-de-Cretot and retracted his constitutional oath. For this, he was arrested and imprisoned in Rouen for three months until the judgment of the department's criminal tribunal set him free.[20] The old Maurist's arrest represented the exception and not the rule. At the local level, the 3 *brumaire* An IV pronouncement received little publicity, let alone enforcement. Non-jurers persisted with their devotions (usually unimpeded by local authorities), and, in a tirade to the Directory, a citizen of Rouen deplored not only this lack of enforcement of the law but the participation of local officials at the services of refractories: "The law on the police of worship is tread under foot in many cantons of Seine-Inférieure by your commissioners, by the [national] agents and by the ministers of Catholic worship. The latter sing Masses, vespers, [read] the catechism, and make processions with the cross and extra banners."[21]

In 1796–97, the political pendulum in Paris swung towards the right, and the 7 *fructidor* An V (24 August 1797) act granted all priests amnesty and freedom to exercise their ecclesiastical duties.[22] Refractory clerics hardly had time to take advantage of this benevolent offer when they had to go back into hiding by renewed threats of deportation. The left-wing coup of 18 *fructidor* An V (4 September 1797) put Jacobin sympathizers on the Directory and led to a purge of the right-wing members of the Council of Five Hundred. The day after the coup, the radicalized Council reinitiated the war of oaths; all functioning clerics had to pledge "hatred for the monarchy and anarchy, [and] devotion and fidelity to the Republic and to the Constitution of An III." In order for a cleric to have the right to make such a declaration, however, he first had to prove that he had taken all of the other oaths which various revolutionary governments had demanded of him. In this circumstance, a non-juring priest was damned if he tried to swear the hatred of monarchy oath and damned if he did not. Any clergyman who did not

---

18. "Bureau de police administrative civile et militaire," ADSM, L 2089.

19. ADSM, L 1255; Ledré, *Le Diocèse de Rouen,* 21, 36; Aston, *Religion and Revolution,* 281.

20. "État nominatif et numérique des prêtres qui ont été en réclusion depuis le 26 mars 1793 (époque de l'établissement de cette maison) jusqu'au 18 ventôse An V qu'ils on été définitivement mis en liberté," BMR, Ms p 110.

21. AN, F7 7265.

22. Aston, *Religion and Revolution,* 283–84; Ledré, Le Diocèse de Rouen, 24, 34.

appear before his local administration with proof of his constitutional oath and who did not show his "hatred for the monarchy" was proscribed by the law and, if apprehended, was subject to deportation to the French overseas colonies, or—as later decreed—the islands of Ré and Oléron off the west coast of France.[23]

Among the monks turned constitutionals, Dom Bride led the way in swearing the hatred of the monarchy oath on 25 *fructidor* An V (11 September 1797), followed closely by Dom Letellier two days later.[24] This enabled them to continue their parochial vocations. Although Dom Dabout still ministered to his flock at Lintot, he must not have felt immediately compelled to take this new oath since he waited until 25 *frimaire* An VII (15 December 1798) to do so.[25] The Council of Five Hundred had ordered that only juring priests could swear the new oath. But thirteen ex-Maurists who had neither accepted nor rejected the Civil Constitution also pledged their hatred of the monarchy.[26] In order to prosecute violators, the national government mandated that all cantons answer five questions regarding the oath-taking activities of the clerics in their jurisdictions:

> 1) In the canton or in the communes, are there priests who have been or ought to be deported, in execution of the law of 26 August 1792, or of that of 21 April 1793 (old style) and who have returned or remained in France? 2) Are there priests who have taken with restrictions the oath prescribed by the law of 26 December 1790 or who, after having taken it, have retracted it? 3) Are there ecclesiastics, either secular or regular, lay brothers and *conversi*, who have not taken the oath of liberty/equality . . . or who, after having taken it, have retracted it? 4) Among the individuals included in the two preceding articles, are there any who, having retracted or modified the oath . . . then took it purely and simply? 5) Are there priests or ministers who exercise the functions of worship of whatever kind without having made the declaration prescribed by the law of 7 *vendémiaire* of the previous year?[27]

Local administrations often did not delve too rigorously into their clergy's oaths and most likely viewed the five-question survey as tedious busy-work rather than a matter a national security.[28] The departmental governments tried to remind municipal officials that noncompliant clerics "are harmful, by their turbulence, to the happy harmony which ought to surround all Frenchmen," but this did not ensure enforcement.[29] But not even the threat of deportation muzzled unguarded

23. "Extrait du registre servant à constater la prestation de serment de haine à la royauté et auquel sont tenu les ministres des cultes aux termes de l'article vingt-cinq de la loi du 19 fructidor An V," ADSM, L 1215; AN, F7 7360; Pierre, ed., *La Déportation ecclésiastique*, xxvi; Rousseau, *Moines bénédictins martyrs*, 260, 296; Ledré, *Le Diocèse de Rouen*, 51 f. 39; G., "La Déportation ecclésiastique sous le directoire," 362.
24. ADSM, L 1205.
25. ADSM, L 1212.
26. ADSM, L 1211, 1316, 3259, 1209, 1212, 1210, 1205, 1214, 1207.
27. ADSM, L 1254; Ledré, *Le Diocèse de Rouen*, 22, 44.
28. Ledré, *Le Diocèse de Rouen*, 23.
29. Central administration of Eure to municipal administration of its *arrondissement*, 22 *messidor* An VI (10 July 1798), ADE, 57 L 2, dos. 1790–An VI.

criticism of the new reprisals by clerical opponents of the Directors. In a signed letter to the minister of police, the refractory Dom Blandin mocked the revolutionary penchant for denunciations: "I denounce you, citizen minister, or rather I denounce to your tribunal a circular for the departmental administrations invested with your signature" which ordered the roundup and expulsion of deported or exiled priests who had returned to France. He further accused the entire Directory of violating the will of the Council of Five Hundred, and thus the nation, by passing this legislation to "revive or allow to revive in your name the laws which have caused so many tears to be shed and so much blood to be spilled. . . . You have not consulted the constitution, justice or humanity."[30] The words of the old Maurist may have plucked at the minister's conscience. One month later, his missive to the department administrators on the execution of the recent religious legislation "reminded [them] of the principles of justice and humanity."[31] But if the minister of police did temper in response to Dom Blandin's open letter, he never let the refractory Dom Blandin feel the effects of his concession. He ordered the executive directory of the department of Seine-Inférieure to designate the non-jurer as deserving of deportation. For his part, the ex-monk spent the next few years hiding in the homes of sympathetic Fécamp inhabitants and escaped apprehension and prosecution for his audacious pen.[32]

The reign of the five Directors after the coup of *fructidor* inaugurated a second period of persecution which proved as perilous for the former Maurists as the reign of Terror, but afforded them another opportunity to show that they had not wavered in their commitment to their religious convictions. Constitutional and refractory monks who failed to fulfill every letter of the Directory's mandates concerning the clergy could find themselves reunited on the same prison ships bound for the islands near La Rochelle. Dom Moniez had resigned his curé position at Saint-Clair-sur-les-Montes on 27 *vendémiaire* An II (18 October 1793) and had surrendered the papers of his canonical institution, although he had claimed that he had left his *lettres de prêtrise* in one of the Maurist houses. After 9 *thermidor* he began exercising his ministry in the parish of Lanquetot, but he refused to offer his submission to the laws of the Republic. The Directory issued a mandate for his arrest, but the government of Seine-Inférieure lost his whereabouts after the law requiring the hatred of the monarchy oath. On the night of 12–13 *nivôse*

---

30. Blandin to P. J. M. Sotin de La Coindière, 28 *frimaire* An VI (18 December 1797), AN, F7 7560.

31. ADSM, L 26.

32. Minister of general police of the Republic to the commissioner of the executive directory for the central administration of the department of Seine-Inférieure, 15 *nivôse* An VI (4 January 1798), Caumont of the municipality of Fécamp to Duval commissioner of the executive directory of the department of Seine-Inférieure, 24 *nivôse* An VI (14 January 1798), Duval to the commissioner of the municipal administration of the commune of Fécamp, 14 *pluviôse* An VI (2 February 1798), ADSM, L 342; Minister of general police to the executive directory of the department of Seine-Inférieure, 23 pluviôse An VI (16 February 1798), AN, F7 7560; Martin, *Histoire de Fécamp*, II, 165; Lecrocq, *L'Hôpital de Fécamp*, 312, 384 f. 59, 387 f. 67; Montier, "Les Moines de Fécamp," 199.

An VII (1–2 January 1799), the National Guard apprehended him in the village of Ecretteville-sur-Mer at the home of a local man named Cadinot.[33]

When interrogated, first at the Yvetot prison and then at Rouen's house of detention, Dom Moniez explained that Cadinot had summoned him to set the broken leg of a newborn child. The National Guard and local officials of Ecretteville-sur-Mer, on the other hand, claimed that he had arrived at the house to baptize the baby. The department administration accused him of retracting the constitutional and Liberty-Equality oaths, but he emphatically defied the government to prove this claim.[34] In the end, his steadfast insistence of his innocent, strictly medical motives for being at the Cadinot home convinced no one. The ministry of police convicted him on 14 *floréal* An VII (3 May 1799) of performing religious rituals without adhering to the 19 *fructidor* An V oath law and sentenced him to deportation to the Île de Ré.[35] As one of the thirty-one Benedictines condemned to inhabit the island's Vauban fortress, he remained there for less than a year. After Napoleon Bonaparte's coup of 18–19 *brumaire* An VIII (9 November 1799), he regained his freedom with all the other ecclesiastical prisoners. Although a native of Arras, he returned to Seine-Inférieure under the surveillance of Rouen's mayor and municipal officials, swore his fidelity to the Consular government, and took up residence at Bolbec.[36]

In a similar case, the department of Orne in Lower Normandy arrested the former freemason and Sainte-Trinité monk Dom Bonvoust for failing to take any of the oaths required during the Revolution. A National Guardsman discovered him walking near the cemetery of Almenèche in the middle of the night. Dom

---

33. Mauconduit, Commissioner of the executive directory of the canton of Sassetot to the citizen administrators of the department of Seine-Inférieure, 12 *nivôse* An VII (1 January 1799), ADSM, L 1256; "Du registre de la municipalité de Saint-Sylvestre," ADSM, L 6196; Administration of the department of Seine-Inférieure to minister of general police, 28 *floréal* An VII (17 May 1799), AN, F⁷ 7567. While in prison, Dom Moniez made the acquaintance of fellow ecclesiastical prisoner Abbé Louis Dumesnil whom Dom Legrand had met during the Terror. Dumesnil later memorialized Dom Moniez as part of the incarcerated, clerical "society of respectable persons . . . a consolation which I have deeply felt during this time of suffering; I have a thousand times thanked Providence for it" [Abbé Louis Dumesnil, *Ma Prison ou mes avantures pendant le terreur*, BMR, Mss mm 31; Dumesnil, *Souvenirs de la Terreur,* 142–43; Ledré, *Le Diocèse de Rouen,* 40 f. 10].

34. "Interrogatoire du Monniez [sic] par le directoire du jury d'Yvetot," "Procès-verbal des déclarations de Xavier Fidèle Le Monniez [sic], prêtre insermenté," [Central administration of the department] to the minister of general police, 14 *germinal* An VII (3 April 1799), "Procès-verbal de laquel de la commune d'Ecretteville sur Mer," ADSM, 1 M 639; Unknown to the directory of the jury of the correctional tribunal of Yvetot, 17 *nivôse* An VII (6 January 1799), Queval directory of the jury of the *arrondissement* of Yvetot to the central administration of the department of Seine-Inférieure, 20 nivôse An VII (9 January 1799), ADSM, L 1256.

35. "Extrait des registres des deliberations du directoire exécutive," Minister of general police to the prefect of the department, 8 *ventôse* An IX (27 February 1801), ADSM, 1 M 639; AN, F7 4374; Loth, *Liste des prêtres,* 36–37; Ledré, *Le Diocèse de Rouen,* 52; Rousseau, *Moines bénédictines martyrs,* 88, 269.

36. Minister of general police to the prefect of the department, 8 *ventôse* An IX (27 February 1801), Caudron mayor of Rouen to prefect of the department of Seine-Inférieure, 19 *nivôse* An IX (9 January 1801), ADSM, 1 M 639; Ledré, *Le Diocèse de Rouen,* 56. For a description of the adverse condition under which the deported clergy lived on the islands of Oléron and Ré, see Rousseau, *Moines bénédictins martyrs,* 297–305.

Bonvoust possessed no identification papers, but he carried a sack containing sacred vessels for Mass, vestments, hymnals, and Eucharist wafers. After taking him into custody, the director of the correctional tribunal interrogated him. The old monk maintained that he had done nothing illegal; he asserted that the decrees concerning the constitutional oath did not apply to him, a nonpublic functionary. When questioned about the religious functions he had performed since 1790, the old Maurist answered, "It is true that I have said Mass from time to time: I have not heard anyone's confession. . . . I have also baptized many children, but I have not married anyone since 1796. I can justify myself by the pieces which are in my sack." The contents of his satchel did not substantiate his claim; the interrogator found marriage and baptismal certificates dated after the 19 *fructidor* An V law and bearing Dom Bonvoust's signature, letters asking the ex-monk to perform a wedding, and a document describing the regularization of an illicit marriage.[37]

The tribunal sentenced Dom Bonvoust to deportation on the Île de Ré, but while he awaited this punishment, he was incarcerated at Argentan. The health official for the prison confirmed that the fifty-one-year-old ex-monk suffered from gout, an inguinal hernia on his left side, and blindness in his right eye.[38] He begged the minister of general police in Paris, in light of these maladies, to have pity on his miserable condition and set him free. According to Dom Bonvoust, even the members of the local tribunal did not judge him deserving of such a hideous fate: "After the examination of my papers [they] could not keep from saying before some of their soldiers that if all [prisoners' papers] had been as mine were there would have been a lot less blood spilled."[39] The administration of department must not have shared these sentiments. When the minister of general police requested information about Dom Bonvoust's case, it responded that "it would be dangerous to return him [Bonvoust] to society."[40] In the end, the old Benedictine escaped deportation but certainly not in the way that he had intended; he died in the prison of Alençon on 19 *germinal* An VII (8 April 1799).[41]

Doms Moniez and Bonvoust appear to have acted alone, but local authorities in upper Normandy uncovered at least two substantial groups of nonconforming priests which included Maurists among their numbers. Although Dom

37. ADO, L 1663, as cited in Chaussy, "Les Derniers moines," 257–62; "Arrêté de déportation XXIV," 16 *nivôse* An VI (5 January 1798), Pierre, ed., *La Déportation ecclésiastique,* 121–22; Bellamy, *Bénédictins et Annonçiades,* 28, 78–79 f. 11; Montier, "L'Abbaye de la Sainte-Trinité," 328, f. 25. Since the government had taken over the recording of births and marriages in 1792, possession of baptismal and marriage certificates such as those which Dom Bonvoust carried in his satchel was considered criminal and punishable by deportation [Pierre, ed., *La Déportation ecclésiastique,* xxvii].

38. As cited in Chaussy, "Les Derniers moines," 262.

39. Bonvoust to the minister of general police, 7 *messidor* An VI (25 June 1798), Bonvoust to the minister of general police, 7 *messidor* An VI (25 June 1798), AN, F7 7478.

40. Minister of general police to the central administration of the department of Orne, [29 thermidor An VI (16 August 1798)], Administration of the department of Orne to the minister of general police, 2 *fructidor* An VI (19 August 1798), AN, F7 7478.

41. Rousseau, *Moines Bénédictins martyrs,* 344; Bellamy, *Bénédictins et Annonçiades,* 25; Bellamy, "La Vie religieuse," 50; Chaussy, "Les Derniers moines," 263.

Despinose may have relinquished his letters of priesthood according to Siblot's decree, at some point he retracted his constitutional oath and suffered a brief prison stay during An IV. In the final days of the Directory, the canton of Montiv-illliers arrested him and deported him to the island of Ré for belonging to a nest of seven refractories—who did "more evil than all the satellites of England, and daily threatened the security and public tranquility of the cantons where they re-mained." Upon his release in 1800, he returned to the ministry in upper Normandy as the Concordat curé of Montivilliers.[42]

The cantonal government of Goderville in the district of Montivilliers uncovered the most extensive network of refractories and *non-soumissionaires* to the law of 19 *fructidor* An V. At its heart was none other than the former vicar and clerical prisoner, Dom Monthois. On 13 *nivôse* An VI (26 December 1797), the canton denounced him to the departmental administration, along with his fellow ex-Maurist Dom Pétit (who had moved to Seine-Inférieure with Letellier after the suppression of their abbey at Bonneval), the former Benedictine Dom Martel who had apparently agreed to submit himself to the laws of the Republic but had drawn the line at swearing hatred of the monarchy, several non-juring seculars, and a host of lay men and women including some former members of municipal governments.[43] The department administration had first taken action against this network around Goderville in *frimaire* An VI (November-December 1797) when it mandated the temporary suspension of several municipal and cantonal officials whom it suspected of having "tolerated the violation of the laws on the police of worship." The canton's denunciation confirmed the department's apprehensions. A number of those relieved of their administrative posts were in fact implicated in connection with the Dom Monthois affair. The central administration then or-dered the arrest of "these provocateurs of discord" as well as any laity who may

---

42. "Arrêté de déportation XXXVIII," 8 *frimaire* An VI (28 November 1797), Pierre, ed., *La Dé-portation ecclésiastique,* 66; Municipal administration of the canton of Montivilliers to the minister of general police, 17 *brumaire* An VI (7 November 1797), AN, F7 7293; Loth, *Liste des prêtres,* 36–37; Ledré, *Le Diocèse de Rouen,* 52, 56, 94; Sévestre, *L'Enquête gouvernementale,* 321. Loth listed only two Benedictines deported to Île de Ré, but he perhaps did not include those Maurists who had become constitutional curés [Loth, *Liste des prêtres,* 36–37]. Nigel Aston counted about one hundred juring priests throughout France who were imprisoned during the Directory [Aston, *Religion and Revolution,* 394, f. 13].

43. "Délibération de l'administration municipale du canton de Goderville séance du 13 nivôse An VI," ADSM, L 1253; Ledré, *Le Diocèse de Rouen,* 36–37. Dom André Joseph Petit had remained at Goderville after Dom Letellier assumed control of the constitutional parish at Fécamp. Dom Petit refused to hand over his letters of priesthood and in execution of Siblot's decree was jailed on 28 *germinal* An II (18 April 1794), probably in the same prison as his monastic friend Dom Letellier. There was no indication that Petit swore the oath of 19 *fructidor* An V. He may have been the same Dom Petit which the central administration of the department denounced on 5 *frimaire* An VI (25 November 1797) although the one indicated in the report was a refractory returning from deporta-tion, and there is no evidence that Dom Petit had incurred that punishment before An VI [*Procureur syndic général* to the *procureur syndic* of the district of Montivilliers, 10 May 1791, ADSM, L 2095; "État des prêtres mis en état d'arrestation," ADSM, L 2098; "Formation du tableau des pensionnaires ecclésiastiques," ADSM, L 1316; "Administration centrale 1 vendémiaire An VI—29 ventôse An VI," ADSM, L 26]. Dom Claude Justin Martel had been imprisoned after Siblot's persecution, from 2 *floréal* An III (22 April 1795) to 11 fructidor An III (28 August 1795) [ADSM, L 6380].

have provided lodging to these priests, illegally opened churches for their use, or simply formed part of the congregation at their Masses.[44]

By 24 *ventôse* An VI (14 March 1798), the commandant of Goderville's gendarmerie had followed the instructions of his commander "to use all zeal and intelligence . . . capable for this entire execution" and had taken into custody the ringleaders of this refractory cell. The canton administration produced over seventy witnesses who testified that they had seen the refractories performing religious services or had heard about such activities from their neighbors. Most gave disclosures similar to that of Jean Ferry from Goderville. Although he pointed out that he had never personally attended the service of a non-jurer or *non-soumissionaire*, he had overheard that Doms Monthois, Petit, and the other arrested clerics had said Mass clandestinely in various homes throughout the canton and beyond. Others asserted that these priests had operated more overtly in the area, saying Masses in local churches which sympathizers on the town administrations had unlocked. A fifty-year-old woman from Vilmesnil and a merchant from Annouville alleged that they saw Dom Martel lead a procession out of the church of Auberville-le-Renault. The merchant even claimed that children dressed for their First Communion accompanied the ex-Maurist.[45]

In light of these revelations, the departmental government appeared eager to conceal the true extent of this overt defiance of the Directory's laws. In its report to the police of worship in Paris, the central administration of Seine-Inférieure admitted the existence of "very strong proof of the influence which they [the non-juring and *non-soumissionaire* priests] have had in the operation of a great number of assemblies." It even conceded the rather embarrassing fact that local municipal agents and their assistants had participated in these illegal gatherings. At the same time, it withheld the information about public processions and outdoor Masses and instead painted these refractories as fugitives in hiding: "What can be said is that the care which the dangerous priests took to hide themselves in the shadows proves at least that the law is so respected that it forces its enemies to fear discovery."[46]

As for the priests involved, perhaps the department's efforts to cover up the true extent of this scandal spared the clergy the most severe punishment. By condemning these clerics to deportation, the departmental government in essence

---

44. "Administration centrale 1 vendémiaire An VI–29 ventôse An VI," ADSM, L 26; "Délibération de l'administration municipale du canton de Goderville séance du 13 *nivôse* An VI," Municipal administration of the canton of Goderville to the central administration, 19 nivôse An VI (8 January 1798), ADSM, L 1253; Ledré, *Le Diocèse de Rouen,* 39.

45. Vautier, head of the Third Escadron of the National Gendarmerie to the citizens composing the central administration of the department of Seine-Inférieure, 9 ventôse An VI (27 February 1798), ADSM, L 1253. The record of the witness testimony kept in the departmental archives of Seine-Maritime appears to have been ripped out of a book as there were page numbers from 98r to 112v in the upper right-hand corners.

46. "Compte que rend mois de ventôse et germinal, police des cultes," AN, F[1cIII] II Seine-Inférieure 8, dos. An V–VII.

admitted its own failure to strictly enforce the law.[47] The statements of judgment for Doms Monthois, Martel, and Petit did not appear with the other arrested clerics, so their actual punishment is unknown. However, they must not have endured the harrowing trip to the La Rochelle islands. Abbé Julien Loth, who compiled a list of all the priests deported from Seine-Inférieure, only counted two Benedictines who suffered this fate during the Directory—Doms Despinose and Moniez. Dom Monthois and his company did not appear on Loth's list or any other from Ans V to IX (1796–1801). Furthermore, after the coup d'état of 18–19 *brumaire* An VIII, Dom Monthois petitioned Bonaparte to release him from the prison at Le Havre, whose decrepit state rendered his fate "more unfortunate than those deported to Oléronet [*sic*] or the Isle of Rhe [*sic*]."[48]

A period of religious freedom and toleration accompanied the end of the Terror, and several of the ex-Maurists who had either endured imprisonment or relinquished their letters of priesthood proved their commitment to their vocations by reestablishing their parish ministries. The Directory government began a second phase of clerical persecution, and priests who had not sworn the oath to the Civil Constitution of the Clergy and the hatred of the monarchy oath could once again face the same punishments as the refractory clerics from 1792 to 1794.[49] However, the persecution measures passed by various governments throughout the Revolution allowed ex-Maurists such as Doms Despinose and Monthois to demonstrate that even the threats of imprisonment, deportation, and a wretched death from starvation and disease could not dissuade them from preserving their religious identities.

---

47. "État des jugements rendus par le Tribunal correctionnel de l'arrondissement du Havre, département de la Seine-Inférieure, contre divers prêtres qui ont celebré leur culte, sans s'être conformés à la loi, et dont l'affiche a été ordonnée pour chacun d'iceux," ADSM, L 6421. Mauconduit, Dom Trémauville, and others received sentences of 2 years in prison and fines of 500 francs. For some details on the unequal enforcement of the deportation decree during the Directory, see Pierre, ed., *La Déportation ecclésiastique,* xxxi–xxxiii.

48. Monthois to the first consul of the French Republic, 15 fructidor An VIII (2 September 1800), AN, F7 7780, dos. 39.

49. Pierre, ed., *La Déportation ecclésiastique,* xvii–xviii.

EPILOGUE

THE MAURISTS AND THE CONCORDAT

AMONG THE FORMER MAURISTS who had resumed their ministry after the Terror, some persisted in performing their sacerdotal duties despite the religious persecution renewed under the Directory. Moreover, the anticlerical policies of the Directory also did not prevent a few monks from recanting their constitutional oaths, considered schismatic by the pope, and seeking union with the Church in Rome.[1] Those who wished to could either seek absolution from the papal legate Cardinal Giambattista Caprara or from a non-juring priest appointed by the refractory bishop of the area to lift the censure of schism from the retracting constitutional priests. For example, in addition to reestablishing his ministry at Fécamp, in the shadow of his old abbey, the former Maurist Dom Blandin, as the representative of the refractory archbishop of Rouen in exile, received authorization to absolve the recanting jurers of Fécamp. In this capacity, he tried to convince his fellow ex-Benedictine Dom Letellier to retract, but the latter remained attached to the constitutional church until after Bonaparte's coup of 18–19 *brumaire* An VIII (9–10 November 1799). By 15 July 1801, fifteen former Maurists in upper Normandy administered the sacraments with the blessing of Rome.[2]

While France breathed easier with the end of the Reign of Terror in July 1794, the Directory government proved a poor replacement. The five Directors, mired in corruption scandals and the continual threat of coups, did little to stabilize the nation. France was still at war with its neighbors, and the internal divisions between Jacobins on the left and royalists on the right seemed just as critical as ever. By 1799, the French people had lost confidence in their government and began to look elsewhere for competent leadership. France's armies meanwhile enjoyed greater victories in their conflicts abroad. The French army in northern Italy, led by the young General Napoleon Bonaparte, had defeated the Austrians and

---

1. "Noms des familles des ecclésiastiques qui ont signé leur rétraction depuis le 30 April 1802," ADSM, 1 M 636; ADSM, L 1345;
2. Guéry, *Deux bénédictins normands,* 23, 33.

restored France's military prestige. Bonaparte became a national celebrity, and his success on the battlefield contrasted sharply with the Directors' ineffectiveness. Judging the time ripe for a coup, in 1799 Bonaparte left his army in Egypt, sent there to disrupt British trade routes, and returned to France. With the help of his brother, the president of the Council of Elders, Bonaparte overthrew the Directory on 18–19 *brumaire* An VIII (9–10 November 1799) and set up the Consulate. This new government remained a republic in name but concentrated power in the hands of its chief executive officer, the First Consul. Bonaparte served in that position—making some of his most lasting domestic achievements—until his coronation as emperor in 1804.

As First Consul, Bonaparte made it his goal to conciliate relations between the Church in France and the Church in Rome. To begin this rapprochement, he allowed refractories to return from exile or deportation and released any priests imprisoned under the Directory. He also granted these men permission to perform their priestly functions again. Under the Consul's benevolence, the twice-incarcerated Dom Monthois resumed his ministry in upper Normandy, as did Dom Despinose who had survived deportation. Doms Petit and Outin, who had refused to swear the oath and had never taken positions in the constitutional church, also began serving parishes in the diocese of Rouen.[3] Even more former Benedictines entered the parochial ministry after Bonaparte and Pope Pius VII signed the Concordat on 15 July 1801. This agreement ended the schism begun by the Civil Constitution of the Clergy and represented a compromise for both the juring and non-juring clergy.

All priests—whatever their status regarding the oath—had to resign all claims to diocesan positions in order to receive new appointments in the *concordataire* church. For the constitutional priests, this meant that they did not have to retract their oath (although many in upper Normandy had already done so), but they did have to relinquish their current curates and vicarates. On the other hand, refractory priests could resume their ministries without fear of persecution, but they could not demand their pre-Revolution parishes. The Concordat also stipulated that the laity would no longer elect the clergy. Bonaparte would nominate the bishops, and the pope had the right to approve or reject his choices. Each bishop would then select the parish clergy with the assistance of the local government officials.[4]

Six days after Bonaparte signed the Concordat, his minister of the interior, Jean Antoine Chaptal, requested that the prefect of each department compile

---

3. Monthois to Bonaparte, 15 *fructidor* An VIII (2 September 1800), Minister of justice to the minister of general police, 25 *vendémiaire* An IX (17 October 1800), AN, F⁷ 7780, dos. 39; ADSM, 1 M 636; "Décision," 9 *nivôse* An VIII (30 December 1799), Napoleon I, *Correspondance de Napoléon I,* No. 4486, VI, 44; Guéry, *Deux bénédictins normands,* 27, f. 1. These four are all listed by the concordataire bishop of Seine-Inférieure as having retracted their oaths, although not all of them swore the oath.

4. "Convention entre sa sainteté Pie VII, et le gouvernement français," Caprara, ed., Concordat, 5–9; Aston, *Religion and Revolution,* 324–28. By inserting this stipulation into the Concordat, Bonaparte allowed Pius VII more influence over the French church than a pope had enjoyed since

a list "of the priests [who are] worthy of the confidence of the government" in that area in order to determine which priests to appoint to posts in their dioceses. In addition to the investigation by the prefect, the new bishops appointed after the Concordat (since both constitutional and refractory bishops had to resign) also conducted their own inquiries, and the results of both were used in determining the curés and vicars for the post-Revolution dioceses of France.[5] Each department reported the results of its inquiry differently. For Seine-Inférieure's investigation, punctually performed a month after the Concordat, the prefect Jacques-Claude Beugnot arranged the list of ecclesiastics into three classes: those of the first class were clergy of superior education and morality who ought to receive the highest clerical positions in the diocese; second-class priests had some education and could pastor the faithful in the department's larger towns; the third class included those of limited intellectual ability but whose virtues made them suitable for rural parishes. Next to the names in these three lists, the prefect also provided comments regarding the morality and financial status of each subject.[6]

The nine former Maurists who appeared in Beugnot's inquiry illustrate how the Church in France sought to incorporate all worthy clerics, regardless of their behavior during the Revolution. Two ex-Benedictines became constitutional priests—Dom Bride and Letellier; both warranted first-class entries (although Letellier's bore the comment "able to do good, but elsewhere than Fécamp"). Dom Monthois, who had spent much of the previous ten years in and out of prison and was even convicted as the ringleader for a group of refractories during the Directory, was described as "good religious, useful for the ministry" on the list of second-class priests.[7] The separate investigation undertaken by Seine-Inférieure's *concordataire* bishop, Étienne-Hubert de Cambacérès, included seven more Benedictines who had retracted their constitutional oaths, or in some cases had never sworn one. For each entry on this list, the bishop commented on the suitability of the subject to serve as a pastor, vicar, or *desservant*. These remarks seem to indicate that the bishop did not base a cleric's worthiness solely on his oath status; he described the ever petulant Dom Outin's capacity for the parish ministry as "absolutely none." No ex-Maurist appeared on the department's "List of ecclesiastics of the diocese of Rouen deserving exclusion."[8]

1517. When the first consul realized this, he tried to amend the settlement by issuing the Organic Articles which gave him extensive control over the clergy in France. The pope never accepted the Articles and thus Napoleon initiated his own conflict with the papacy.

5. Jean Antoine Chaptal to the prefect of the department of la Manche, 28 *thermidor* An IX (21 July 1801), AN, F19 866; Aston, *Religion and Revolution,* 323. Bonaparte restructured the administration of France, placing each department under the authority of a prefect. Departments retained their district subdivisions, renamed *arrondissements* (subprefectures), and each of these was headed by a subprefect. The cantonal level of administration was eliminated, but the commune governments were retained.

6. AN, F19 866; Sévestre, *L'Enquête gouvernementale,* 297–98.

7. Sévestre, *L'Enquête gouvernementale,* 299, 303, 309. The other six were Dom Huard in the second class and Doms Lengaigne, Despinose, Grognet, Guesdon, and Trémauville in the third class. Dom Letellier was actually listed twice, in the first class and the third class.

8. ADSM, 1 M 636; Sévestre, *L'Enquête gouvernementale,* 368, 374–76; Lecroq, *L'Hôpital de Fécamp,* 305.

The prefect of Eure, Charles-Armand Masson Saint-Amand, proved more dilatory in responding to Chaptal's request. He finally sent the minister of the interior the list of his department's clergy on 17 *vendémiaire* An X (9 October 1801). Rather than dividing the clerics according to classes, Masson Saint-Amand chose to group them by *arrondissements* and included comments regarding character and financial status with each entry.[9] Since fewer Eure Maurists had opted to continue their ecclesiastical functions either in the constitutional church or as refractory priests, the prefect indicated only seven who currently resided in that department. The prefect did label each of these worthy candidates for positions in the Church. The former constitutional curé of Rouvray, Dom Claude-Auguste Troussel, even earned the special distinction of inclusion on the prefect's separate list of twenty individuals whose particular excellence rendered them deserving of the highest offices. "Modest and educated on diverse subjects of science, [he is] esteemed in his rural commune. . . . He will obtain more consideration in a large commune where he will have the occasion to develop and to make known his good qualities of heart and spirit."[10] The investigation conducted by the episcopal vicars of Eure turned up nine Maurists, but only four of these deserved consideration.[11] Nevertheless, the presence of former monks among the clergy appointed to positions in the Church of both departments illustrates that at least a few former monks preserved their religious (if not their monastic) vocations throughout the Revolution and during the Consulate regime.

As monks had done during the Revolution, some former Maurists perpetuated their Congregation's reputation for outstanding intellectual achievements by taking jobs in academia during the Napoleonic era. Dom Blandin became a private tutor for a wealthy Catholic family in Le Havre, and his former monastic brother, Dom Louis Dominique Lecomte, tried to persuade him to join the faculty of the *École Secondaire* in Bayeux. A Maurist from Saint Wandrille, Dom Pierre Guillaume Berthaux, received an appointment as a professor of mathematics at the college of Lisieux.[12] Of course, the most illustrious son of the Congregation to pursue a career in the intellectual realm remained Dom Gourdin, the librarian of the city of Rouen and of the department of Seine-Inférieure. He continued to accumulate books for the library and undertook the task of producing a handwritten catalog of the nearly one million volumes which it contained. The department also commissioned him to establish a library for its public school. And for the city of Rouen, in 1803 he played a pivotal role in reconstituting the *Académie de Rouen* which had been disbanded during the Revolution. Among these contributions to Norman scholarship, Dom Gourdin never forgot his attachment to his religious

---

9. AN, F19 865.
10. Sévestre, *L'Enquête gouvernementale,* 96.
11. Ibid., 98–131. Maurists from upper Normandy also appeared among the *concordataire* clergy for other departments, but this study has only examined those remaining in the departments of Eure and Seine-Inférieure.
12. Guéry, *Deux bénédictins normands,* 33, f. 1, 37–38; Lohier, "L'Inventaire," 160, f. 18.

vocation. In his 1807 letter to Dom Grappin, he proudly declared that he had resumed his sacerdotal duties, said Mass for a reconstituted convent of Benedictine
nuns, and had begun to wear his habit again.[13]

Of those who had secularized and married after vacating the cloister,
Dom Gobard and others took advantage of reconciled relations between France
and Rome to regularize their marriages and seek forgiveness for the scandal which
their actions may have caused.[14] Although the former Fécamp monk and local engineering and mechanical d'savant, Dom de Maurey, had pronounced in 1790 his
desire to preserve his commitment to the common life, he traded his brown habit
for workman's clothes and left the communal life shortly after his declaration.
However, he put his Maurist scientific education to good use during the Revolution by inventing a machine to spin wool. In 1803, he begged forgiveness from
Cardinal Caprara for the scandal which he may have caused by marrying in 1795.
He protested that he had only taken a wife because he needed help with his experi-
ments. Although he and his lab assistant had already produced two children, in
addition to the spinning machine, he promised to refrain from conjugal relations.
The cardinal granted him absolution, and Dom de Maurey's brother, the *concordataire* curé of Incarville in the department of Eure, blessed the marriage.[15]

The former constitutional curé of Yvetot, Dom Legrand, proved as vigi-
lant a defender of the clergy in his capacity as subprefect of the *arrondissement*
of Yvetot during the reign of Napoleon as he had when the Terror had threatened
his clerical brothers. His duties as subprefect included reporting to the prefect
on the religious sentiment and public opinion in his area as well as submitting
a list of the worthy clerics as part of the prefectural inquiry conducted after the
signing of the Concordat. At the top of this delineation, Legrand recommended
his fellow ex-Maurist Dom Bride for the curate of his *arrondissement*'s *chef-lieu*,
Yvetot.[16] Although this designation for his former monastic brother demonstrated
Legrand's persistent respect and attachment for those who had shared his former
vocation, in 1815 he provided the most corroborative evidence that he had never
fully disavowed his cenobitic life. In his response to critics who lambasted him
for never seeking reconciliation with the Church, he emphatically stated, "I will
always pride myself to have belonged to that order of Benedictines, where I was
found worthy to study rhetoric and belles-lettres for twenty-four years."[17]

---

13. Gourdin to Grappin, 19 March 1807, Dantier, ed., *Rapports sur la correspondance,* 195;
Deries, "La Vie d'un bibliothécaire," 226–37.
14. Chaussy, "Les Derniers moines," 257; ASWF (1980), 14; Lohier, "L'Inventaire," 160, f. 20,
161, f., 27.
15. Montier, "Les Moines de Fécamp," 211–15; Bellamy, *Bénédictins et Annonçiades,* 78, f. 10;
Chaussy, "Les Derniers moines," 257; Bellamy, "La Vie religieuse," 50.
16. AN, F¹ᶜᴵᴵᴵ Seine-Inférieure 8 dos. An VIII–XIII; Legrand to the prefect of the department of
Seine-Inférieure, 8 *prairial* An X (28 May 1802), "État indicatif des ecclésiastiques presentés par le
sous-préfet de l'arrondissement d'Yvetot pour plusieurs paroisses et succursales de son arrondissement," ADSM, VII 28; ADSM, 1 M 159, 3 M 1; Tougard, *La Révolution à Yvetot,* vol. 2, 13, f. 20, 18.
17. As cited in Tougard, *La Révolution à Yvetot,* vol. 2, 13, f. 20.

During Napoleon's reign as Emperor of the French, a commission appointed to investigate the reestablishment of the male religious orders concluded that "the contemplative communities are useful to society." Yet, despite the commission's recommendation and a deluge of petitions, including one from Dom Outin, for the return of the orders, the emperor decided against reinstituting the Congregation of Saint-Maur or any other branch of the Benedictine order.[18] Benedictine monasticism finally returned to France in 1833 when Dom Prosper Guéranger reopened the abbey of Solesmes, but not under the rule of the Congregation of Saint-Maur. By that time, most of the monks forced out of their cells by the Revolution had died. Guéranger did invite one of the remaining Maurists of upper Normandy, Dom Blandin, to join the Solesmes revival, but the septuagenarian's health prevented him from traveling. Thus, none of the Maurists of upper Normandy ever reentered the monastic life after they had left their cloisters during the Revolution.[19] They had, however, in various ways, maintained connections with their Benedictine roots throughout the Revolution and even after the Concordat.

18. AN, F¹⁹ 6246, dos. Congrégations religieuses: documents divers; AN, F¹⁹ 352.
19. Lecroq, *L'Hôpital de Fécamp*, 385; Montier, "Les Moines de Fécamp," 200.

CONCLUSION

A STUDY OF THE RELIGIOUS HISTORY of eighteenth-century society requires consideration of both the ancien régime and the Revolution in their entirety. Applying this methodology to the Benedictines of the Congregation of Saint-Maur in upper Normandy calls into question the idea of a progressive secularization of monastic society culminating with the French Revolution. The Catholic Church, and in particular the regular clergy, faced external and internal challenges in the eighteenth century, but as the Maurists of upper Normandy illustrated, a religious order of savants could still attract young novices who continued to produce quality scholarship in the fields of science, history, and philosophy. The Maurists' connections with secular society, which increased in the eighteenth century, were not symptomatic of a discontent with the monastic vocation. Rather, men like Dom Gourdin corresponded with lay scholars and joined intellectual societies like the *Académie de Rouen* to further their academic pursuits in the fulfillment of their Benedictine *labora*. Furthermore, as the monks and freemasons at Fécamp demonstrated, Maurists could assist the less fortunate of secular society in their collaborations with important laymen. In turn, the cahiers and letters to the National Assembly from these towns testify to the good relations which these monks had fostered with the local laity and the latter's desire to continue this cooperation. This hardly indicates a pervasive distaste for the communal life, either among those in the abbey or those in the outside world.

During the elections of the Estates-General in 1789, the First Estate of upper Normandy evidenced its esteem and respect for the Congregation by electing the Maurist, Dom Davoust, as one of its representatives to Versailles. As the debates over the elimination of the regular clergy began in the National Assembly, the monks from various Norman abbeys petitioned for their survival. But, their pleas fell on the deaf ears of the National Assembly's deputies, already bent on the elimination of the religious orders. The actions of the monks, after the suppression decree in February 1790, further reveal the fallacy of viewing the Revolutionary religious legislation as a culmination of secularization or of assuming that these policies were universally accepted and obeyed throughout France. The declarations of attachment to their monastic vows and the desire "to live and die in that state which [they] had voluntarily and so solemnly embraced" certainly do

135

not indicate a willingness to conform to the Assembly's pronouncements.[1] Even those, such as Dom Trémauville, who chose to discontinue the communal life, left their abbeys "with great sorrow."[2] The monks of the Congregation had expressed their disapproval of the suppression schemes proposed in the National Assembly, and they certainly did not welcome the one passed on 13 February 1790. Thus, the connections of the Norman Maurists with the world beyond their abbey walls must not have resulted from discontent with their vows and the wish to leave the monastery at the first opportunity.

Tracing the lives of these monks after the suppression further refutes the notion that the regular clergy had degenerated beyond hope of reform and therefore deserved, and even desired, the elimination of their monastic lifestyle. On the contrary, most Maurists, regardless of their declarations, continued to maintain connections with their former Benedictine roots after leaving their monasteries. A few refused to abandon their monastic lifestyle and sought temporary refuge in the houses of union at Bec and Jumièges, while others took up residences near their former monastic abodes. Together with other ex-Maurists, these men continued to live in the area through the Napoleonic era and beyond, sitting on town governments, fulfilling their priestly duties and, in the case of Dom Catelain at Saint-Wandrille, even becoming the town mayor. Men who appeared to shed their ecclesiastical garb altogether also maintained ties to their pasts by vigilantly defending religion and especially their former fellow clergymen. Dom Legrand's heroic exploits during the Terror and his solicitation for the proper functioning of religious worship in his subprefecture of Yvetot exemplify the ways in which even laicized monks could preserve some links to their religious identities.

About thirty former Maurists from upper Normandy pursued their religious vocations by entering the ranks of the secular clergy as constitutional priests. After swearing their loyalty to the government, Doms Bride, Bricque, Levacque, and others performed their pastoral ministries and tried to reconcile obedience to the state and Christian devotion. By serving in local, departmental, and national governments, these ex-monks also sought to protect the interests of their parishes (as Ruault did during the Yvetot famine of 1793) or the prerogatives of the Church by saving statues and sacred articles from destruction.

The Terror and the de-Christianization phase of the Revolution forced these men to abandon the last aspect of their religious vocations, their priesthood, but their attachment remained. Some monks, both those who swore the constitutional oath, such as Dom Letellier, and those who did not, such as Dom Lebrun, provided the ultimate proof of their steadfast character by suffering the rigors of imprisonment, deportation, and even death rather than betray their religious

---

1. ADE, 57 L 24.
2. "Tableau dressé conformément à l'article quatre du titre 1 de la loi du 14 Octobre 1790 sur décret concernant les religieux contenant les noms, âge, date de profession et déclaration faites par les religieux bénédictins, cordeliers, jacobins, et capucins," ADE,116 L 2.

loyalties. At the same time, some who did temporarily suspend their sacerdotal duties and relinquish their *lettres de prêtrise* resumed these functions during the Directory, despite a new wave of persecution in An VI–VIII (1797–99). After the Concordat, the names of both the Maurists who endured prison and exile and those who had abandoned their sacred ministry to escape punishment appeared on the prefectural lists of worthy clerics in the dioceses of Eure and Seine-Inférieure. Thus, the actions of these men before, during, and after the French Revolution reveal that the Catholic Church in eighteenth-century France could still produce worthy clerics in spite of challenges, conflicts, and increased interaction between the spiritual and secular realms.

APPENDIX A

MAURISTS WHO WERE PRESENT IN UPPER NORMANDY IN 1790[1]

LAST NAME	FIRST NAME	MONASTERY	AGE
Alleaume de Tréfforêt[2]	Marie Aimé Augustin	Bec	36
Allix	Charles Matthieu	Jumièges	64
Andri	Louis Antoine Joseph	Lyre[3]	30
Aubin	Jean Charles Joseph	Saint-Ouen[4]	43
Bacon	Jean François Joseph	Préaux	67
Banse	Michel Nicolas	Jumièges	41
Bardel	François Laurent	Fécamp	27
Baron	Louis	Bec	34
Bautier	Thomas	Bonne-Nouvelle	58
Beaussart	Louis Alexandre	Ivry	50
Benoit	Louis Julien	Bec	36
Berguesse	Louis Philippe	Bernay	48

1. Unless otherwise noted, all information comes from AN, D XIX, 10, no. 147.
2. His name only appears in the list provided by the Revue Mabillon ["Les Religieux de la Congrégation" 55 no. 219 (January-March 1965): 48].
3. Monk of Notre-Dame-de-Lyre but living at another monastery in 1790 ["Religieux de l'abbaye de Notre-Dame-de-la-Vieille-Lire [sic]," ADE, 166 L 4].
4. Also listed as residing at Notre-Dame-de-Bonne-Nouvelle [AN, F19 6113].

LAST NAME	FIRST NAME	MONASTERY	AGE
Bernès, *convers*	Bernard	Bec	59
Berthaux	Pierre Guillaume	Saint-Wandrille	30
Besserve	Jean Jacques Henry	Lyre	45
Billard	Jean Baptiste	Bonne-Nouvelle	63
Blanchard	Charles Antoine	Bec	53
Blanchet	André	Bonne-Nouvelle	70
Blandin	Louis Ambroise	Fécamp	30
Bonnard	Augustin Joseph	Tréport	46
Bonnard	Norbert	Aumale	33
Bonvoust	Charles Jean	Fécamp	43
Bourdon	Nicolas	Bec	64
Bourlier	Pierre	Aumale	50
Bréant	Louis	Saint-Taurin	77
Bricque	Jean Denis	Conches	43
Bride	Jean Pierre	Saint-Ouen	70
Bride	Pierre Armand	Saint-Ouen	50
Brixier	Mathurin François	Saint-Wandrille	63
Broncquart	Antoine Joseph	Jumièges	32

LAST NAME	FIRST NAME	MONASTERY	AGE
Broucqsault[5]	Ignace François	Ivry	37
Cadet	Olivier Joseph	Préaux	39
Cambier	Louis Joseph	Valmont	39
Capelle	Jean	Bec	73
Capperon[6]	François	Saint-Wandrille	30
Cartault	Pierre Alexis	Fécamp	79
Cartier	Jean Martin	Tréport	60
Catelain[7]	Emmanuel	Saint-Wandrille	23
Chahau	Jean Antoine	Préaux	57
Chesnon	Henry	Tréport	73
Collibeaux	Jean	Fécamp	48
Coquil	René Guillaume	Bec	39
Cotté	Jean Louis	Saint-Ouen	70
Courbet	Jean Nicolas	Jumièges	66

5. His name only appears in the list provided by the Revue Mabillon ["Les Religieux de la Congrégation" 56 no. 224 (April-June 1966): 44].

6. His name does not appear in Archives nationales list [AN, D XIX, 10, no. 147], but it does appear in the declarations from Saint-Wandrille ["Procés Verbal des effets de l'abbaye de Saint-Wandrille dressés par les officiers municipaux dudit lieu," AN, F19 6113].

7. Refer to note 6, above

LAST NAME	FIRST NAME	MONASTERY	AGE
Crespin	Jacques François Alexis	Préaux	55
Dabout	Guillaume François	Boscherville	61
Dabout	Jean François	Saint-Ouen	51
Daguin	François	Bec	74
Danne	Jean Jacques	Bec	51
Darras	Pierre Louis Joseph	Bec	61
David	Pierre Charles	Bec	51
Davoust	Alexis	Saint-Ouen	63
Dechy	Antoine François	Saint-Wandrille	45
de Laperche	Jacques	Préaux	42
Delaplace	Denis	Tréport	56
Delarue	Jacques Nicolas	Bonne-Nouvelle	77
Delénable	François Robert	Bonne-Nouvelle	54
Deleyris	Placide	Saint-Ouen	50
Delobel	Jean François	Saint-Ouen	73
de Maurey	Jacques Antoine	Fécamp	31
de Mésanges	Louis Charles	Jumièges	76
de Montigny	Jean Jacques	Jumièges	46

LAST NAME	FIRST NAME	MONASTERY	AGE
de Quane	Charles	Jumièges	47
de Rancher	Pierre Antoine Casimir	Bec	28
de Recusson	Michel	Saint-Ouen	35
Dergny	Laurent François	Saint-Taurin	69
Derouvroy	Jean Charles	Saint-Ouen	50
Desmares	Pierre	Fécamp	29
Despinose	Thomas Antoine Jean	Jumièges	58
Destruissart	Thomas	Saint-Ouen	32
d'Huldebert	Pierre René Robert	Bec	25
Droulez	Louis Joseph	Bec	50
du Bocquet	Alexandre Joseph	Lyre	43
Dubois	Nicolas	Fécamp	40
Dubrez, *commis*	Alexis	Fécamp	51
Dubuisson	Jean Louis	Saint-Ouen	58
Dubust	François Eléonor	Conches	76
Dufour	Bruno	Boscherville	56
Duhamel	François	Saint-Ouen	25
Dupont	Olivier	Saint-Ouen	66

LAST NAME	FIRST NAME	MONASTERY	AGE
Dupont	Philippe Nicolas	Boscherville	58
Durel	Jean François	Jumièges	74
Durieux	Albert Joseph	Bec	36
Duriez	Leonard Dominique	Boscherville	56
Duval, commis	Charles	Bec	56
Duvrac	Pierre Michel	Lyre	42
Evrard[8]	Jean Jacques	Bec	44
Fillaut	Guillaume François	Bec	77
Follin	François	Saint-Taurin	66
Fontaine d'Épreville	Jacques Pierre	Fécamp	76
Fortier	Antoine Joseph	Saint-Ouen	31
Fossé	Charles	Boscherville	55
Foulon	Pierre	Bec	30
Francke[9]	Pierre Sévère Joseph	Lyre	29
Froger	Armand Jean	Saint-Ouen	30

8. Living at Notre-Dame-du-Bec in 1790 by lettres de cachet of the king, his name appears on the declarations from that abbey [ADE, 57 L 1 and 95 L 1, dos. Premier Cahier].

9. Monk of Notre-Dame-de-Lyre but living at another monastery in 1790 ["Religieux de l'abbaye de Notre-Dame-de-la-Vieille-Lire [sic]," ADE, 166 L 4].

LAST NAME	FIRST NAME	MONASTERY	AGE
Garnier	Jean François	Conches	45
Gautherot	Emeric	Saint-Ouen	32
Gobard	Gaspard Léon	Jumièges	32
Gobard	Michel Barthélemy	Saint-Wandrille	33
Goulliart	Antoine Joseph	Saint-Ouen	26
Gourdin	François Philippe	Jumièges	51
Govart	Charles Joseph	Bec	54
Grognet	Louis Nicolas	Saint-Wandrille	46
Guesdon	Jean Pierre	Jumièges	31
Hautement	Michel Jean Baptiste	Bec	76
Herment	Jean Marie	Fécamp	58
Heutte	Nicolas Benôit	Saint-Taurin	71
Hommeril	Pierre	Lyre	47
Huard	Jacques François	Boscherville	56
Hubert	Henri	Jumièges	25
Hubert	François Michel	Saint-Ouen	33
Julien	Louis	Fécamp	66
La Batte	Jean Baptiste Paul	Lyre	29

LAST NAME	FIRST NAME	MONASTERY	AGE
Labigne	Jean Baptiste	Lyre	54
Lainé	Adrien	Fécamp	61
Lamache	Charles François	Conches	54
Langlois	Louis	Saint-Ouen	66
Lartois	Edme Nicolas	Lyre	45
Lavieuville	Marie Antoine	Saint-Ouen	25
Leborgne	François	Saint-Ouen	32
Lebrun	Louis François	Saint-Wandrille	46
Le Carpentier	Jean Nicolas	Bec	70
Le Chevallier	Étienne François	Préaux	56
Lechevallier	Gilles	Préaux	50
Lecomte	Louis Dominique	Bec	30
Leconte	Martin	Bec	58
Lefevre	Jean Jacques	Valmont	45
Lefevre	Vindicien	Fécamp	44
Lemache	Jean François Gilles	Conches	57
Lemaire	Jacques Alexis	Fécamp	50
Lengaigne	Louis François Joseph	Saint-Wandrille	31

LAST NAME	FIRST NAME	MONASTERY	AGE
Lentrain	Jean Baptiste	Jumièges	24
Lepicard	Léonard Nicolas	Fécamp	54
Le Riche	Noël	Fécamp	46
Lestievetz	François Louis Joseph	Saint-Wandrille	48
Levacher	Jean Louis	Saint-Taurin	26
Levacque	François Joseph	Saint-Taurin	48
Le Vasseur	Jean Pierre Marie	Lyre	50
Levesque	Philippe François	Préaux	70
Locoge	Jean-Baptiste	Saint-Ouen	29
Maillon, *commis*	Jean-Baptiste	Jumièges	62
Marais	Pierre	Bernay	35
Martin	Omer	Boscherville	58
Marye	Pierre	Bec	52
Maselinne	Laurent Alexandre	Bec	50
Massey	René Julien	Bec	48
Meigniot	Philippe Antoine Joseph	Valmont	39
Meslin	Thomas Louis	Conches	50
Mesnard	Nicolas Joseph Louis	Saint-Ouen	32

LAST NAME	FIRST NAME	MONASTERY	AGE
Moniez	Xavier Fidele	Bec	57
Montéage	Georges Eloy Vallery	Jumièges	30
Monthois	Placide Joseph	Valmont	44
Mullet	Étienne Joseph	Conches	51
Mullet	Pierre Martin	Conches	42
Nicolle	André Jérôme Joseph	Fécamp	30
Nicolle	Jean Baptiste Noël	Fécamp	27
Outin	Toussaint	Jumièges	55
Painblanc	Pierre Joseph Florentin	Jumièges	33
Parisel	Nicolas	Bernay	63
Pataillier	Jacques Augustin	Fécamp	66
Perceval	Jean Marie	Bec	58
Picheré	Guillaume	Fécamp	74
Pichonner	Jacques Antoine Michel	Préaux	42
Podevin	François Joseph	Saint-Ouen	27
Quennouel	Jacques Joseph Louis	Fécamp	42
Raoullet	Jean Michel	Bec	24

LAST NAME	FIRST NAME	MONASTERY	AGE
Reserve[10]	Unknown	Lyre	Unknown
Richer	Jean Dominique	Valmont	71
Rivart	Jacques Joseph	Tréport	55
Rogissart, *convers*[11]	Jean Baptiste Bruno	Bec	Unknown
Ruault	Alexandre Jean	Saint-Wandrille	44
Rungette	François André	Bec	31
Sarrazin	Charles Noël	Fécamp	30
Sta	Pierre Jean François	Valmont	33
Surmont	Philippe André Joseph	Tréport	41
Trehet	Guillaume Jean Julian	Saint-Wandrille	43
Trémauville	Étienne Alexis	Saint-Taurin	40
Valincourt	Louis	Jumièges	72
Vanizac	Louis François	Aumale	55
Vigneron	Charles	Bernay	61

10. His name does not appear in Archives nationales list [AN, D XIX, 10, no. 147], but only his last name appears in the list of declarations from Notre-Dame-de-Lyre ["Religieux de l'abbaye de Notre-Dame-de-la-Vieille-Lire [sic]," ADE, 166 L 4].

11. "Former Camaldule, added to the community of Bec by capitular act on 27 March 1774," AN, D XIX, 10, no. 147.

APPENDIX B

DECREE OF THE NATIONAL ASSEMBLY, 13 FEBRUARY 1790

Article 55: Letters patent of the King, which prohibits in France the monastic vows of one or the other sex. Given at Paris on 19 February 1790.

Louis, by the grace of God, etc.,

Decree of 13 February 1790.

The National Assembly decrees the following:

First Article: The constitutional law of the kingdom no longer recognizes the solemn monastic vows of persons of one or the other sex: declares, as a result, that the regular orders and congregations in which one makes such vows, are and will remain suppressed in France, without the possibility of reestablishing them in the future.

Second Article: All individuals of one or the other sex, living in the monasteries and religious houses, can leave, while making their declaration before the municipality of the area; and it will indefinitely provide for their future by a suitable pension. Likewise there will be indicated some houses where the religious who do not want to profit by the disposition of the present decrees can retire.

Declare besides that nothing will change, at present, in regard to the houses designated for public education and charitable establishments; and that, until a party has been made for these services.

Third Article: The religious can remain in the houses where they are today, except for the article which obliges the religious to reunite many houses into one.

Let us mandate and ordain to all the tribunes, etc.[1]

---

1. Assemblée nationale constituante, Collection complète, I, 198–99.

APPENDIX C

DECLARATIONS OF MAURISTS
FROM UPPER NORMANDY IN 1790[53]

LAST NAME	MONASTERY	DECLARATION
Alleaume de Tréfforêt	Bec	Leave without conditions
Allix	Jumièges	Stay with conditions
Andri	Lyre	Leave without conditions
Aubin	Saint-Ouen	Leave with conditions
Bacon	Préaux	Leave with conditions
Banse	Jumièges	Leave without conditions
Bardel	Fécamp	Undecided Leave without conditions Leave without conditions
Baron	Bec	Leave without conditions
Bautier	Bonne-Nouvelle	Leave without conditions
Beaussart	Ivry	Leave without conditions
Benoit	Bec	Undecided
Berguesse	Bernay	Leave without conditions

---

53. The declarations of the Maurists from upper Normandy have been grouped into the following categories: Stay (in the communal life) without conditions, Stay with conditions, Leave (the communal life) without conditions, Leave with conditions, Undecided, Did not declare, Absent, Unknown, Deceased. The multiple declarations of some monks are listed with the first declaration at the top and the last declaration at the bottom.

LAST NAME	MONASTERY	DECLARATION
Bernès, *convers*	Bec	Leave without conditions
Berthaux	Saint-Wandrille	Leave without conditions
Besserve	Lyre	Stay without conditions
Billard	Bonne-Nouvelle	Leave with conditions
Blanchard	Bec	Leave without conditions
Blanchet	Bonne-Nouvelle	Stay with conditions
Blandin	Fécamp	Undecided Leave without conditions
Bonnard, Augustin	Aumale	Unknown
Bonnard, Norbert	Tréport	Leave without conditions[54]
Bonvoust	Fécamp	Undecided Leave without conditions Leave without conditions
Bourdon	Bec	Stay without conditions
Bourlier	Aumale	Leave without conditions
Bréant	Saint-Taurin	Stay with conditions
Bricque	Conches	Unknown
Bride, Jean	Saint-Ouen	Stay without conditions
Bride, Pierre	Saint-Ouen	Stay with conditions

54. The declarations of the monks of Tréport were not recorded in the municipality's inquiry on 4 May 1790 [AN, F19 6113].

LAST NAME	MONASTERY	DECLARATION
Brixier	Saint-Wandrille	Leave without conditions
Broncquart	Jumièges	Absent [Leave without conditions]
Broucqsault	Ivry	Leave without conditions
Cadet	Préaux	Leave with conditions
Cambier	Valmont	Stay with conditions
Capelle	Bec	Stay without conditions
Capperon	Saint-Wandrille	Leave without conditions
Cartault	Fécamp	Did not declare Did not declare
Cartier	Tréport	Leave without conditions[55]
Catelain	Saint-Wandrille	Leave without conditions
Chahau	Préaux	Stay with conditions
Chesnon	Tréport	Leave without conditions[56]
Collibeaux	Fécamp	Did not declare Stay without conditions
Coquil deslongchamps	Bec	Leave without conditions
Cotté	Saint-Ouen	Undecided
Courbet	Jumièges	Leave without conditions
Crespin	Préaux	Leave with conditions

55. Refer to note 54, above.
56. Refer to note 54, above.

LAST NAME	MONASTERY	DECLARATION
Dabout, Guillaume	Bosherville	Leave without conditions
Dabout, Jean	Saint-Ouen	Leave without conditions
Daguin	Bec	Leave without conditions
Danne	Bec	Leave without conditions
Darras	Bec	Did not declare
David	Bec	Leave without conditions
Davoust	Saint-Ouen	Absent [Leave without conditions]
Dechy	Saint-Wandrille	Leave without conditions
De Laperche	Préaux	Leave with conditions
Delaplace	Tréport	Leave without conditions[57]
Delarue	Bonne-Nouvelle	Leave with conditions
Delénable	Bonne-Nouvelle	Leave with conditions
Deleyris	Saint-Ouen	Undecided
Delobel	Saint-Ouen	Undecided
de Maurey	Fécamp	Absent Leave with conditions Leave without conditions
de Mésanges	Jumièges	Stay with conditions
de Montigny	Jumièges	Stay with conditions

57. Refer to note 54, above.

LAST NAME	MONASTERY	DECLARATION
de Quane	Jumièges	Leave without conditions
de Rancher	Bec	Leave without conditions
de Recusson	Saint-Ouen	Leave without conditions
Dergny	Saint-Taurin	Undecided
Derouvroy	Saint-Ouen	Undecided Leave with restrictions
Desmares	Fécamp	Absent Leave without conditions Leave without conditions
Despinose	Jumièges	Absent [Leave without conditions]
Destruissart	Saint-Ouen	Absent Leave with conditions
d'Huldebert	Bec	Leave without conditions[58]
Droulez	Bec	Leave without conditions
du Bocquet	Lyre	Stay without conditions
Dubois	Fécamp	Undecided Leave without conditions Leave without conditions Leave without conditions[59]
Dubrez, *commis*	Fécamp	Did not declare
Dubuisson	Saint-Ouen	Stay without conditions

58. Declaration made at Saint-Wandrille ["Procès Verbal des effets de l'abbaye de Saint-Wandrille," AN, F19 6113; "Extrait du procès-verbal dressé par les officiers municipales de la paroisse de Saint-Wandrille ce 28 avril de la presente année [1790]," ADSM L 1327].
59. Refer to note 58, above.

LAST NAME	MONASTERY	DECLARATION
Dubust	Conches	Unknown
Dufour	Boscherville	Unknown
Duhamel	Saint-Ouen	Leave without conditions
Dupont, Olivier	Saint-Ouen	Undecided
Dupont, Phillippe	Boscherville	Unknown
Durel	Jumièges	Stay with conditions
Durieux	Bec	Leave without conditions
Duriez	Boscherville	Unknown
Duval, *commis*	Bec	Leave without conditions
Duvrac	Lyre	Leave without conditions
Evrard	Bec	Leave without conditions
Fillaut	Bec	Stay without conditions
Follin	Saint-Taurin	Stay with conditions
Fontaine d'Épreville	Fécamp	Stay with conditions Stay with conditions Stay with conditions
Fortier	Saint-Ouen	Undecided Leave with conditions
Fossé	Boscherville	Unknown
Foulon	Bec	Leave without conditions
Francke	Lyre	Leave without conditions

LAST NAME	MONASTERY	DECLARATION
Froger	Saint-Ouen	Stay with conditions
Garnier	Conches	Unknown
Gautherot	Saint-Ouen	Undecided
Gobard, Gaspart	Jumièges	Leave without conditions
Gobard, Michel	Saint-Wandrille	Leave without conditions
Goulliart	Saint-Ouen	Leave with conditions
Gourdin	Jumièges	Stay with conditions
Govart	Bec	Leave without conditions
Grognet	Saint-Wandrille	Leave without conditions
Guesdon	Jumièges	Leave without conditions
Hautement	Bec	Stay without conditions
Herment	Fécamp	Did not declare Stay with conditions
Heutte	Saint-Taurin	Leave without conditions
Hommeril	Lyre	Leave without conditions
Huard	Boscherville	Unknown
Hubert, François	Saint-Ouen	Undecided Leave with conditions
Hubert, Henri	Jumièges	Leave without conditions
Julien	Fécamp	Undecided Stay without conditions Stay without conditions

LAST NAME	MONASTERY	DECLARATION
La Batte	Lyre	Leave without conditions
Labigne	Lyre	Stay without conditions Leave without conditions[60]
Lainé	Fécamp	Undecided Stay without conditions Stay with conditions
Lamache	Conches	Unknown
Langlois	Saint-Ouen	Leave with conditions
Lartois	Lyre	Stay without conditions
Lavieuville	Saint-Ouen	Leave with conditions
Leborgne	Saint-Ouen	Undecided Leave with conditions
Lebrun	Saint-Wandrille	Leave with conditions
Le Carpentier	Bec	Stay without conditions
Le Chevallier	Préaux	Leave with conditions
Lechevallier	Préaux	Leave with conditions
Lecomte	Bec	Leave without conditions
Leconte	Bec	Leave without conditions
Lefevre, Jean	Valmont	Stay with conditions
Lefevre, Vindicien	Fécamp	Undecided Stay without conditions Leave without conditions

60. Refer to note 58, above

LAST NAME	MONASTERY	DECLARATION
Lemache	Conches	Unknown
Lemaire	Fécamp	Undecided Leave without conditions Leave without conditions Leave without conditions[61]
Lengaigne	Saint-Wandrille	Leave without conditions
Lentrain	Jumièges	Leave without conditions[62]
Lepicard	Fécamp	Stay without conditions Stay without conditions Stay without conditions
Le Riche	Fécamp	Undecided Leave with conditions Stay without conditions
Lestievetz	Saint-Wandrille	Leave without conditions
Levacher	Saint-Taurin	Leave without conditions
Levacque	Saint-Taurin	Stay without conditions Leave without conditions
Le Vasseur	Lyre	Leave without conditions
Levesque	Préaux	Stay with conditions
Locoge	Saint-Ouen	Absent Leave with conditions
Maillon, *commis*	Jumièges	Leave without conditions
Marais	Bernay	Leave without conditions
Martin	Boscherville	Deceased

61. Refer to note 58, above.
62. Refer to note 58, above.

LAST NAME	MONASTERY	DECLARATION
Marye	Bec	Undecided
Maselinne	Bec	Leave without conditions
Massey	Bec	Leave without conditions
Meigniot	Valmont	Leave without conditions
Meslin	Conches	Unknown
Mesnard	Saint-Ouen	Stay with conditions
Moniez	Bec	Leave without conditions
Montéage	Jumièges	Leave without conditions
Monthois	Valmont	Stay with conditions
Mullet, Étienne	Conches	Unknown
Mullet, Pierre	Conches	Unknown
Nicholle, André	Fécamp	Undecided Leave with conditions Absent [Leave without conditions]
Nicolle, Jean	Fécamp	Undecided Leave with conditions Absent [Leave without conditions]
Outin	Jumièges	Stay with conditions
Painblanc	Jumièges	Stay with conditions
Parisel	Bernay	Leave without conditions
Pataillier	Fécamp	Did not declare Stay without conditions Leave without conditions

LAST NAME	MONASTERY	DECLARATION
Perceval	Bec	Leave without conditions
Picheré	Fécamp	Stay without conditions Stay without conditions Stay without conditions
Pichonner	Préaux	Leave with conditions
Podevin	Saint-Ouen	Undecided Leave without conditions
Quennouel	Fécamp	Undecided Stay with conditions Leave without conditions
Raoullet	Bec	Leave without conditions[63]
Reserve	Lyre	Leave without conditions
Richer	Valmont	Stay with conditions
Rivart	Tréport	Unknown[64]
Rogissart, *convers*	Bec	Leave without conditions
Ruault	Saint-Wandrille	Leave without conditions
Rungette	Bec	Leave without conditions
Sarrazin	Fécamp	Undecided Stay with conditions Leave without conditions
Sta	Valmont	Stay with conditions
Surmont	Tréport	Leave without conditions[65]

63. Refer to note 58, above.
64. Refer to note 54, above.
65. Refer to note 54, above.

LAST NAME	MONASTERY	DECLARATION
Trehet	Saint-Wandrille	Absent [Leave without conditions]
Trémauville	Saint-Taurin	Leave without conditions
Valincourt	Jumièges	Stay without conditions
Vanizac	Aumale	Unknown
Vigneron	Bernay	Stay without conditions[66] Leave without conditions

66. Declaration made at Bec [ADE, 95 L 1, dos. 1790–An III].

APPENDIX D

MAURISTS WHO APPEAR
IN UPPER NORMANDY AFTER 1790

LAST NAME	FIRST NAME	MONASTERY
Aubry	Jean Baptiste	Saint-Martin-de-Séez
Borel	Jean Baptiste	Saint-Denis-en-France
Bricque	Louis Charles François	Unknown
Cardon	Charles Gabriel	Saint-Lucien-de-Beauvais
Caron	Amand Fidèle Constant	Saint-Martin-de-Pontoise
Chevallier	Louis Antoine	Saint-Martin-de-Séez
Daspres	Louis Hippolite	Montreuil Bellay
Delépine	André François Marie	Unknown
de Noyelle	Henri François de Paule	Saint-Florent-de-Saumur
Depoix	Jacques	Saint-Serge-d'Angers
de Saulty	Antoine Joseph	Saint-Étienne-de-Caen
de Soulbieu	Charles	Saint-Florentin-de-Bonneval
Dubois	Luc Pierre Joseph	Unknown
Duvillard	Jean Baptiste François	Saint-Étienne-de-Caen
Ferey	Jean-Baptiste	Sainte-Trinité-de-Lessay
Ferrand	Pierre Julien	Notre-Dame-de-Josephat

Girard	Jacques	Notre-Dame-de-Coulombs
Gouilliart	Norbert Joseph	Sainté-Trinite-de-Lessay
Guillotte	Jacques Michel	Saint-Germer-de-Flay
Huart	Jean-Baptiste	Saint-Germer-de-Flay
Legrand	François Henry	Saint-Évroult
Lelaisant (dit Castel)	Nicolas Jean François	Saint-Robert-de-Cormillon
Letellier	Guillaume Dominique	Saint-Florentin-de-Bonneval
Leturgez	Joseph	Saint-Martin-de-Pontoise
Martel	Claude Justin	Notre-Dame-de-Coulombs
Mauger	Étienne Joseph	Saint-Étienne-de-Caen
Petit	André Joseph	Saint-Florentin-de-Bonneval
Pottier	Louis Honorat Magloire	Saint Jacut
Tissier	Étienne	Notre-Dame-de-Josaphat
Troussel	Claude Auguste	Saint-Nicaise-de-Reims
Villeroy	Antoine François	Saint-Martin-de-Seez

APPENDIX E

AMOUNT OF PENSIONS FOR RELIGIOUS WHO CHOSE TO SECULARIZE[1]

AGE	AMOUNT OF PENSION (in livres)
Choir monks	
under 50 years	900
50 to 70 years	1,000
over 70 years	1,200
Lay brothers and _conversi_	
under 50 years	300
50 to 70 years	400
over 70 years	500

---

1. "Lettres patentes du roi, sur un décret de l'assemblée nationale, qui fixent le traitement des religieux qui sortiront de leurs maisons; données à Paris le 26 février 1790," p. 2, ADE, 56 Edt 5 p.

APPENDIX F

AMOUNT OF SALARY FOR CONSTITUTIONAL CURÉS[1]

PARISH POPULATION	SALARY OF CURÉS (in livres)
Paris	6,000
More than 50,000	4,000
10,000–50,000	3,000
3,000–10,000	2,400
2,500–3,000	2,000
2,000–2,500	1,800
1,000–2,000	1,500
Less than 1,000	1,200

1. "Traitements des curés et vicaires constitutionnels," ADSM L 2097.

APPENDIX G

AMOUNT OF SALARY FOR CONSTITUTIONAL VICARS[1]

PARISH POPULATION	SALARY OF FIRST VICAR (in livres)	SALARY OF SECOND VICAR (in livres)	SALARY OF THIRD VICAR (in livres)
Paris	2,400	1,500	1,000
More than 50,000	1,200	1,000	800
3,000–50,000	800	700	
Less than 3,000	700		

1. "Traitements des curés et vicaires constitutionnels," ADSM L, 2097.

APPENDIX H

EX-MAURISTS WHO BECAME CONSTITUTIONAL CLERGY

EX-MAURIST	PARISH	POSITION
Bourlier, Pierre	Villers-sur-Aumale	*desservant*
Bricque, Louis Charles François	Saint-Sylvestre Saint-Jean-de-Folleville	curé curé
Bride, Pierre Armand	Bolbec	curé
Brixier, Mathurin François	Rançon	*desservant*
Dabout, Jean François	Lintot	curé
de Montigny, Jean Jacques	Heurteauville	*desservant*
de Quane, Charles	Bielleville	curé
Despinose, Thomas Antoine Jean	Saint-Aubin-de-Cretot	curé
Durieux, Albert Joseph	unknown	curé
Duvrac, Pierre Michel	Beuzevillette	curé
Ferey, Jean Baptiste	Lanquetot	curé
Fortier, Antoine Joseph	Beuzevillette	vicar
Gobard, Gaspard Léon	Saint-Quentin-des-Isles	curé
Grognet, Louis Nicolas	Auzbosc	curé
Hubert, Henri	Bouville	curé
Legrand, François Henry	Yvetot	curé
Lengaigne, Louis François Joseph	Autretot	curé
Lestievetz, François Louis Joseph	Boishimont	curé
Letellier, Guillaume Louis Dominique	Fécamp, Sainte-Trinité	curé
Levacque, François Joseph	Allouville	curé
Mauger, Étienne Joseph	Saint-Wandrille	*desservant*
Mesnard, Nicolas Joseph Louis	Yvetot Saint-Marie-des-Champs	vicar curé

EX-MAURIST	PARISH	POSITION
Moniez, Xavier Fidèle	Saint-Clair-sur-les-Montes	curé
Monthois, Placide Joseph	Auberville-la-Renault	vicar
Mullet, Pierre Martin	Tilleul-Dame-Agnès	*desservant,* curé
Parisel, Nicolas	Launay	curé
Ruault, Alexandre Jean	Yvetot	curé
Sta, Pierre Jean François	Valmont	curé
Surmont, Philippe André Joseph	unknown	curé
Tissier, Étienne	Saint-Antoine-la-Forêt	curé
Trémauville, Étienne Alexis	Ecretteville-sur-les-Baons Cléville	curé curé
Troussel, Claude Auguste	Rouvray	curé

BIBLIOGRAPHY

In this bibliography, there are two newspapers: *Journal de Paris* and *Moniteur.*

Abbreviations for Archival Sources

ADE	**Archives départementales de l'Eure**
ADO	**Archives départementales d'Orne**
ADSM	**Archives départementales de Seine-Maritime**
AMY	**Archives municipales d'Yvetot**
AN	**Archives nationales de France**
ASWF	**Abbaye de Saint-Wandrille de Fontenelle, *Des Curieuses recherches de Fontenelle* (1946, 1949, 1951, 1967, 1980, 1989, 1991)**
BN	**Bibliothèque nationale de France**
BMR	**Bibliothèque municipale de Rouen**

Primary sources are in bold.

Archives départementales de l'Eure. *État sommaire des documents conservée aux archives du département de l'Eure.* Évreux: Imprimerie Hérissey, 1939.

Assemblée nationale constituante. *Journal des débats et des décrets.* Versailles: [n. p.], 1789–1815.

———. *Collection complete des lois promulguées sur les décrets de l'assemblée nationale, depuis le 3 novembre 1789.* 15 vols. Paris: Imprimerie nationale, 1791.

Aston, Nigel. *Religion and Revolution in France* 1780–1804. Washington, DC: The Catholic University of America Press, 2000.

Aubert, Roger. "La Restauration monastique dans l'Europe occidentale du XIXᵉ siècle." *Revue bénédictine* 83 (1973): 9–39.

Aulard, François-Alphonse. Christianity and the French Revolution. Translated by Lady Frazer. London: E. Benn, 1927. Originally published as Le Christianisme et la Révolution française (Paris: F. Rieder, 1925).

———, ed. *La Révolution française et les congrégations: Exposé historique et documents.* Paris: E. Cornély, 1903.

Barruel, Abbé Augustin. *Mémoires pour servir à l'histoire du jacobinisme.* Hambourg: Fauche, 1798–99.

Baston, Abbé Guillaume-André-René. *Mémoires de l'Abbé Baston Chanoine de Rouen.* Paris: A. Picard et Fils, 1897.

Baudot, Marcel. *Normandie bénédictine.* Pacy-sur-Eure: Imprimerie de la Vallée d'Eure, 1979.

171

Beaunier, Dom. *Recueil historique des archevêchés, évêchés, abbayes et prieurés de France*. Ligugé: Abbaye de Saint-Martin, 1906.

Bellamy, David. *Bénédictins et Annonçiades à Fécamp sous la Révolution*. Maromme: Qualigraphie, 1989.

———. "La Vie religieuse à Fécamp sous la Révolution à travers les exemples de l' abbaye des bénédictins et du couvent des annonciades." *Révolution et mouvements révolutionnaires en Normandie: Actes du XXIVe Congrès des sociétés historiques et archéologiques de Normandie* (1990): 43–52.

Bellenger, Dom Aidan. "'Superstitious enemies of the flesh'? The Variety of Benedictine Responses to the Enlightenment." In *Religious Change in Europe 1650–1914*, ed. Nigel Aston, 149–60. Oxford: Clarendon Press, 1997.

Besnard, A. *Monographie de l'église et de l'abbaye Saint-Georges de Boscherville*. Paris: Librairie historique des provinces, 1899.

Beugnot, Jacques-Claude, Comte. *Mémoires du Comte Beugnot: Ancien Ministre (1783–1815)*. 2 vols. Paris: E. Dentu, 1866.

Blanchet, François. "Le Fonds de Jumièges aux archives départementales de la Seine-Inférieure." *Congrès Scientifique du XIIIe centenaire de Jumièges* (1955): I, 373–78.

Bled, Chanoine O. "Les Origines de la Bibliothèque de Saint-Omer et ses deux premiers conservateurs." *Mémoires de la Société des antiquaires de la Morine*, 31 (1912–13): 208–17.

Boivin-Champeaux, Louis. *Notice pour servir à l'histoire de la révolution dans le département de l'Eure*. Évreux: P. Huet, 1864.

Bonnenfant, Chanoine Georges and Georges Huard. *Histoire générale du diocèse d'Évreux*. 2 vols. Paris: Auguste Picard, 1933.

Bonnet de Viller, Dom François. "Les Derniers moines de Jumièges." *Congrès Scienti fique du XIIIe centenaire de Jumièges* (1955): II, 837–45.

Boudet, Marcel. "Moines et familiers de Jumièges d'après les registres paroissiaux." *Congrès Scientifique du XIIIe centenaire de Jumièges* (1955): II, 831–36.

Bourienne-Savoye, Anne. "Les Fécampois et leur abbaye." *Révolution et mouvements révolutionnaires en Normandie: Actes du XXIVe Congrès des sociétés historiques et archéologiques de Normandie* (1990): 81–84.

——— and Marie-Hélène Desjardins-Menegalli. *Marins, moines, citoyens Fécampois dans la Révolution*. Fécamp: Musées municipaux de Fécamp, 1990.

Brette, Armand. *Les Constituants: Liste des députés et des suppléants élus à l'Assemblée constituante de 1789*. Paris: Au Siège de la société, 1897.

Bugner, Monique. "Les Bâtiments de la congrégation de Saint-Maur." *Sous la règle de Saint-Benoît: Structures monastiques et sociétés en France du moyen âge à l'époque moderne* (1982): 539–54.

Camou, Hélène and Philippe Maillard. *La Loge de la Triple Unité de Fécamp*. Fécamp: Musée municipaux de Fécamp, 1991.

Caprara, Cardinal Giambattista, ed. *Concordat et recueil des bulles et brefs de N. S. P. Le pape Pie VII, sur les affaires actuelles de l'église de France*. Paris: Chez Le Clere, 1802.

Chaline, Olivier and Gérard Hurpin, ed. *Vivre en Normandie sous la Révolution: Documents*. 2 vols. Rouen: Société de l'Histoire de Normandie, Archives de la Seine-Maritime, 1989.

Charles, J., M.-C. de La Conté, and C. Lannette. *Répertoire des abbayes et prieurés de l'Eure*. Évreux: Archives départementales de l'Eure, 1983.

Charpillon, Caresme Anatole. *Dictionnaire historique de toutes les communes du département de l'Eure: Histoire, géographie, statistique*. Second edition. 2 vols. Paris: Guénégaud, 1966.

Charvin, Dom G. "Un épisode des controverses jansénistes dans la Congrégation de Saint-Maur en 1745." *Revue Mabillon* 44 (1954): 45–66.

Chaussy, Dom Yves. *Les Bénédictins de Saint-Maur*. 2 vols. Paris: Études Augustiniennes, 1989.

———. "Les Derniers moines de Fécamp." *L'Abbaye Bénédictine de Fécamp: Ouvrage scientifique du XIIIe centenaire* (1960): II, 253–66.

———, ed. **Matricula Monachorum: Professorum Congregationis S. Mauri in Gallia Ordinis Sancti Patris Benedicti ab initio eiusdem Congregationis, usque ad annum 1789. Paris: Librairie Perrée, 1959.**

Clérembray, Félix. *La Terreur à Rouen 1793, 1794, 1795*. Paris: Office d'édition du livre d'histoire, 1994.

Cochin, Auguste. *La Révolution et la libre-pensée: La socialisation de la pensée (1750–1789), la socialisation de la personne (1789–1792), la socialisation des biens (1793–1794)*. Paris: Plon, 1924.

Colloque de la faculté de théologie de l'Université catholique de Lyon. *Religieux et religieuses pendant la révolution (1770–1820)*. 2 vols. Lyon: Profac, 1995.

Comité de salut public. Recueil des actes du Comité de salut public, avec la correspondance officielle des représentants en mission et le registre du Conseil exécutif provisoire. 27 vols. Edited by François-Alphonse Aulard. Paris: Imprimerie nationale, 1889.

Congrès des sociétés historiques et archéologiques de Normandie. *Révolution et mouvements révolutionnaires en Normandie*. Le Havre: Centre havrais de recherche historiques, 1990.

Cooney, Mary Kathryn, " 'I Have Not Compromised Myself in Anything': Dom François Philippe Gourdin and the Suppression of Monasticism in France." *Consortium on Revolutionary Europe: Selected Papers* (2005): 25–33.

———. "Très Chers Frères: Freemasonry and the Benedictines of the Congregation of Saint-Maur." *Consortium on Revolutionary Europe: Selected Papers* (2002): 173–83.

Cousin, Patrice. *Précis d'histoire monastique*. Paris, Bloud et Gay, 1959.

Dantier, Alphonse, ed. Rapports sur la correspondance inédite des Bénédictins de Saint-Maur, addressés à S. Exc. le ministre de l'instruction publique et des cultes. Paris: Imprimerie impériale, 1857.

Daoust, Abbé Joseph. "L'Activité littéraire de Jumièges aux XVIIe et XVIIIe siècles." *Congrès Scientifique du XIIIe centenaire de Jumièges* (1955): II, 655–62.

de Beaurepaire, Georges. *Fécamp pendant la Révolution: 1792–1795*. Rouen: Imprimerie Cagniard, 1911.

de Boüard, Michel. *L'Abbaye bénédictine de Fécamp*. Fécamp: L. Durand et Fils, 1959.

———. *Histoire de la Normandie*. Toulouse: Édouard Privat, 1970.

——— and Jean Merlet. *L'Abbaye du Bec-Hellouin*. Paris: Caisse nationale des monuments historiques, 1964.

de Chastenay, Victorine. *Mémoires de Madame de Chastenay: 1771–1815.* 2 vols. Paris: Librairie Plon, 1896.

de la Bunodière, M. *Derniers jours de l'abbaye de Saint-Ouen de Rouen: Discours de M. de La Bunodière et réponse à ce discours par Mgr. Loth, président.* Rouen: Imprimerie Cagniard, 1909.

de la Varende, Jean. *L'Abbaye du Bec-Hellouin.* Paris: Plon, 1951.

de Loucelles, F. *Histoire générale de la franc-maçonnerie en Normandie 1739–1875.* Dieppe: Imprimerie du F. Émile Delevoy, 1875.

de Mathan, Chanoine. "Deux abbayes voisines: Fécamp et Valmont." *Les Abbayes de Normandie: Actes du XIIIe Congrès des sociétés historiques et archéologiques de Normandie* (1979): 307–13.

Denis, Dom P. "Les Bénédictins de la Congrégation de Saint-Maur: Originaires de l'ancien diocèse de Séez." *Bulletin de la Société historique et archéologique de l'Orne* 31 (April 1912): 293–318.

Deries, Léon. "La Vie d'un bibliothécaire: Dom Gourdin, ex-bénédictin de l'abbaye de Saint-Ouen à Rouen." *Revue Mabillon* 18 (1928): 209–39.

de Rochemonteix, Camille. *Les Congrégations religieuses non reconnues en France 1789–1881.* 2 vols. Le Caire: Imprimerie Polyglotte, 1901.

Deshayes, C.-A. *Histoire de l'abbaye royale de Jumièges.* Rouen: F. Baudry, 1829; reprinted Brionne: Gérard Monfort, 1980.

de Viguerie, Jean. "Les Abbayes mauristes normandes." In *Histoire Religieuse de la Normandie,* 209–20. Chambray: C. L. D., 1981.

Dubuc, André. "Bibliothèque et œuvres d'art dans les abbayes supprimées à la Révolution en Seine-Inférieure." *Les Abbayes de Normandie: Actes du XIIIe Congrès des sociétés historiques et archéologiques de Normandie* (1979): 141–55.

―――. "Les Difficultés financières de Jumièges à la fin de l'ancien régime." *Congrès Scientifique du XIIIe centenaire de Jumièges* (1955): II, 115–22.

Duchet-Suchaux, Gaston and Monique Duchet-Suchaux. *Les Ordres religieux: Guide historique.* Paris: Flammarion, 1993.

Dumesnil, Abbé Louis. *Souvenirs de la Terreur: Mémoires inédits d'un curé de campagne.* second edition. Edited by Baron Erouf. Paris: Didier et Cie, 1873.

Dupuy, Pascal. "Ordre et désordre en révolution: Le Cas d'une région typique, la Haute-Normandie (1789–1800)." *Consortium on Revolutionary Europe 1750–1850: Selected Papers* (1994): 458–69.

Eude, Robert. "L'Église de la Sainte-Trinité de Fécamp et ses curés pendant la période concordataire (1804–1096)." *L'Abbaye Bénédictine de Fécamp: Ouvrage scientifique du XIIIe centenaire* (1960): II, 267–97.

Évrard, Fernand. "L'Esprit public dans l'Eure." *La Révolution française* 66 (1914): 122–59, 405–26, 521–52.

Fallue, Léon. *Histoire de la ville et de l'abbaye de Fécamp.* Rouen: Imprimerie de Nicétas Periaux, 1841.

Fauvel, Daniel. "Les Projets de réunion de paroisses dans le district de Montivilliers de 1790 à 1792." In *Révolution et mouvements révolutionnaires en Normandie: Actes d XXIVe Congrès des sociétés historiques et archéologiques de Normandie* (1990): 173–80.

Fournée, Jean. "Abbayes, prieurés et couvents généralités sur les ordres religieux." *Les Abbayes de Normandie: Actes du XIIIᵉ Congrès des sociétés historiques et archéologiques de Normandie* (1979): 27–55.

Fromentin, Alexandre. *Essai historique sur Yvetot et coup d'œil jeté sur ses environs Valmont, Saint-Wandrille, Caudebec.* Rouen: A. Péron, 1844.

Furet, François. *Interpreting the French Revolution.* Translated by Elborg Forster. Cambridge: Cambridge University Press, 1981. Originally published as *Penser la Révolution française* (Paris: Editions Gallimard, 1978).

G. "La Déportation ecclésiastique sous le directoire." *Revue bénédictine* 13 (1896): 359–66, 459–70.

Gasnault, Pierre. "La Correspondance des mauristes aux XVIIᵉ et XVIIIᵉ siècles." *Sous la règles de Saint-Benoît: Structures monastiques et sociétés en France du moyen âge à l'époque moderne* (1982): 293–304.

Goube, Jacqueline. "Les Attributions d'abbayes aux paroisses à la Révolution dans le département de la Seine-Inférieure." *Les Abbayes de Normandie: Actes du XIIIᵉ Congrès des sociétés historiques et archéologiques de Normandie* (1979): 157–62.

Goujon, A. *Histoire de Bernay et de son canton touchant à l'histoire générale de la Normandie.* Brionne: Le Portulan, 1970.

Gourdon de Genouillac, H. *Histoire de l'abbaye de Fécamp et de ses abbés.* Fécamp: A. Marinier, 1875.

Guéry, Abbé Charles. *Deux bénédictins normands: Dom Louis-Ambroise Blandin et Dom Louis-Charles-Magne Fontaine.* Évreux: Imprimerie de l'Eure, 1914.

———. *Histoire de l'abbaye de Lyre.* Évreux: Imprimerie de l'Eure, 1917.

Hébert, Abbé P., ed. *La Révolution à Rouen et dans le pays de Caux: Extraits de la correspondance de M. le Marquis de Bailleul et de M. Toustain, son secrétaire (à Rouen), avec quelques lettres de MM. Bard et Bellet, régisseurs des châteaux de Bailleul et de Croixmare.* Évreux: Imprimerie de l'Eure, 1903.

Hérissay, Jacques. *Les Pontons de Rochefort: 1792–1795*: Paris: Le Livre d'histoire, 1925; reprinted 2000.

Hyslop, Beatrice Fry. *A Guide to the General Cahiers of 1789 with the Text of Unedited Cahiers.* New York: Columbia University Press, 1936.

Jouen, Chanoine Léon Alfred. *Jumièges: Histoire et légendes, ruines et reliques.* Rouen: Lecerf, 1937.

Journal de Paris.

Julia, Dominique. "Les Bénédictins et l'enseignement aux XVIIᵉ et XVIIIᵉ siècles." *Sous la règle de Saint-Benoît: Structures monastiques et sociétés en France du moyen âge à l'époque moderne* (1982): 345–91.

Kessler, M. Verona, O.S.B. "The Suppression of the Benedictine Order in France during the Revolution." MA thesis, Creighton University, 1957.

Lamare, Philippe. *Mémorial de Philippe Lamare: Secrétaire de Dom Gouget Bénédictin de l'abbaye de Fontenay (1774–1788).* Caen: Louis Jouan, 1905.

Langlois, E.-Hyacinthe and Espérance Langlois. *Essai historique et descriptif sur l'abbaye de Fontenelle ou de Saint-Wandrille et sur plusieurs autres monuments des environs.* Paris: J. Tastu, 1827; reprinted Saint-Wandrille: Éditions de Fontenelle, 1991.

Lannette, Claude. *Guide des Archives de l'Eure*. Évreux: ADE, 1982.

Laporte, Dom Jean. "Jumièges et Saint-Wandrille." *Congrès Scientifique du XIIIe centenaire de Jumièges* (1955): I, 191–98.

La Révolution à Yvetot et dans le pays de Caux. Yvetot: Centre culturel des Vikings, 1989.

La Révolution en Haute-Normandie, 1789–1802. Rouen: Éditions du P'tit Normand, 1988.

La Rochefoucauld, Dominique de. *Ordonnance de M. le Cardinal de La Rochefoucauld, Archévêque de Rouen, au sujet de l'élection faite le 20 mars 1791, de M. Charrier de la Roche, par MM. les électeurs du département de la Seine-Inférieure, en qualité d'évêque métropolitain dudit département.* **Paris: Crapart, 1791.**

Laurain-Portemer, Madeleine. "L'Habit des mauristes au XVIIIe siècle." *Sous la règle de Saint-Benoît: Structures monastiques et sociétés en France du moyen âge à l'époque moderne* (1982): 124–135.

Lecocq, Georges. *Les Congrégations religieuses en 1789*. Paris: Librairie Centrale H.-E. Martin, 1880.

Lecomte, Maurice. *Les Bénédictins et l'histoire des provinces aux XVIIe et XVIIIe siècles.* Vienne: Abbaye Saint-Martin de Ligugé, 1928.

Lecroq, Dom Gaston. *L'Hôpital de Fécamp et sa communauté des bénédictines hospitalières.* Caen: Société d'impression de Basse-Normandie, 1939.

Ledré, Charles. *Le Diocèse de Rouen et la législation religieuse de 1795 à 1800.* Paris: Lefebvre-Filleau, Jean-Paul. *Moines Francs-Maçons du pays de Caux.* Nanterre: Chlorofeuilles Communication, 1991.

Le Grand, Léon. *Les Sources de l'histoire religieuse de la révolution aux archives nationales.* Paris: Librairie Ancienne Honoré Champion, 1914.

Le Hodey de Saultchevreuil, Étienne. *Journal des États généraux convoqués par Louis XVI, le 27 avril 1789; Aujourd'hui Assemblée nationale permanente.* **35 vols. Paris: Chez Devaux and Gattey, 1789–91.**

Lekai, Louis J. "Cistercian Monasteries and the French Episcopate on the Eve of the Revolution." *Analecta Cisterciensia* 23 (1967): 66–114.

———. "The Cistercian Order and the 'Commission des Réguliers' (1766–1783)." *Analecta Cisterciensia* 23 (1967): 179–225.

———. "French Cistercians and the Revolution, 1789–1791." *Analecta Cisterciensia* 24 (1968): 86–118.

Lemaire, Suzanne. *La Commission des réguliers 1766–1780.* Paris: Société anonyme de Recuil Sirey, 1926.

Lemaitre, Jean. "Aperçu sur la Franc-maçonnerie à Fécamp." *Association des amis du vieux Fécamp et du pays de Caux bulletin* (1984–85): 25–28.

Lemaitre, Louis Nicolas. *Journal de route de Louis-Nicolas Lemaitre: Prêtre émigré originaire du pays d'Ouche.* **Edited by Gisèle Tellier, C. Mesnil, and Y. Mannevy. Bernay: Société historique les amis de Bernay, [n. d.].**

Lemarchand, Guy. "Les Monastères de Haute-Normandie au XVIIIe siècle: Essai d'un bilan économique." *Annales historiques de la révolution française* 179 (1965): 1–28.

Lemoine, Dom Robert. *Le Monde de religieux.* Paris: Editions Cujas, 1935.

Le Parquier, E., ed. *Cahiers de doléances des paroisses du bailliage de Neufchatel-en-Bray, secondaire du bailliage de Caux (1789).* Rouen: imprimerie Cagniard, 1908.

Les Archives de la France pendant la révolution: Introduction à l'inventaire du fonds d'archives dit les monuments historiques. Paris: Imprimerie de J. Claye, 1866.

"Les Religieux de la Congrégation de Saint-Maur pendant la révolution." *Revue Mabillon* 55 no. 219–57 no. 232 (January-March 1965–April-June 1968): 45–72, 101–68, 157–219, 219–50, 253–91.

Lohier, Dom Fernand. "Dom Étienne Mauger." *Revue Mabillon* 8 (1912): 339–80.

———. *Dom Louis-François Le Brun: Moine de Saint-Wandrille.* Saint-Wandrille: Abbaye de Saint-Wandrille, [n. d.].

———. "L'Inventaire de l'abbaye de Saint-Wandrille en 1790: Le Départ des moines." *Bulletin de la société des antiquaires de Normandie* 41 (1933): 155–92.

Loth, Abbé Julien. *Histoire du Cardinal de La Rochefoucauld et du diocèse de Rouen pendant la Révolution.* Évreux: Imprimerie de l'Eure, 1893.

———. *Les Conventionnels de la Seine-Inférieure.* Rouen: Espérance Cagniard, 1883.

———. *Liste des prêtres déporté de Rouen, morts sur les ponts, en rade de Rochefort pour la foi, en 1794.* Rouen: Imprimerie Mégard, [1866?].

Mage, Lily Diana. "Public Spirit and Public Opinion in Auvergne Before and During the French Revolution." Ph.D. dissertation, Columbia University, 1963.

Maltier, Dom Jacques. "Les Prieurs mauristes de Jumièges." *Congrès Scientifique du XIIIe centenaire de Jumièges* (1955): II, 817–30.

Marle, Anne. "État des monastères bénédictins de la congrégation de Saint Maur de Normandie en 1790." DEA mémoire, Université de Paris IV Sorbonne, 1994.

Martène, Dom Edmond. *Histoire de la Congrégation de Saint-Maur.* **9 vols. Paris: A. Picard, 1928.**

Martin, Alphonse. *Histoire de Fécamp illustrée.* 2 vols. Fécamp: L. Durand et Fils, 1894.

———. *Notes pour servir à l'histoire de l'abbaye de Valmont.* Fécamp: Imprimerie de L. Durand, 1876.

McMahon, Darrin M. *Enemies of the Enlightenment: The French Counter-Enlightenment and the Making of Modernity.* Oxford, Oxford University Press, 2001.

Moniteur.

Montier, Jean. "L'Abbaye de la Sainte-Trinité de Fécamp au XVIIIe siècle." *L'Abbaye Bénédictine de Fécamp: Ouvrage scientifique du XIIIe centenaire* (1959): I, 17–86.

———. "Les Derniers jours de Jumièges." *Congrès Scientifique du XIIIe centenaire de Jumièges* (1955): I, 123–45.

———. "Les Moines de Fécamp pendant la Révolution." *L'Abbaye Bénédictine de Fé camp: Ouvrage scientifique du XIIIe centenaire* (1961): III, 133–222.

———. *Martial de Loménie dernier abbé de Jumièges et son oncle Loménie de Brienne ministre de Louis XVI.* Fécamp: L. Durand et Fils, 1967.

Muller, Claude. *Les Bénédictins d'Alsace dans la tourmente révolutionnaire.* Langres: Dominique Guéniot, 1990.

Napoleon I, emperor of the French. *Correspondance de Napoléon I, publiée par ordre de l'empereur Napoléon III.* **32 vols. Paris: Imprimerie impériale, 1859–69.**

Nortier, Michel. "Les Sources de l'histoire de Jumièges à la bibliothèque nationale." *Congrès Scientifique du XIIIe centenaire de Jumièges* (1955): I, 379–99.

Pierre, Victor, ed. *La Déportation ecclésiastique sous le directoire: Documents inédits recueillis et publiés pour la Société d'histoire contemporaine.* **Paris: A. Picard et Fils, 1896.**

Pigout, Jean. *Bolbec pendant la Révolution (1789–1799): À travers les registres des délibérations municipales.* Bolbec: Imprimerie Ferric, 1989.

———. *La Révolution en Seine-Maritime: Bolbec: 1789–1794.* Luneray: Imprimerie Bertout, 1989.

Plongeron, Bernard. *Les Réguliers de Paris devant le serment constitutionnel: Sens et conséquences d'une option 1789–1801.* Paris: Librairie Philosophique, 1964.

——— and Paule Lerou, ed. *Le Piété populaire en France: Répertoire bibliographique.* Vol. 1, *Normandie, Picardie, Nord-Pas-de-Calais,* by Jean Fournée. Histoire Religieuse Modern et Contemporaine Séries. Paris: Éditions du Cerf, 1984.

Porée, Chanoine. *Histoire de l'abbaye du Bec.* 2 vols. Évreux: Imprimerie de Charles Hérissey, 1901; reprinted Bruxelles: Éditions culture et civilisation, 1980.

———, **ed. "Lettres de quelques bénédictins de la fin du XVIIIe siècle."** *Revue Bénédictine* **19, no. 14 (1902): 171–82.**

Répertoire des abbayes et prieurés de Seine-Maritime. Rouen: Archives départementales, 1979.

Rivet, Auguste. *Traité des congrégations religieuses: 1789–1943.* Paris: Éditions Spes, 1944.

———. *Traité du culte catholique et des lois civiles d'ordre religieux.* 2 vols. Langres: Gillot, 1950.

Rousseau, François. *Moines bénédictins martyrs et confesseurs de la foi pendant la Révolution.* Paris: Abbaye de Maredsous, 1926.

Saunier, Eric, ed. *Encyclopédie de la Franc-maçonnerie.* La Pochothèque, 2000.

———. *Révolution et sociabilité en Normandie au tournant des XVIIIe et XIXe siècles: 6000 francs-maçons de 1740 à 1830.* Rouen: Universités de Rouen et du Havre, 1998.

Savalle, E. *Les Derniers moines de l'abbaye de Jumièges.* Rouen: [n. p.], 1867.

Sévestre, Emile. *L'Enquête gouvernementale et l'enquête ecclésiastique sur le clergé de Normandie et du Maine de l'an IV à l'an XIII.* Vol. 1, *Les Enquêtes de Normandie.* Paris: A. Picard et Fils, 1918.

———. *Le Personnel de l'église constitutionnelle en Normandie (1791–1795).* Paris: A. Picard et Fils, 1925.

Sicard, Abbé Augustin. *Le Clergé de France pendant la Révolution.* 3 vols. Paris: Librairie Victor Lecoffre, 1912.

Simon, Abbé G.-A. "Réforme de Saint-Maur en Normandie." *Normannia* 2, no. 1 (1929): 249–99; 2, no. 2 (1929): 449–80; 2, no. 3 (1929): 583–624.

Soboul, Albert, ed. *Dictionnaire historique de la Révolution française.* Paris: Presses Universitaires de France, 1989.

Sueur, Gabrielle. "De l'attitude différente de trois prêtres de la Seine-Inférieure lors de la promulgation de la constitution civile du clergé." *Révolution et mouvements révolutionnaires en Normandie: Actes du XXIVe Congrès des sociétés historiques et archéologiques de Normandie* (1990): 369–74.

Suissa, Jean-Luc. *Le Département de l'Eure sous le consulat et l'empire (1798–1815).* Évreux: Association normande de documentation et d'information culturelles, 1983.

Tackett, Timothy. *Religion, Revolution and Regional Culture in Eighteenth-Century France: The Ecclesiastical Oath of 1791*. Princeton, NJ: Princeton University Press, 1986.

Tassin, Dom René Prosper. *Histoire littéraire de la Congrégation de Saint-Maur.* **Bruxelles: Chez Humblot, 1770.**

Theiner, Augustin. *Histoire des deux concordats de la république française et de la république cisalpine.* Paris: E. Dentu, 1869.

Thibault, Anne Alexandre Marie and Sigisbert Étienne Coster. *Les Séances des députés du clergé aux États généraux de 1789: Journal du curé Thibault et du Chanoine Coster.* **Paris: Au Siège de la Société, 1916.**

Thiron, J. "Les Moines de Saint-Wandrille pendant la révolution." *Revue Mabillon* 58, no. 244 (1971): 93–96.

Tougard, Robert. *La Révolution à Yvetot.* 2 vols. Yvetot: Imprimerie nouvelle, 1988.

Treilhard, Jean-Baptiste. *Rapport fait au nom du comité ecclésiastique, le jeudi 17 décembre 1789, sur les ordres religieux.* **[n. p.], [n. d.].**

Tribout de Morembert, Henri. *La Révolution dans l'Eure: Le Journal d'un curé d'Évreux 1788–1792.* **Évreux: Imprimerie de l'Eure, 1934.**

Tulard, Jean, ed. *Dictionnaire Napoléon.* 2 vols. Paris: Fayard, 1987.

Un Religieux bénédictin de la Congrégation de St. Maur. *Histoire de l'abbaye royale de Saint-Pierre de Jumièges.* Edited by Abbé Julien Loth. 3 vols. Rouen: Ch. Métérie, 1885.

Van Kley, Dale K. *The Religious Origins of the French Revolution: From Calvin to the Civil Constitution, 1560–1791.* New Haven, CN: Yale University Press, 1996.

Vaultier, Frédéric. *Souvenirs de l'insurrection normande dite du fédéralisme, en 1793.* **Edited by Georges Mancel. Caen: Le Gost-Clérisse, 1858.**

Vernier, J.-J. *La Seine-Inférieure à l'époque de la Révolution.* Rouen: Imprimerie Lecerf Fils, 1914.

Veuclin, Ernes-Victor. *Fin de la célèbre abbaye du Bec-Hellouin: Documents inédits.* Brionne: Imprimerie V. Daufresne, 1885.

———. *Notices sur la période révolutionnaire à Bernay et ses environs.* Saint-Aubin-les-Elbeuf: Les Éditions page de garde, 1997.

Vimont, Jean-Claude. *Punir Autrement: Les Prisons de Seine-Inférieure pendant la Révolution.* Rouen: Le Centre Régional de Documentation Pédagogique de Haute-Normandie, 1989.

Voltaire. *Dictionnaire de la pensée de Voltaire par lui-même.* **Bruxelles: Éditions complexe, 1994.**

Vovelle, Michel. *The Revolution against the Church: From Reason to Supreme Being.* Translated by Alan José. Columbus: Ohio State University Press, 1991. Originally published as *1793: La Révolution contre l'Église: De la raison à l'être suprême* (Lausanne: Editions Complexe, 1988)

———. *Piété baroque et déchristianisation en Provence au dix-huitième siècle: Les attitudes devant la mort d'après les clauses des testaments.* Paris: Plon, 1973.